STATE OF GIVING

State of Giving

STORIES OF OREGON VOLUNTEERS, DONORS, AND NONPROFITS

Greg Chaillé & Kristin Anderson

Oregon State University Press   Corvallis

The paper in this book meets the guidelines for permanence and durability of the Committee on Production Guidelines for Book Longevity of the Council on Library Resources and the minimum requirements of the American National Standard for Permanence of Paper for Printed Library Materials Z39.48-1984.

Library of Congress Cataloging-in-Publication Data

Chaillé, Greg.
State of giving : stories of Oregon volunteers, donors, and nonprofits / Greg Chaillé and
   Kristin Anderson.
   pages cm
   Includes index.
   ISBN 978-0-87071-772-7 (original trade pbk. : alk. paper) — ISBN 978-0-87071-773-4
   (e-book)
   1. Voluntarism—Oregon. 2. Volunteer workers in community development—Oregon.
3. Nonprofit organizations—Oregon. 4. Endowments—Oregon. 5. Humanitarianism—
Oregon. I. Title.
HN79.O73V6434 2015
302'.14—dc23
                        2015002332

Oregon State University Press
121 The Valley Library
Corvallis OR 97331-4501
541-737-3166 • fax 541-737-3170
www.osupress.oregonstate.edu

Contents

Preface
Toward a Better Oregon

For over thirty years, I had the great fortune to work for the Oregon Community Foundation (OCF), and for twenty-five of those years, I was its president. This job—this vocation, really—took me to the four corners of Oregon and to most places in between, and in my travels, I saw firsthand the needs of Oregon and the people working with commitment, passion, and pride to address those needs. This book tells some of their stories and celebrates the impact that these donors, volunteers, and nonprofits have made in their communities and across Oregon as a whole.

I have had the pleasure of working with many of the great philanthropists of Oregon. In using the word *philanthropist*, I don't just mean the rich and well known: I mean steadfast, generous, and hardworking people of all demographics and geographies, people who volunteer their time and energy as well as their money. Working with these Oregonians meant I found myself among grey suits, in wood-paneled boardrooms, drinking burnt coffee on one day; on the next, it could be mill yards, a horse trek, or a farmhouse kitchen with conversations lubricated by Jameson or potent homebrews. But in both boardrooms and kitchens, Oregonians were coming together, commitments were being made, and *things were getting done*.

In my experience both as someone who knows our state intimately and who, as a long-ago transplant, can see with clarity what makes it exceptional,

I know that Oregonians of all types have an extraordinary commitment to improving their communities. This community spirit may have an equal in other states, but what's crucial is that it is vibrant and strong here, among both native Oregonians and those of us who have chosen to make Oregon our home. Despite our state's purported disapproval of transplants (epitomized, perhaps, by Tom McCall's infamous invitation to "visit . . . but for heaven's sake, don't move here"), Oregon is a welcoming place, and newcomers don't have to live here very long before they are drawn into our communities.

This book celebrates natives and newcomers alike as people who, having benefited from Oregon's warmth and welcome, then return the favor by using their time and insights to provide solutions to some of our state's most pressing challenges. *State of Giving* is overflowing with visionaries and idealists who are young and old, urban and rural, black, white, Asian, Native American, Hispanic, liberal, conservative, gay, straight, male, female, wealthy, impoverished, and everyone in between. It tells the stories of people who have fulfilled needs within their communities and people who have looked outside of their communities and fulfilled needs there too.

It's a book populated with people like Anna Jones, the almost-nonagenarian who emigrated to Clackamas after her family was bombed out of Naples during the war and who still volunteers twice a week at the community service center she helped found almost four decades ago. Like Pete and Mary Mark, who infused money, influence, and enthusiasm into Oregon's cultural scene; like Kayse Jama, a Somalian refugee whose push for solidarity and equity among Portland's ethnic minorities has changed policies and lives. It's filled with local leaders such as Leo Adler of Baker City, who donated everything from steak dinners for the town's firefighters to a $22 million endowed scholarship fund for the town's youth; or Dave Hatch, who teaches Native American kids not only about the importance of the salmon to their cultures but about the importance of science education, too. It's filled, in short, with ordinary people who have done extraordinary things for our state.

These visionary civic leaders, nonprofit directors, donors, and volunteers are out there right now, working to preserve and improve others' lives. They are key contributors to everything that we know and admire about Oregon today, and they are also fascinating, driven individuals whose personalities and projects make for riveting stories. The everyday heroes whose stories are recounted in this book—and those countless others (of whom you may be one) whose stories also deserve to be told—are for me a constant source of inspiration. They are to my co-author, Kristin Anderson, too: her perspective has helped structure this book into a wide-ranging survey, and I am grateful to her for her intelligence, her passion, and for the breadth and depth of her insights. We hope that these organizations and individuals will inspire you as they have us. Their stories are rallying cries, calls-to-arms for wider civic engagement across our state, and reminders of how much of a difference an individual can make.

STATE OF GIVING: OVERVIEW, INTENTS, AND PURPOSE

Our principal arguments in this book are straightforward. First, we suggest that donors, volunteers, and nonprofits have contributed and are contributing invaluably to many aspects of our lives and deserve recognition for their impact. Second, we argue that all Oregonians have the capacity to do likewise: if you have passion for a cause or love for your community, then you have what it takes to be a philanthropist.

Our methods and aims in this book are similarly accessible: we highlight and summarize several key challenges facing Oregon; we narrate how philanthropists, volunteers, and nonprofits have worked together to help redress these problems and improve our communities; and we call for even wider civic participation in the future. In titling the book *State of Giving*, we make the argument that, although there is something exceptional that brings Oregonians together for the common good, Oregon could afford to be even more exceptional: there are a great many needs as yet unmet. *State of Giving* is also, then, a state-of-the-union—a survey of present accomplishments and a declaration of future needs. Our emphasis is very much on the present and recent past, and our target audience is broad: it should appeal to anyone interested in Oregon's culture and communities.

In the Introduction, we share a broad overview of Oregon philanthropy and volunteerism since about 1980 and discuss our state's current rates and trends of giving. In subsequent chapters, we explore those problems whose urgent resolution we feel to be essential to Oregon's survival and prosperity: the urban-rural divide, education inequity, hunger and homelessness, environmental degradation, minority communities' marginalization and disempowerment, and the decline of arts, cultural, and heritage funding. The final chapter zooms out to discuss challenges and opportunities for Oregon philanthropy, nonprofits, and volunteerism more broadly, including building community-wide efforts, engaging the next generation of leaders, and learning from new models of giving. It is this chapter that consolidates the book's message: Oregon's prosperity is in every Oregonian's hands.

In each chapter, our goal is not to survey the full breadth of efforts against these challenges, but to profile a diverse range of people and nonprofits working to surmount them, and to use their successes as examples to inspire us all in our own future work. Volunteerism and other forms of civic engagement weigh equally with monetary philanthropy in this book: these chapters show multiple ways to make a difference within your community.

Photo by Kristin Anderson.

We acknowledge, too, the philanthropic sacrifice that nonprofit workers make: most are underpaid, overworked, and endure these conditions because they are devoted to the cause. For nonprofit professionals, we hope that this book is not only validating but useful: it will give you greater insight into why and how people donate and volunteer, as well as highlight some outstanding nonprofit organizations' strategies and impact.

We should clarify, however, that *State of Giving* is not intended to be an objective history or technical analysis, although there are elements of both in subsequent chapters. There are also some philanthropic/nonprofit categories that we decided were best covered elsewhere: for example, philanthropy to religious organizations or to universities isn't discussed extensively in *State of Giving* (although both religious organizations and universities should be congratulated for their role in creating a national culture of philanthropy). Nor, save in a few instances, do we profile corporate philanthropy. Nonprofits are increasingly relying on foundations and individuals for their funding, and our aim in part is to highlight acts of giving and causes that might otherwise remain under the radar. Finally, it is simply not possible for us to be as exhaustive as we would like in our profiles of nonprofits, volunteers, and donors—this is just a representative sampling. There are many others (including some of Oregon's biggest names) who deserve acclaim and go unmentioned here. Your name very likely deserves to be included: please forgive us if it's not.

This book aims to show a variety of pathways into philanthropy—into the giving of time, talent, or money. Someone may have helped pay for a new community center, but someone else may have volunteered to help paint or staff it. Some people, like Mary Farrell of Medford's Maslow Project, find something they care about and start a new nonprofit, often with their own savings. Some, like Maslow donor Roger Stokes, contribute major gifts to an institution or cause. Some give through private or community foundations, like OCF. Others donate small amounts through Kickstarter campaigns or participate in fundraising runs or donate their ancient car to Oregon Public Broadcasting or their clothes to St. Vincent de Paul. Many register their weddings with charities instead of department stores or give time or money to local advocacy organizations or to politicians who are advancing something they believe in. Still others volunteer their time or expertise to individuals in need—an elderly family member, a person needing pro bono legal assistance—or to schools, nonprofits, and other organizations across the state. In many cases, people donate to their communities through estate gifts and will never see the good work funded through their generosity.

Accordingly, a main argument of this book is that anyone can be a philanthropist—you don't have to be Bill Gates or Phil Knight. Moreover, the areas in which you can have a positive impact on your community are myriad and eclectic: philanthropy and volunteerism aren't only about fulfilling urgent needs but are also about sustaining the quieter, qualitative things—free concerts, cultural exchanges, hiking trails, scenic viewpoints—that make life worth living.

GIVING BACK:
SHARED REWARDS, STRONGER COMMUNITIES

All of the people and organizations discussed in this book believe that a more unified, equal, and resilient Oregon is not only desirable but necessary and possible, and all of them have worked to make it so. These people are not wholly selfless: indeed, many of these donors, nonprofit workers, and volunteers speak of the significant personal rewards of giving back. If there is one recurring theme in these people's stories, it is that philanthropy is mutually beneficial. Whether you were born in Oregon or moved here, giving back to the community draws you closer to it, making it more of a spiritual and emotional home. It adds value to your own joys, satisfaction to your own work, and a sense of purpose that otherwise may not be so clearly understood. Time after time, people have told us that they donate or volunteer because they want to give something back to the community that has given so much to them. Ultimately, philanthropy isn't so much a material act as a mindset, a way of life: an obvious, reflexive response to living with and among others.

No matter who you are, we hope that you will find inspiration within these stories to look around you, to see what could be better, and to start— with your time, your money, your ideas, or all three—to make it so. Oregon is a passion-inspiring place, a "remarkable enclave and blessed corner of this planet," as Jonathan Nicholas has remarked, but it has extensive and urgent troubles, too, and we cannot sit back expecting others to fix them for us.

Everyone has something to offer, be it passion or hours or dollars or elbow grease. After all, we are all working toward the same goal: a better Oregon.

Art patron and philanthropist Arlene Schnitzer once said, "We've got a great thing going here—we just can't let our guard down. We have to keep believing that we have the most wonderful state in the country and keep working toward making it so." So find what you care about, figure out what you can give, and start giving. Oregon—all of us—will be the richer for it.

GREG CHAILLÉ

Columbia River Gorge. Photo by Kristin Anderson.

Introduction
Philanthropic Oregon: An Overview

"We have learned that vision and imagination are priceless qualities. . . . Have we not learned to plunge a little, to take a chance or two, to bank on the future?"
—Mary Frances Isom, Oregon librarian, community leader, and philanthropist, 1920

"Ever since the days of the pioneer-era barn raises, philanthropy and neighbor-helping-neighbor have been proud parts of Oregon's history."
—Kerry Tymchuk, Director of the Oregon Historical Society, 2013

It has been said that Oregon philanthropists are a retiring sort, the kind of people who drive Chevrolets rather than Cadillacs and who donate at similarly modest levels. But you don't have to look far into Oregon's past to learn that our anemic philanthropic reputation isn't deserved. Oregon's history is rife with individuals whose contributions to our state may not have been widely recorded but were nevertheless invaluable: church members who fed impoverished neighbors, landowners who donated acreage for public parks, volunteers who helped with harvests, charitable professionals who used their expertise for pro bono work, the unnamed African American widow who in 1917 donated $250 of the money she earned as a cleaner to Salem Hospital. Other contributors are better documented, such as the Pendleton Foundation Trust, the state's second community fund,[1] which was established in 1928 just in time to help ease townspeople's Depression-era distress; Dr. Bernard Daly of Lakeview, who started a scholarship fund in 1922 that has helped put more than two thousand local students through college; or Mary Frances Isom, whose time and passion led to the creation of the magnificent central library in downtown Portland and to the reform of libraries throughout the state.

And many of us are familiar with Oregon's bigger philanthropic names, such as Asahel Bush of Salem; the Astors of Astoria; Abigail Scott Duniway, whose effort and activism helped win women suffrage in 1912; and of course Simon Benson of Portland, who helped develop the Columbia River Highway

and installed Portland's cheerful bronze "bubblers." These members of the philanthropic old guard were often part of a generation of transplanted industrial and civic leaders who began to measure Oregon's communities by East Coast standards and to realize that charitable investments and activism would help make Oregon flourish, a vision that more recent generations of volunteers, small donors, and well-known philanthropists—Bill and Patricia Wessinger, Ken Ford and Hallie Brown Ford, Phil and Penny Knight, Ken and Joan Austin, Thomas Autzen, Glenn Jackson, and countless others—have sustained enthusiastically. The introduction tells the story of some of Oregon's philanthropic greats, those who paved the way for the donors (both large and small), nonprofits, and volunteers that populate the rest of *State of Giving*.

Simon Benson, alongside one of his famous "bubblers." Courtesy the Oregon Historical Society.

A PHILANTHROPIC RENAISSANCE

Even though Oregon has a lengthy and eminent philanthropic lineage, recent decades have produced a great philanthropic flourishing, made all the more magnificent because it has been sustained throughout several economic downturns. The late 1970s and early 1980s were a period of recession, high interest rates, high unemployment, and "stagflation," and the recession hit Oregon especially hard, putting the timber industry into a tailspin. On top of this came severe cuts to federal social programs, and in 1976, the federal government eliminated charitable deductions for non-itemized tax returns, a major blow for philanthropy and the nonprofits that relied upon it. However, these economic clouds had a silver lining. Because charities had to scramble harder to attract donors, the nation's nonprofits became more adaptable, developing personalized strategies for fundraising that helped mitigate an otherwise adverse economic climate and that prepared them well for years to come.

This period also saw the rising influence of what Tom Brokaw has called the "greatest generation." Many of these individuals had endured the Depression and World War II and had benefited from public welfare and education initiatives that helped make them the wealthiest and best-educated generation in the nation's history. As a result, they had a strong desire to give back to the society that had given them a leg up, and their high rates of charitable giving advanced philanthropy even as America's tax law and economy disincentivized such acts. In Oregon, this philanthropic upwelling emerged at all levels of giving and was augmented by the legacy of community-minded and optimistic political leaders like Senator Mark Hatfield and Governor Tom McCall. Regardless of its causes, however, Oregon's last three or more decades have seen an incredible amount of charitable giving everywhere from Ashland to Zumwalt.

Portland's Arlene Schnitzer Concert Hall (formerly the Paramount Theater). Photo by Kristin Anderson.

Oregon's renaissance arguably began with two grand philanthropic acts, both in the early 1980s. One was Harold and Arlene Schnitzer's gift of $1 million to help transform the dilapidated Paramount Theater into a concert hall for the new Portland Center for the Performing Arts complex. It was a game-changing gift, one of the larger philanthropic pledges in Oregon history and one of the most catalytic, chiefly because the deal's broker, Bob Scanlan, convinced the Schnitzers to put their name on the building in order to revitalize a stalled capital campaign. Down the Willamette Valley in Eugene, Nils and Jewel Hult's contribution of $3 million for the construction of the Hult Center for the Performing Arts had a similarly catalyzing effect.

These were breakthrough moments. First, they were large donations, profound contributions to the improvement of public life in Oregon. As Arlene Schnitzer herself noted, such donations "raised expectations and set a new standard." They were also *acknowledged* donations. As anyone who has heard of Carnegie Hall, the Guggenheim Museums, or the Smithsonian knows, the tradition of honoring philanthropists with named buildings is well established, dating back beyond Renaissance patronage to classical times and beyond. But despite many existing examples in Oregon (Autzen Stadium, for one), at that particular moment in Oregon's history, the idea of naming public buildings after living donors sparked much discussion about the role and prominence of philanthropy. Some saw such attributions as distasteful—too East Coast, not Oregonian enough.

However difficult these controversies proved for the Schnitzers and the Hults (in both cases, public debate grew ugly very quickly and proved upsetting to both families), the long-term result of this media coverage was positive. The donations from the Schnitzers and the Hults meant that philanthropy was being talked about, that visionary leaders were being celebrated for their generosity, and that the floodgates had been opened for new waves of philanthropic contributions inspired by these vanguard donors. The Oregon Community Foundation's growth reflected that optimism. In 1987, OCF had an endowment of $44 million; today, it is over $1.6 billion and growing. Other private and community foundations have celebrated similar growth, a result of donations both large and small.

AN OREGON CORNERSTONE: PHILANTHROPY FROM THE FORESTS

There are many facets of Oregon philanthropy and volunteering that deserve recognition, but any overview of the subject should begin with timber: the story of Oregon's giving tradition is rooted first and foremost in its forest products. Many of Oregon's greatest donors earned their fortunes in the woods and mills. For example, the Collins Foundation began at a southern Oregon mill, and Bill Swindells, who founded the Oregon Community Foundation in 1974, was a timber man as well. The Hult family started in forest products and diversified into real estate; the Hayes family have found their livelihoods and passions in timber and silviculture; and Stuart Shelk, founder of Ochoco Lumber, his wife Pauline, and their family have been huge contributors in eastern Oregon.

Many of these big donors had very humble beginnings, which perhaps contributed to their philanthropic natures. For example, during the Depres-

sion, Ken Ford started collecting scrap lumber for firewood and later became one of Oregon's "gyppo" loggers, the owner of a small, hand-to-mouth operation. His talent and ambition soon propelled him on to bigger things: he invested in timberlands that were being sold at rock-bottom prices, and he eventually created Roseburg Forest Products, today one of the five largest companies in Oregon. He and his wife, Hallie Brown Ford, created a foundation in 1957 to benefit Oregon's timber communities. This grew to become the Ford Family Foundation, officially founded in 1996, which is particularly known for its scholarship program for students who are often the first generation in their families to attend college. They receive mentoring in addition to their tuition grants, and twice a year, all Ford scholars gather for a

Ken Ford. Courtesy the Oregon Community Foundation.

leadership development program, so that they in turn can give back to their communities. The Ford Family Foundation also created the Ford Leadership

Institute, which recruits delegates mostly from communities of fewer than five thousand people.

Another superb example of timber-driven philanthropy is L. L. "Stub" Stewart, the CEO of Bohemia Lumber. He was about as traditional a lumberjack as you could find, at least in appearance. Although somewhat diminutive in stature (hence the nickname), Stub was hardworking, straightforward, and determinedly informal. He was also an OSU graduate who realized the need to support a broad range of nonprofits in his community in order to strengthen it. A devout believer in public service, Stub served in the state legislature and spent thirty years on the State Parks and Recreation committee, advocating tirelessly for the expansion and preservation of state parkland and becoming a founding father of the Beach Bill to preserve public access to Oregon's coastline. When not working as a public servant, Stub was socializing, working hard to bring people together and to forge the kind of private/public friendships that help grease the cogs of both social progress and commercial development. (In Stub's hands, these were usually overlapping goals.)

Stub Stewart. Courtesy the Oregon Parks and Recreation Department.

Stub was famous for his annual steelhead fishing trips on the Rogue River. No one stayed in the same boat for the full trip: one of Stub's goals was for everyone to shuffle from raft to raft getting to know each other. A few participants suspected that the trips were not solely for fun and games—if you were invited, Stub probably wanted to lobby you on some issue—but he also seemed to have a more altruistic goal. He would carefully pick who came so that the most diverse interests and concerns were represented, and so that, over evenings of storytelling, pinochle, and plenty of whiskey, diverse perspectives could find alignment in that intimate, edgy setting. His favorite campfire story told of his ancestors, who had been shipwrecked on the Oregon coast and hacked their way through thick forests, dining on shoe leather, until they eventually reached Cottage Grove. However mythologized the tale, Stub told it brilliantly, and the pioneering follies of the Stewart clan seemed appropriate to the community forging that occurred on his river trips.

Most of Stub's efforts were more visible, however: little deeds—like paying for a flagpole to be erected on Eugene's Skinner Butte—and larger ones, like purchasing a prominent and ugly railroad yard in downtown Cottage Grove, cleaning up its industrial waste, and transforming it into a fourteen-acre heritage park for the town. What was most remarkable about Stub was that, like many of Oregon's timber barons, there was a well-rounded man and active civic leader hidden behind rugged features and open-collared shirts. An industrious lumberman, you would expect that he wouldn't have much time for community, and yet he devoted his spare time almost entirely to serving it and could confidently spar and barter with US senators and governors. When Stub died, he left money to organizations across many regions and sectors, as well as leaving a public legacy so substantial that a new state park was created in his honor, featuring a network of mountain bike trails that he never would have used but that he certainly would have appreciated.

As is perhaps apparent, the history of Oregon's forest products industry, like the established history of Oregon's business culture more broadly, is largely a masculine one. Donna Woolley represents a rare exception. Another classic Oregon story of entrepreneurship, intrepidity, and civic spirit, Donna grew up in a family of small-scale turkey farmers in Drain. Her mother forbade her from wearing trousers, so even when she was feeding the birds or controlling squirrels with a .22 rifle (her father paid her five cents a skin), she looked like a Hollywood starlet.[2] (It may have been her early years shooting vermin that led her, in later years, to become one of the top ten trapshooters in the United States.)

Donna Woolley. Courtesy Dolly Woolley.

In 1953, she married Harold Woolley, a timber man. When he died in a tractor accident in 1970, she was forced to decide whether to continue his business while also raising their three children. She accepted the challenge, and despite being one of the only women in a male-dominated sector, she expanded Woolley Logging Company so that, at its peak, it operated three mills and employed five hundred workers. That placed her in a position to give back. She donated money and time to the University of Oregon; she served on Umpqua Community College's board and donated land for its Harold Woolley Center; she gave copious time and money to the World Forestry Center in Portland; and she donated to many other causes besides. Baseball was a particular passion of hers. The Woolley Logging Company sponsored the Drain Black Sox, who became Oregon's first and only National Baseball Congress champions, and she was also a big supporter of the Springfield team, known as the "Woolley Bullies." In 1980, the University of Oregon gave her their Pioneer Award; in 2000, Eugene appointed her their First Citizen; and in 2001, she was given the Howard Vollum Award for philanthropy. Meanwhile, Donna travelled internationally with a group from the World Forestry Center, ostensibly to investigate the world's forests but really to seek a bit of adventure. (Which they found: they were caught on the Volga River during the Soviet coup against Gorbachev in 1991.) With typical bluntness, she attributed her philanthropy not to her business successes but to her own personal code of ethics. In a column for the *Eugene Register-Guard* that was later cited in her obituary,[3] she summarized her ideology, as humble as it is gung-ho: "Once you know where your passion lies, take advantage of the many ways to give—hands-on volunteer work, charitable donations and support of scholarship funds, for instance. . . . Those involved in philanthropic giving—including individuals, families, organizations and businesses—can't imagine life without it."

Donna Woolley's *compulsion* to give back, her assertion that it would be difficult to envision a world in which she wasn't contributing hours or funds, is a common theme among Oregon's donors and volunteers. However, for some people, philanthropy and volunteerism become an essential part of their lives only through learned practice. Hampton Lumber's John and Carol Hampton, whose patronage of Oregon's arts and heritage organizations has had a tremendous and lasting effect, represent opposite pathways into giving. Their son Jamey Hampton says that his mother Carol was a painter herself and had always supported the arts, but it took a nudge to get John to give as a matter of habit. As Jamey tells it: "Peter Koehler, who was on the board of the Portland Opera, invited my dad along to a performance and asked him to donate some money. I don't think my dad had ever given much money to anything before: it's not that he wasn't generous, but I don't think it had ever occurred to him that he was now in position to give. He offered Peter $50, and that was the beginning. The amount he contributed only went up from there, and he always used to jokingly blame Peter for his new habit."

John soon considered opera to be the perfect art form and became one of Portland Opera's biggest supporters. Carol, meanwhile, remained close to the visual arts, continuing as a patron to up-and-coming artists and even purchasing a $1 million Robert Rauschenberg mixed-media work to give to the Portland Art Museum, a contribution that also supported the local nonprofit Blue Sky Gallery from which she had purchased it. They were both dedicated volunteers, too, with Carol working quietly behind the scenes and John—always flamboyant—advocating exuberantly for his causes, once even appearing at a fundraising event in full doublet and hose to perform a

John and Carol Hampton. Portland, 1997. Courtesy Hampton Family.

duet with a *real* opera singer. While his singing was not, perhaps, as polished or as tuneful as his partner's, it was enthusiastic and hilarious . . . and consequently was a charmingly effective fundraising tool.

Another forest products philanthropist who followed an unusual pathway into giving was William Swindells, the founder of the Oregon Community Foundation. Swindells had married into the Gerlinger family, who owned the

Willamette Valley Lumber Company (which later became Willamette Industries). Swindells joined the family business and became its leader after his wife Irene's father, George Gerlinger, died in 1948. At its peak in the 1990s, Willamette Industries owned or managed 1.7 million acres of forestland and operated more than 100 wood products facilities in 23 states and in Ireland, France, and Mexico.

Bill Swindells cared deeply about both his community of Dallas, Oregon, and his region. He had always been philanthropic, giving to local causes, but it took a nudge from his sister-in-law, Jean Gerlinger Doyle, to take it to the next level. She was on the board of the San Francisco Foundation and told Bill that Oregon ought to have a community foundation as well. In 1973, he took $63,000 from his own private foundation and donated it as the first fund in the new Oregon Community Foundation. A community foundation operates under the promise that when donors pool their money together under shared management, they make their money stretch further, give more knowledgeably, and consequently have greater impact while retaining their individual giving priorities. Bill threw himself into OCF with all of the impatience, forcefulness, and diligence he normally reserved for the boardroom. There were no secrets to fundraising, he often said: all it took was good hard work. The early discipline and energy provided by Bill (along with capable and charismatic leadership by Ned Look, OCF's first president) caused the community foundation to grow quickly, and by example, Swindells helped trigger Oregon's philanthropic rejuvenation.

Bill Swindells, Sr. Courtesy the Oregon Community Foundation.

Ultimately, whether through Ken Ford's quiet planning, Donna Woolley's constancy and community ethics, or John Hampton's chutzpah, timber philanthropy has helped lay the cornerstones for many of the key organizations and initiatives upon which Oregon and Oregonians have come to rely. A dominant force in Oregon's economy for over a century, timber money—and the volunteer commitments of those for whom timber provided a strong livelihood—had, and continues to have, a tremendous impact on our state's social growth.

Mt. Hood National Forest. Photo by Kristin Anderson.

TECH TITANS, PROPERTY DEVELOPERS,
AND OTHER PHILANTHROPIC TRENDSETTERS

However, as most Oregonians know, timber is a boom-and-bust industry, and while forest products money helped Oregon acquire many of the cultural and social treasures we now consider purely "Oregonian," new sources of community giving have emerged to help compensate for slowdowns in the timber economy.

Mike and Sue Hollern of Bend are representatives of a later generation of timber folk, a generation that has seen timber decline and that has helped Oregon's economy diversify and its communities find new sources of income and giving. After working for the vice president of finance at his alma mater, Stanford University, Mike Hollern was invited in 1965 to join his mother's family's company, the Minnesota-based Brooks-Scanlon, whose mill in Bend needed a manager.

At the time, the company owned nearly 300,000 acres of timberland in central Oregon, and Sue, Mike, and their kids quickly discovered a deep appreciation for its communities and countryside. Then, many mills were still humming, although all the sawmills in nearby Sisters had already closed.[4] There was still a great optimism about Oregon's economy and its future, an optimism that translated into a high level of community giving. In Bend, under Mike Hollern's leadership, Brooks-Scanlon became a key donor to central Oregon, and he and Sue also donated very generously from their own pockets. Then, as work at the mills began to slow due both to environmental concerns and wider economic trends, the need to broaden Oregon's financial foundation became increasingly apparent. Revenue sources would need to diversify, and sources of charitable giving would have to as well.

Under Mike's leadership, Brooks-Scanlon formed Brooks Resources, a property development and real estate subsidiary responsible for the creation of Black Butte Ranch and other well-known resorts and developments, which helped bring tourist dollars to an area now devoid of sawmills. These days, four decades after the Hollerns' arrival in Oregon, they have become pillars not just of central Oregon's new economy but of its communities. Under Mike's leadership, Brooks Resources has pledged to give at least 3 percent of its pre-tax income to charities including the Bend Foundation, which Hollern founded. Moreover, the company is also instilling this philanthropic passion in its employees: at Mike's direction, Brooks Resources will match employees' charitable contributions up to $1,000 per employee per annum, and employees can also earn donations for their chosen nonprofits by cycling or walking to work.

Sue and Mike Hollern. Courtesy the Hollerns.

Loren Irving, a colleague and longtime friend of Mike's, describes Hollern as having "a gentle manner, a huge heart, and an incredible vision and integrity." Irving recalls Hollern welcoming him into the company in 1969 with the words, "Welcome aboard. One thing I want you to keep in mind is that as a member of our team, you will be expected to choose an organization in the community and volunteer. The company will be behind you whoever you decide to support in order to make this community a better place to live." It is, Irving notes, "an incredible corporate attitude, and it started a lifetime of community involvement for me."

Brooks Resources' corporate charity is mirrored in the personal donations of Mike and Sue Hollern, who together have helped build up central Oregon's cultural assets—education, theater, music, the High Desert Museum, the Art in Public Places initiative—and also its social service nonprofits, helping the hungry, homeless, and jobless find fresh starts. Their goal, Hollern says, is to create a resilient economy by making central Oregon a more well-rounded and diverse place. They want to lure a creative class to Bend to ensure the area's survival in the downturns of industry and forestry. And their efforts have been effective: "I think Bend has about six hundred nonprofits now," Loren Irving notes, "and there would be very few not touched in a very positive way by Mike and Sue Hollern." When asked what motivates him to do all of this, Mike Hollern's answer is simple: "I love Bend, I love the community."[5]

Bend's struggles to move from timber into more resilient industries mirror the struggles of much of the rest of Oregon. Some regions are already diversified, some are becoming more so, and many are still fighting to find a place in a post-timber economy. New industries, some lured into the state through low corporate tax rates and amenable community agreements, have brought with them a rejuvenated real estate and property development market. From these sources, a philanthropic optimism that was once rooted in timber money has spread out new tendrils.

Nike and Columbia Sportswear both grew enormously during the last three decades, as did philanthropic giving from the Bowerman and Knight families (Nike's co-founders), and from Gert Boyle and her son Tim, who together rescued Columbia Sportswear from bankruptcy after the death of Gert's husband, Neal. Intel brought a wave of up-and-coming young professionals into the Portland area and with it a modest swell in charitable donations. And Doug Strain, who founded Electro-Scientific Industries (ESI), Keith Thompson of Intel (who deserves credit for bringing Intel here in the first place), Scott Gibson (from Intel and later Sequent computers), Norm Winningstad from Tektronix, and many others from the "Silicon Forest" have contributed invaluably to Oregon's philanthropic needs.

Howard Vollum and M. J. "Jack" Murdock, co-founders of Tektronix, and Vollum's wife, Jean, were some of Oregon's biggest givers, although they took very different paths in their philanthropy. Jack Murdock, who died in 1971 in a plane crash on the Columbia, created the M. J. Murdock Charitable Trust, now valued at over $800 million, which has been a funding mainstay for nonprofits in the Pacific Northwest over the years. Howard Vollum, on the other hand, didn't create a permanent fund but gave extensively during his lifetime and bequeathed large sums to a dozen or so nonprofits to spend at their discretion. His wife Jean continued his philanthropic legacy until her own death, funding the Oregon Symphony and giving over $2.5 million to Ecotrust, which she had helped found years earlier.

Of course, Oregon's charitable contributions are not merely the result of wealth emerging out of its timber, technology, and sportswear industries, as dominant as these sectors may seem. For example, the rise of Native American tribal foundations and funds has also significantly enriched Oregon's philanthropic landscape. Oregon's nine recognized tribes all have giving programs that benefit both tribal and non-tribal communities. Six of the nine tribes in Oregon have formally organized foundations with boards, grant priorities, and application procedures: the Spirit Mountain Community Fund, the Siletz Tribal Charitable Fund, the Three Rivers Foundation, the Cow Creek Umpqua Indian Foundation, the Coquille Tribal Community Fund, and the Wild Horse Foundation. Combined, the six tribal foundations have given over $100 million in grants and scholarships since 1997, the year the first foundation (Spirit Mountain) was formed.

Individuals from other business sectors have also helped lead the way. Duncan Campbell, for instance, began as an accountant for Arthur Andersen and later founded a timber investment firm, The Campbell Group. Having endured an abusive and solitary childhood—his parents were negligent and alcoholic—Campbell vowed that if ever he became wealthy, he would use his money to aid abused, impoverished, and neglected children. In 1993, he turned over the running of his investment firm and created Friends of the Children. His organization matches committed mentors with five- and six-year-old kids with the goal of giving them long-term stable guidance through high school and beyond. "My parents never helped me with homework, never came to any games. . . . I was always alone," Duncan recounted in an interview with the nonprofit advocates Encore.org.[6] Now, Friends of the Children employs eighty-two mentors who help over seven hundred children in Portland, Klamath Falls, Seattle, San Francisco, Cincinnati, Boston, and New York. "We select the children who have accumulated the most heartache and trouble in their young years," Campbell explains. "Our vision is that this will be how our community, our society, will care about children."[7]

Another visionary philanthropist, Eugene patron Carolyn Chambers was a media and construction powerhouse at a time when women were seldom power players in either industry. At twenty-five years old, Carolyn borrowed $100,000 from her father, a Chevrolet dealer, to launch Liberty Communications, which in turn started KEZI-TV, a station that flourished under her leadership for fifty years. After her husband Richard died in 1986, she also took over his construction business, an industry that also boasts few women. She was supremely generous, donating to the University of Oregon, the Hult Center for Performing Arts, the Sacred Heart Medical Center at RiverBend, and to their own family foundation, which has donated millions to local nonprofits.

Carolyn Silva Chambers. Courtesy the Chambers Family Foundation.

Ever the pragmatist, Carolyn brought her business acumen to her giving: she wanted to see concrete, detailed, realistic proposals, and she was prolific in offering sound guidance to help a nonprofit or university develop its programs. She did nothing half-heartedly: once she became involved with a project, she supported it with a great deal of time and money, including lobbying her influential friends to support projects alongside her. Through her philanthropy and her powerful advocacy, Carolyn became a potent example of what was possible. In Chambers' obituary, Jeanne Staton, president of a Eugene demolition firm, noted, "[s]he was very innovative and ahead of her time. And she blazed the way for other women. It's extremely important to have role models like that. Even though women are breaking that glass ceiling, it's still darned hard to be respected. Someone like Carolyn . . . makes young women think 'She did it, maybe I can, too.' And she [taught that] it's very important to give back to the community."[8]

With the exception of a couple of major economic downturns, real estate has been booming since the eighties across areas of Oregon, in part thanks to growth in high-tech and retail industries, and in part because Oregon has become a prime tourist destination and a desirable place to relocate or buy a second home. While much of rural Oregon still struggled in the wake of mill closures and other declines in natural resources industries, there were pockets of property development all over the state, which in turn led to new waves of philanthropy. The Hollerns of Bend, the Schneiders of Ashland, Mike Keiser in Bandon (the developer of Bandon Dunes Golf Resort and a prominent south coast philanthropist), and many others have left a lasting legacy in Oregon's communities, building their fortunes in real estate only to return their profits to the communities that helped them thrive.

Joe Weston. Courtesy the Oregon Community Foundation.

One of Oregon's most prominent property developers, Joe Weston, is a sterling example of this philanthropic trend. Joe is an opinionated, genial man fond of eye-catching ties—he favors big wide ties that provide a full view of their subject matter, always on one of two themes: Americana (bald eagles, flags, and such) or varieties and patterns of roses, thus staking out his identity as both a patriot and a Portlander. Joe Weston's is the archetypal rags-to-riches story. In high school, he worked as a soda jerk. Noticing that his boss was doing very well as a rental landlord, he began to invest modestly in property, in due course expanding his holdings and diversifying his interests. Now in his mid-seventies, Weston has a vast and varied portfolio of properties and has accumulated tremendous wealth. He has used some of these assets to start a $100 million charitable foundation with OCF, and he intends to bequeath his huge remaining fortune to his foundation in support of Oregon's communities. This largesse is inspired by his Catholicism and the tradition of giving he learned during his years at Portland's Central Catholic High School. He uses his foundation to provide grants to some of his favorite causes, including education and services for senior citizens and the working poor. Between 2010 and 2014, his foundation distributed almost $15 million dollars to charities as diverse as OMSI, Meals-on-Wheels, the Tillamook YMCA, Oregon Public Broadcasting, the Jewish Family and Child Service Center,

the Cascade AIDS Project, and the ALS Association of Oregon and Southwest Washington, as well as to many different Catholic schools and groups.
Despite having one of the largest foundations in Oregon and an outsized
personality, Weston's approach to philanthropy is humble:

> Charitable giving has always been a part of my life. I was born
> into a poor family, but even though they didn't have money, my
> parents shared what they had, giving their food and time to the
> community. There were a lot of people that influenced me to
> give—for example, our local pharmacist offered discounts on
> prescriptions to people who couldn't afford them. I was fortunate
> that I was able to make a lot of money. Because of the values I
> learned growing up, I wanted to give back to the poor and needy.

Although hard-edged in business, Weston clearly has a soft side, as
evidenced through his philanthropy, his ties, and also through his practice of
painting one of his favorite motifs—roses—onto the sides of his properties.
These roses, named after those to whom he is close or appreciates, are a touch-
ing honor for all those who have been celebrated in such a beautiful way.

Two of Portland's best-known philanthropists, Arlene and Harold
Schnitzer, also emerged from real estate and property development. Much
of their wealth, energy, and time has been dedicated to supporting diverse
organizations throughout their community. "Both Harold and I learned philanthropy from our families," says Arlene, and through their
faith: "charity is inherent in Judaism, it's to do with taking
care of community," she adds. Their intrinsic empathy has
long been evident: after Harold's death in 2011, he was
remembered by US Senator Ron Wyden as "one of those
really rare individuals you'd call a vintage Oregonian . . .
who almost always says when you talk to him, 'What can I
do to help?'"[9]

Arlene and Harold Schnitzer.
Courtesy the Schnitzer Family.

Arlene has continued their family tradition of giving
back to a broad range of philanthropic causes, ranging from
the Oregon Zoo to the founding of a Judaic Studies program
at Portland State University. However, Arlene's main passion
is also the one for which the couple is most famous: arts
funding. She has been supporting the arts since the 1960s,
when she owned one of Portland's first major galleries and
nurtured the careers of many now well-known Northwest artists. Beyond the
renovated concert hall that bears Arlene's name, the Schnitzers have donated
to the Portland Opera, to the Oregon Ballet Theatre, and to countless other

Photo by Kristin Anderson.

organizations, and they also have contributed large sums and many important works of art from their own collections to the Portland Art Museum.

For Arlene and many others, this commitment to the arts is essential to our state's maturation and growth. "I think a community's major vitality comes from keeping its young people there so they don't have to rush off to the big cities," Arlene declares. "And the only way you can do that is by having professionalism abound in your city. If you have good music, good museums, good opera, good galleries, that's the way you keep young people in an area and keep a city vital. I want Portland to be a vital community, and a community can't be vital without the arts." Her philanthropic strategy is pitched accordingly: while the Schnitzers have certainly contributed to capital campaigns and programs, much of their giving is more regular, providing annual operating support to the organizations they value. "You have to have a community that's well fed both physically, intellectually, and spiritually," Arlene concludes. "And if you believe that, as I do, you have to put your money where your mouth is."

COMMUNITY NEED, COMMUNITY OBLIGATION:
GIVING BACK AT EVERY SCALE

It seems that many Oregonians agree with Arlene Schnitzer. Certainly, as these profiles have shown, Oregon has a strong collection of big-name, big-giving philanthropists. But while pockets of wealth and reinvestment are present across the state, it is important to remember that these decades of philanthropic renaissance were not limited just to booming areas and to wealthy people.

Dr. Walter Reynolds is a perfect example: the first African American graduate of University of Oregon's medical school (which would become OHSU), Dr. Reynolds ran a clinic in one of Portland's poorer neighborhoods.

For him, philanthropy was an everyday activity. Portland's most destitute sat alongside the middle class in his waiting room, and while 30 percent of his patients were on Medicare and Medicaid, many more had no insurance at all. In his eyes, however, all patients were equal, and those who couldn't pay weren't asked to. Dorothy Jamison, who worked for him in the 1980s, wonders how he managed: "I don't know how he kept operating. . . . I don't think he ever turned anyone down," she says with admiration. For Dr. Reynolds—"a soft-spoken man and a good listener," according to Dorothy—providing treatment democratically was his duty as a doctor and as a community member who had experienced his own share of hardship and prejudice: his high school guidance counselor told him not to bother trying pre-med, and his mentor, Dr. DeNorval Unthank, was for a long while Oregon's only black doctor.

Dr. Walter Reynolds. Courtesy Oregon Historical Society (Org Lot 563).

"We need basic medical care for everyone in this country," Dr. Reynolds declared in a 1996 interview. In the absence of that, he took it upon himself to help fill the gaps.[10] Passionate about the prejudice that still haunts our society, he spoke of the need to create a culture of service to others and to spread "cultural competency"—knowing yourself and your society in order to diagnose and mend those areas where weaknesses, injustices, and bigotry linger.[11] Oregon Health Sciences University (OHSU) honored him in 2009 by naming one of their two landmark aerial tram cars after him. Dr. Reynolds embodies a culture of service, and his barrier-shattering generosity and advocacy deserve universal recognition.

As Dr. Reynolds and many of those profiled in subsequent chapters demonstrate, Oregon has a proud philanthropic lineage across its socio-economic and professional spectrum, and since the 1980s, philanthropic giving even from within some of our most economically depressed communities has grown tremendously. We currently rank above both Washington and California in our average rates of giving—a fact which is a testament to Oregon's civic spirit at *all* levels of giving.[12] Rates of volunteerism have ascended in pace with rates of monetary giving. In 2012, Oregon ranked eleventh nationally in the percentage of citizens who volunteer (34.1 percent); volunteers contributed an astonishing $3.6 billion of service that year.[13] And the nonprofit sector—an essential pillar of our civic structure—has profited from this growth: today, we have over fifteen thousand 501(c)3 nonprofits in Oregon.[14] This is a good thing, says Jim White, the director of the Nonprofit Association of Oregon. "In order to have a vibrant civil society, you need those three legs of the stool: government, to provide safety and security and other key services; a robust and thoughtful private sector, to create jobs and drive economies; and an impartial and independent third sector, to make sure that our communities have the aspects of life, liberty, and happiness that make life worth living." Through contributions of time and money, this philanthropic renaissance and the nonprofit growth it has generated have improved Oregon immeasurably.

In the early 1980s, Oregon was nationally regarded as a nondescript western state known for its trees and its Trail. Outside the United States, most people assumed Oregon was somewhere in the Midwest. But philanthropy and nonprofits have helped change all of that, catalyzing a number of projects that have put Oregon firmly on the map: Oregon has become a *destination*. For example, the nonprofit Friends of the Columbia Gorge, spearheaded by John Yeon and led by Nancy Russell, campaigned to protect the Gorge, leading to its designation as a National Scenic Area in 1986. The organization also bought up miles of threatened nearby land. Around the same time

- the Oregon Shakespeare Festival added the Allen Pavilion to its Elizabethan stage and started the Portland company that would become Portland Center Stage;
- the Oregon Coast Aquarium opened in Newport;
- the Astoria Column was renovated after a multiyear community fundraising drive;
- Pioneer Courthouse Square opened in Portland, providing the city with a scenic central "living room";
- the Warm Springs tribes contributed $3.26 million in mostly small donations to the building of the Museum at Warm Springs;

Photo by Kristin Anderson.

- volunteer-driven clean-up organizations such as SOLVE worked hard to ensure our natural splendors were unsullied by human use;
- across the state, individuals and nonprofits were restoring historic buildings, founding new cultural and arts institutions, starting festivals, and revitalizing main streets.

All these privately supported initiatives (as well as thousands more) not only rejuvenated communities but also encouraged tourism, now one of Oregon's biggest income generators. Today, Oregon has a recognizable national and international identity.

Most of all, philanthropy has helped Oregonians to build a better *home*, helping us hone our own sense of culture, belonging, and place. For example, in response to Measure 5's education cuts and other governmental belt-tightening, community groups stepped forward with programs to fill the gaps: Start Making a Reader Today (SMART) was founded to help increase literacy across the state; and Boys and Girls Clubs, funded by local philanthropists and driven by volunteer power, opened in Albany, Coos Bay, Bend, and elsewhere. Other projects responded to different needs: low-income health centers and food pantries sprouted in high-risk areas; salmon habitat restoration programs began in watersheds across Oregon; the HHOPE (Harney Helping Organization for Personal Emergencies) domestic abuse help center opened in Burns; parks were landscaped, basic rights campaigns launched, scholarships founded, and soup kitchens, warming shelters, and animal welfare societies opened their doors.

These projects arose through an upwelling of various philanthropic streams. Nonprofits often speak of the three *T*s—time, talent, and treasure. Donations of time are critical for organizational development and strategy as well as for programming and operational support; donated talent—pro bono expertise—aids these areas as well. And treasure is, of course, also essential for many projects to become reality. This convergence of time, talent, and treasure is a great civic force: it is arguably responsible for most of what we value about our state today—for the works, institutions, and places that attract visitors to our state and that make our lives here more rewarding.

THE PHILANTHROPIC PRESENT

In recent years, there have been a few gifts that have raised the philanthropic bar to new heights, most notably Phil and Penny Knight's $500 million challenge grant to the OHSU Knight Cancer Research Center in October 2013, which OHSU will receive only if it can raise another $500 million in just two years—a remarkable challenge that, at time of publication, they look set to

Photo by Kristin Anderson.

meet. If the match is met, not only will our state receive a world-class cancer research center, but we also will have jumped up to a new level of sophistication in philanthropy, which in turn may translate into new domestic, national, and even international donors for Oregon. This means that whether or not you are involved with OHSU, we all have a stake in the outcome.

But with the exception of Knight's challenge grant and a handful of other landmark gifts, the huge wave of giving in the 1980s, 1990s, and early 2000s has ebbed. Philanthropy and volunteerism in Oregon today fall short of where they could and should be. The timber industry, which fueled some of Oregon's biggest philanthropic gifts, has contracted; years of recession have left their mark on our high tech and other industries; and Oregon now hosts only two Fortune 500 companies. But while Oregon's traditional sources of philanthropy may have diminished, there is cause to be optimistic about Oregon's future. New businesses and sources of funding and innovation are emerging constantly; much of Oregon is caught up in a wave of artisanal craftsmanship, creativity, and localism; and above all, Oregonians seem more committed than ever to seeing their communities, and their state, thrive.

Currently, our monetary giving is solidly middle-of-the-road. Although we may score higher than our neighboring states, we only rank seventeenth in the nation in percentage of income donated.[15] Similarly, Oregon's rank of eleventh in rates of volunteering may seem laudable until you consider that America is a country with modest volunteering rates compared with other developed nations.[16] Oregonians have benefited from the philanthropic investments of the past. It is our turn to give back to the state that has already given so much to us. We read in the papers and talk around coffees and beers about Oregonians' loyalty, eccentricity, pride, and love of place. It is time to act on what we feel: the economy is rebounding, there's optimism in the air again, and the mood seems ripe for another philanthropic renaissance.

The burden of need in our communities can be borne by multiple players, and the more of us that get involved, the smaller our burden and the stronger our community fabric will be. Retired scholarship administrator Sherrill Kirchhoff once described philanthropy as like a quilt: the more beautiful the quilt, the smaller and more multitudinous its patches. In looking at present levels of giving, our message is simple: our state is pretty good now, but if every Oregonian began engaging with and contributing to their communities, imagine how much more resilient our state could be. *State of Giving* celebrates the stories of people who believe this, and who are working against great odds, and against some of Oregon's most entrenched and enduring problems, to strengthen Oregon.

1
Bridging the Urban-Rural Divide

"We believe that there is value in the notion of 'One Oregon.' . . . In every corner of Oregon [people] care deeply about this place where they live. We believe their passion can be harnessed in service to a common good."
—Editors of *Toward One Oregon: Rural-Urban Interdependence and the Evolution of a State*

Some people know how to cut Oregon's expanses down to size; Bob Chandler was one of those people. Endowed with a strong frame and an unimpeachable sense of justice, Bob was a feared newspaper editor known for his straight-talk, no-nonsense approach to politics and community affairs. A resident of Bend and a longtime philanthropist and OCF board member, Bob could spend forty-five minutes in his Cessna 175 Skylark to traverse distances it would take five hours to drive, a useful option for someone whose interests spanned most of Oregon.

There is a saying in rural Oregon that it takes twice as long to travel from Portland to "you name the rural town" as it takes to go the opposite direction. Rural communities often feel that they have to make all the effort to reach out to urban leaders and to participate in statewide activities. Unfortunately, such sentiments are often based on real experience, and with the decline in timber and other rural industries, such experiences are commonplace: rural

Photo by Kristin Anderson.

communities are becoming increasingly isolated and marginalized in state-wide discussions, a situation detrimental both to these communities and to Oregon as a whole.

THE WIDENING GAP

While Oregon's large geographical expanses keep the state physically divided, economic and social bonds have always linked urban and rural communities. Rural areas provide food, energy, natural resources, ecological diversity, and recreation to urban areas. In turn, urban areas provide jobs, commercial and investment markets, entertainment, centralized governance and infrastructure, and specialized services, such as health care and higher education. It is an interdependent model, in which town and county rely upon each other.

In earlier economies, this interdependence was widely understood, if not always appreciated, by both town and country, and while there have always been inequities and friction, in general the model held. However, during the last few decades, as the decline of timber and other natural resource–based industries weakened rural economies, as agricultural markets have shifted from regional to global, and as urban areas have embraced post-industrial high-tech and creative sectors, the divide between urban and rural communities has grown.

Urban Oregon—which takes up 1 percent of the state's landmass but constitutes 69 percent of its population[1]—is the dominant voice in statewide politics, aided not only by geography but by its greater economic leverage and higher tax base. Rural concerns and needs are often marginalized or understated as a result. Add to this the widening political divide between urban progressivism and rural conservatism (a divide exacerbated by shifting demographics and changing economic circumstances), and Oregon's rural regions have seldom seemed more distant from its metropolitan areas.

These disparities are interrelated and therefore difficult to resolve independently. Nearly 14 percent of rural residents have not completed high
school, compared with 10 percent of urban residents. The flow of high school
students to the state's universities reflects this gap, with 22 percent of urban
students but only 16 percent of rural students attending public universities.
In recent decades rural Oregon's Latino population has grown to the point
where several rural counties now are over 25 percent Latino. Their presence
bolsters the rural workforce and often lowers the median age but also intro-
duces issues of integration, tolerance, and service provision to communities
with little infrastructure for managing such shifts. There is also a technology gap: in 2010, 70 percent of urban households had access to broadband
Internet, while only 57 percent of rural households did. Per capita personal
income differed dramatically between urban and rural Oregon: annual income in urban Oregon averaged $39,719, whereas in rural Oregon average
income was only $30,733—a difference of $8,986. An aging rural population
exacerbates this economic gap.[2] In 2010, the average age of a Multnomah
County resident was 35.7; the average was much higher across Oregon's rural
counties, with several counties averaging above 45; Wallowa County had an
average age of 50.[3] All of these disparities aggravate the widening political
gap between urban progressivism and rural conservatism. They also weaken
the state as a whole. Less rural tax income and lower levels of educational
attainment means less investment in infrastructure, education, and innovation statewide, and ultimately that means that fewer Oregonians will have the
knowledge, networks, and experience to advance Oregon's future economy,
cultural life, and civic structures.

Gretchen Pierce, a Eugene businessperson, philanthropist, and longtime advocate for a more unified Oregon, identifies a key problem that results
from the urban-rural divide: a perceived lack of shared interests. "There are
lots of reasons why Oregon is a tough state," she notes. "When we are talking
to representatives from the I-5 corridor, we're all talking the same lingo, but
there's a huge chunk of our population on the coast and in central and eastern
Oregon whose concerns also need to be addressed. We need to try to keep
these communities healthy. Instead, everybody in the valley is thinking only
about themselves, about their own community." In order to move toward a
more united Oregon, she believes, we must push people to identify shared
interests and ensure that everyone's concerns are being heard.

Efforts to unite urban and rural interests require creative solutions
and a great deal of adaptability, two traits that Oregon's nonprofits—supported by donors and volunteers—readily offer. Working in partnership
with, and often as a catalyst for, government and commercial investment,
nonprofit and philanthropic efforts can be uniquely broad in their strategies

and organization: some are grassroots and local, working from within rural communities to improve their situation and their connections; and some are urban or statewide, working from the center to direct resources where they're needed. Aided by its diversity, Oregon's philanthropic community helps to ensure that those who are underrepresented are given greater voice in statewide decision-making. In the words of one philanthropist, the goal is to "bring rural folks back to the table."

The urban-rural divide is arguably *the* preeminent challenge facing Oregon in the twenty-first century, largely because so many other social problems are exacerbated by it. The people profiled in this chapter range from rural middle-school teachers to cycling enthusiasts to steel tycoons to biologists. They are just a few of the civic leaders who are opening lines of communication, finding points of commonality, and investing time, thought, energy, and resources into bridging Oregon's great divide.

BOB CHANDLER: GIVING VOICE TO RURAL OREGON

One of rural Oregon's more vocal and determined champions was Bob Chandler, whose attentiveness to the growing disparities between Oregon's metropolitan and rural populations was matched by the vehemence with which he struggled to reunite them. In appearances, Bob was not your typical fighter: in his middle years long sideburns stretched toward his shirt collar, which was always too tight; in his later years suspenders, a bow tie, and large wire-rimmed bifocals gave him a jolly, avuncular air. But his mild-mannered appearance hid a great passion: he was one of Oregon's most fervent and outspoken unifiers, and urban-rural interdependence was something that Bob had pursued unswervingly since moving to Oregon in the 1950s.

Originally from northern California, after World War II Chandler began working as a reporter and then as a bureau manager for various papers and agencies. In 1953, he bought the *Bend Bulletin*, a local paper based in what was then a small central Oregon mill town. From there, he built up a local newspaper empire that stretched across the state from Baker City to Brookings, becoming what the *Seattle Times* called "one of the nation's most prominent small-town newspaper editors."[4] His editorials were his pride and joy, and he used them to advocate for moderation, governmental and corporate transparency, and most of all for regional solidarity and development. He was highly regarded nationally as well as locally, had friends and contacts across the state and the country, and was, among other honors, a Pulitzer Prize juror and a senior fellow of Columbia University's Freedom Forum Media Studies Center. Despite the accolades, he never called himself anything more than the editor of the *Bulletin*, an assertion that understates his impact on the state as a whole.

Although he lived in Bend, all of Oregon was his home. With his Cessna and his insider's knowledge of small-town Oregon, Bob whittled the state down to a manageable scale, travelling up and down the state, talking to locals, writing his editorials, and learning about problems common to many communities. Due to his connections in Portland and across the country, he had a strong sense of urban and national socioeconomic trends, and he was adept at linking these trends to rural concerns and encouraging mutually beneficial arrangements. Bob knew that what binds communities together is greater than what divides them, and he was, in many ways, an ambassador and vanguard of the "one Oregon" philosophy.

Bob's efforts to improve the bonds between rural and urban populations operated on several fronts. In his newspaper editorials, he zealously defended small-town interests. But he also was a mentor to many young journalists who moved from Bob's smaller-town papers to higher-circulation metropolitan papers. Not only did these young writers keep his papers' reporting fresh and relevant, but, once they had moved on, they also served an evangelical function: the more young writers who could communicate expertly about issues facing rural Oregonians, the more knowledgeable metropolitan Oregon would become about the rural parts of the state.[5]

Robert W. Chandler, newspaper publisher. Courtesy the Oregon Community Foundation.

The Oregon Community Foundation was one beneficiary of his reform: as its board chair in the 1980s, he put the "Oregon" back into OCF, making it a truly statewide foundation by guiding the creation of regional leadership councils consisting of citizen volunteers. These councils provided local insights into each community's specific needs and problems, and in turn helped direct and prioritize statewide resource allocation. Sally McCracken, a prominent Portland philanthropist, recalls "how tickled Bob was when we started the planning for the leadership council in Central Oregon. He was right there at the first meeting suggesting people to be on it." In particular, Bob was determined to make sure that every community had equal representation, including the Warm Springs tribal community. As OCF board chair, Bob also decided that individual philanthropic donations would be invested more effectively if pooled with others' donations. The idea was symbolic as well as pragmatic. It meant that, through philanthropy as well as through dialogue, Oregon was uniting: people from Portland, Prineville, Ontario, and Ashland were all donating into a shared investment fund, and their money was being redistributed just as evenly with the advice of local councils.

Beyond his outreach and his work with OCF, Bob also funded over fifty scholarships for underprivileged children, lobbied for regional development programs, helped woo job-creating companies to his region, advocated for improved regional healthcare options, and secured funding for local education and training efforts. As a result, Bob was widely known as an advocate for the disadvantaged. He contributed substantially to the Bill Healy low-income housing development in Bend and promoted a more lasting solution to rural educational inequity by advocating for and donating to Central Oregon Community College and other regional educational institutions. (Unafraid to voice unpopular sentiments, he even defended transplanted Californians: "They work in factories or stores, or on farms or ranches. They send their kids to school and pay their taxes," he wrote, perhaps self-consciously.[6]) As a member of government commissions and task forces, his promotion of rural Oregon's interests was unwavering. And through his work with the Judicial Review Commission, he helped ensure more equal provision of justice throughout the state. His philanthropic and civic efforts were as wide-ranging as his editorial topics, and all of them hinged around one central concept: that a unified Oregon was better than a divided one, and that individuals could make a difference.

Bob loved central Oregon, but he also loved Oregon as a whole—its landscape, its people, its potential. For Bob, an essential characteristic of Oregonians was their philanthropic spirit—a pioneering, creative ability to see a problem and work on behalf of others to fix it. A few years before his death in 1996, he celebrated the "hundreds of citizens who give their time to Oregon for nothing, or for very little, . . . the people who have helped make Oregon . . . what it is now."[7] Although he never would have admitted as much, he topped that list, which was, perhaps, why he was named Oregon Philanthropist of the Year in 1990.

Bob Chandler's calls for civic engagement, unification, and rural investment resonated in many corridors, and while his blend of local knowledge and statewide influence was unusual, it was certainly not unprecedented. But although many philanthropists and nonprofits have a foot in both rural and urban communities, most base their efforts in one or the other: some focus on statewide initiatives founded in centers of governance and commerce, and some start off locally and built up from there, in turn working to bridge the urban-rural divide from its respective sides.

Gretchen Pierce notes that effective advocacy needs people in both camps: "it takes people working in urban centers to bring rural folks in from the cold," she says, just as "it takes rural folks to tell the urban ones what their needs are and what they can offer, to be spokespeople for their communities and regions." The remainder of this chapter will talk about a few iconic people and organizations working on each side—at local and regional levels to strengthen rural communities and at statewide levels to find systemic solutions.

LOCAL VISIONARIES

Oregonians have always been an innovative bunch—independent, resilient, eccentric, and demonstrating an ad hoc resourcefulness. Or so the stereotype goes. But there is some truth in it: these qualities are particularly evident in local donors and activists whose grassroots efforts improve the smaller communities in which they live, giving those communities a greater voice. Their creativity and willingness to roll up their sleeves are essential to the pursuit of a more united Oregon.

KATHY DEGGENDORFER OF SISTERS AND THE AMERICANA PROJECT

That emphasis on community, civic responsibility, and creativity is certainly what drives Kathy Deggendorfer, who makes her home in the picturesque central Oregon town of Sisters. Nestled at the foot of Black Butte, with a wooden-framed main street decked out with flags and false fronts, Sisters looks out onto the Three Sisters mountains for which it was named. Idyllic though it is, like many small towns it has its problems.

When Kathy moved to Sisters in 1994, she quickly realized that even though it was an interesting community filled with interesting people, they had little in common to bring them all together. Sisters has a small-town mixture of young families, artists, ranchers and farmers, retirees, and residents of second-home developments like Black Butte Ranch. Kathy felt that the community needed something to link these diverse groups, to get them interested in each other. "It's too small of a place to compartmentalize people," she says. "We needed something to put Sisters on the map, but also to make it a respectful and engaged environment for residents." She knew that Sisters had an older-than-average population: as of the 2010 census, the median age was 41.4 years. She also noticed that the local school's arts programs were underfunded, in part because of the area's struggling economy, and that local interest in improving the school system was limited because not enough people knew children of school age.

There was already a movement afoot to create something around which Sisters' residents could rally. Jim Cornelius and Dick Sandvik of Paulina Springs Books (one of the best independent bookstores in the state) had founded the Sisters Folk Festival in 1995 as a music fest and chili cookout. Once Kathy had attended her first festival, which she said "felt like you were sitting in someone's kitchen and had access to everyone," she realized not only its unifying potential to an artistic community like Sisters but also its educational and economic benefit. She joined the organization and began working to expand its program, adding a role for Sisters' many visual artists (a quest dear to her own heart, as she is a well-known Oregon painter) and linking the festival more closely to the wider community's social, civic, and educational needs. In 2000, she asked Brad Tisdel, a local musician and education consultant, to help create and direct the Americana Project, an educational outreach program of the festival. Kathy and Brad initiated the project's annual fundraising event, My Own Two Hands, in 2002. The event relies upon the community's visual artists to donate pieces for auction. It is a popular model, Kathy found, because "we don't ask for money to start with, just time and art—that's the key. Whatever you do for your particular art, that's what you can give."

The auction quickly became one of central Oregon's premier arts events, and it raises significant amounts of money for the Americana Project, which in turn has invigorated music and the arts in the school system by providing local students with musical instruments, visual art materials, and instruction. The project also showcases musical and artistic compositions by students alongside works by local and touring professionals and has given birth to the Americana Song Academy, a music-driven residential camp held at Caldera on Blue Lake that encourages students to explore their creative sides in a nonjudgmental, affirming environment. The academy grants camp and program scholarships to students of all ages, as well as to teachers, who bring their newfound knowledge back into their classrooms.

As Kathy says, the Americana Project is "so much more than music education. It teaches American history and culture, creative writing, and visual arts, and it also teaches kids to have respect for one another and to participate in their own community. Some of them can't carry a tune in a bucket but other students react like they're at a Bob Dylan concert. These kids are taught to perform, to produce, to create . . . they're ambassadors for their community both within and outside of it." It's not just the students who become ambassadors for their community: the project's structure is innovative precisely because they have had great success in leveraging the talents of the community at large, recruiting local musicians, artists, and other experts into the schools to teach master classes and workshops. The Americana Project enables retired scientists, writers, artists, and musicians in Sisters to share their expertise and passion with students, integrating them into the community and enhancing kids' educational experiences. While the programs rely on philanthropy for their funding, volunteers are clearly equally at their heart.

Kathy points out that the Americana Project solves many problems at once. It brings comprehensive art and music programs to schools that otherwise wouldn't be able to afford them, while also endowing students with self-confidence and a community ethos. It capitalizes on the local and regional success of the Sisters Folk Festival to champion local issues, to raise

(Left) Kathy Deggendorfer (back right) emceeing at the annual My Own Two Hands fundraiser in support of the Americana Project in Sisters. Artwork shown by Dennis McGregor. Courtesy the Sisters Folk Festival. (Right) Students at Sisters Elementary School learn violin from Americana Project guest artist Kelly Thibodeaux. Photo by Brad Tisdel.

statewide awareness of local needs, and to consolidate Sisters' own sense of community. Just as importantly, it helps confirm Sisters' reputation as an Oregon arts center and inspires kids to become future festival musicians and advocates, thereby ensuring the continuation of an event that brings valuable tourist dollars into a town that can no longer be dependent on timber and ranching.

The Americana Project provides an example of how small-town resources can be leveraged to create local, statewide, and even interstate impact. And as Kathy notes, it's an exportable model that has been successfully replicated in several communities throughout Oregon and one in Colorado. "There's a national, often rural resource of people out there with great ideas, people who want to be part of their community, but who've just never been asked correctly," Kathy says. "Sisters is just the right size to serve as a petri dish" for this kind of holistic, systematic approach to community engagement and improvement, she says. "Whatever you bring to the table—your art, your expertise, your passion, or even your money," Kathy adds, "what counts is that you're making the effort to get involved."

Kathy has certainly made that effort. She and her mother, Gert Boyle, chairperson of Columbia Sportswear, have donated extensively to the Sisters Folk Festival, the Americana Project, and the Americana Song Academy. Brad Tisdel, now the executive director of the festival, lauds Kathy for her contribution to Sisters' artistic growth and statewide reputation. "She's really been a driving force here for honoring and recognizing the power of cultural events and tourism and has been a passionate supporter of anything that builds community and that increases appreciation for the arts. She's been that person whose networks and creativity can build bridges between different entities, who is constantly driving us forward and saying 'yes we can.'"

Kathy's personal motto could serve as the theme of this book: as she states, "it's up to each of us to create the kind of community we want to live in."

CHARLES ROUSE'S BAKER CITY ADVOCACY

Five hours east of Sisters, Baker County abuts the Idaho border, a line demarcated by the Snake River as it winds its way toward Hells Canyon. The Wallowa Mountains extend into the county's northern reaches, and the mixture of snowy peaks, arid uplands, and grassy valleys makes for a striking confluence of terrains. About half of Baker County's forests and rangelands are owned by the federal government, and, with only 16,134 people (according to the 2010 census) and an expanse larger than any Willamette Valley county, it is one of Oregon's most sparsely populated regions. More than 300 miles from the I-5 corridor, it is also one of the most remote. Its remoteness has only added to its recent troubles: while a hundred years ago Baker County boomed with mining, industry, and agriculture, by the mid-1980s, as resource-based economies across the state faltered and as remote rural areas became increasingly left behind by manufacturing and technology development, Baker County had the highest unemployment rate and one of the lowest income rates in Oregon.

In spite of this bleak picture, native son Chuck Rouse has faith in the region's potential. Sandy-haired, with a constant tan from being outdoors, Chuck spent his youth throwing hay bales and doing other farm work. He speaks warmly of a childhood spent riding across the high desert sagebrush and up into the Wallowas, a pastime that gave him not only a deep appreciation for his community but an abiding love of landscape, of *place*. As a young man, he left the area, first attending Oregon State University, then working in Seattle and Portland before moving back to eastern Oregon to run a furniture store in Baker City, where he quickly discovered that working in small-town Oregon was very different from working in bigger cities. As he observed, businesses in "these small communities depend much more closely on the overall vitality of the community we were living in and servicing."

Chuck Rouse with four-legged friends. Courtesy Chuck Rouse.

Baker City had some big problems, and it occurred to Chuck that as a local business owner, he could "step up and try to help the overall economy as much as possible—after all, business leaders are the ones who have their hands on the dice, much more so than politicians." For Chuck, improving the local economy meant trying to level the playing field for Baker City and other rural communities. He had knowledge of "all of Oregon from a regional economic standpoint" and could see the economic disparity between urban and rural. So he committed himself to working within Baker City to increase dialogue with urban areas and to empower and enliven the local community.

Like so many activist-philanthropists, Chuck threw himself into a number of projects to help build his community's prosperity, donating both time and money to the causes. He chaired the development commit-tee for the Oregon Trail Interpretive Center, which was built in 1992 on a hilltop five miles east of Baker City, creating a regional destination that not only helped increase Baker City's tourist economy but also informed visitors about local communities and concerns. Chuck also worked with the Chamber of Commerce, the Oregon Trail Coordinating Council, and the Miners' Jubilee organizing committee, all of which helped to bring business to Baker City.

Soft-spoken and polite, Chuck is nevertheless a confident advocate for the area. He speaks passionately about the importance of a healthy ru-ral economy and forcefully about redressing the inequalities between the Willamette Valley and the rest of the state. In an interview with the Meyer Memorial Trust, he summarized the issue bluntly: "We get a lot of lip service but as long as Portland and the Interstate-5 corridor are happy, they're will-ing to let the rest of us continue to just barely survive."[8] Chuck believes that philanthropists can play a key role in creating a more equal state and must cooperate with corporations to work for improvements to rural economies. "Philanthropists tend to donate to causes that they know about, and if most of Oregon's money is being made in Portland, that means most of Oregon's philanthropy goes to benefit metropolitan causes," he declares with frustra-tion. If the level of Oregon's philanthropic giving could be raised slightly, adds Chuck, and if people became more comfortable with the idea of giving money into managed statewide funds, like the Oregon Cultural Trust or the OCF Oregon Fund, which distribute grants across the state rather than to an individual's favorite charity, much more could be done to improve the lot of rural Oregonians and to ensure that the rural economy can begin to flourish once more. In turn, rural economies could begin to feed back into Oregon's overall economic health—to turn, as Chuck puts it, "rural Oregon from be-ing a tax liability to a tax payer."

Chuck also believes that statewide and regional corporations have a similarly important role to play in supporting rural Oregon. "If you're an Oregon company and start thinking about what that *means*, you can help the economic vitality of the state by reinvesting in the rural economy, which in turn will strengthen the state's economy as a whole and help your business. Investing widely across the region has a domino effect on a company's health." If a company thinks holistically about the happiness of their employees and the sustainability and ethics of their corporate model, he says, that call center

Northeastern Oregon farmland. Photo by Kristin Anderson.

in Bangladesh could be repatriated to Redmond or that factory in China brought home to La Grande. What Oregon needs, he says with certitude, is a committee of twenty or so Oregon CEOs who can sit down and talk with each other, who can motivate each other and other business leaders to move toward more community-focused corporate policies and Oregon-wide investment strategies. The economics would make sense for them—and for rural Oregon, it could make all the difference.

Much of Chuck's work is directed toward communicating this dual phil-anthropic/corporate message. His efforts have been largely successful: he has worked with Governors Goldschmidt and Kitzhaber on regional economic development; he has helped increase and direct the flow of philanthropic contributions to his region; and he has facilitated the establishment of a bur-geoning tourism infrastructure in Baker City, the community on which his philanthropic interests remain resolutely centered. One of Chuck's proudest achievements is also one of his most recent and most local—acquiring nearly $170,000 from the Meyer Memorial Trust, the Ford Family Foundation, the Leo Adler Foundation, and OCF in order to convert a closed elementary school in his hometown of Richland into a low-income senior residence, library, and community center. "We're so excited about this," he said. "Four of the largest foundations in the Northwest recognized what our community is trying to do."[9]

Chuck's work to develop his own community has been a game-changer for Baker City and for nearby Richland, where he lives. But his advocacy for a broader, pan-Oregon definition of community, and of civic and corporate responsibility, is also inspirational. "It's human nature that we focus on our own lives, our own communities," Chuck says. "We need to widen that focus."

DON KERR AND THE HIGH DESERT MUSEUM

In efforts to bridge the urban-rural divide, community philanthropy can take many forms—from advocating for corporate investment to voicing local concerns at regional forums. One particularly successful way to increase the prosperity of Oregon's rural communities is to improve their tourist appeal, thereby facilitating cultural exchanges, raising statewide awareness of rural and small-town issues, bringing money into the local economy, and consolidating local pride and communal identity. Often driven by nonprofit and philanthropic initiatives, and often powered by volunteers, programs such as these have helped bring Oregonians closer together and have made us more empathetic across regional lines.

One highly successful effort to use tourism to bridge the urban-rural divide is the High Desert Museum, a prominent Bend-area tourist attraction created through the determination and passion of Donald Kerr. Don had been an instructor at the Oregon Zoo and chief biologist for the Oregon chapter of the Nature Conservancy, but he was a self-described "desert rat" and soon adopted Bend as his home. He loves central Oregon with a native's passion, and his work as a biologist made him appreciate all the more its unusual and beautiful ecosystems. In the 1970s, Bend was not a tourist destination. Even though Sunriver Resort was nearby and the Hollerns were driving local philanthropy forward, the town was trying to survive on a declining timber industry. Yet Don saw what the area had to offer—ponderosa forests and sage-colored plains, volcanic peaks, rushing rivers, basaltic andesite and obsidian flows, crystalline lakes and moraines, blue skies, an incredible diversity of flora and fauna, and everywhere striking evidence of geological cataclysms.

Don Kerr with owl. Courtesy the High Desert Museum.

Don knew that in order for the region to prosper, others needed to experience it too. Quiet and gentle, Don was nevertheless persistent in advancing his idea: the community needed an interpretive center that would improve local and statewide knowledge of the high desert region, its peoples, and its ecosystems. It would be a place to give voice to high desert issues and to lure out-of-towners into learning more about local and regional concerns. The plan was to build a facility that would convene ordinary Oregonians to celebrate this unique region's worth and history. The idea behind it, Don said, was "[s]imple: the better people know this region, the better equipped they will be to decide the course of its future."[10]

One of the first people Don approached was Bob Chandler, who was initially skeptical but soon saw the value of such a project and threw his considerable influence behind it. Mike and Sue Hollern were principal backers,

(Left) Lava Butte, near the High Desert Museum. (Right) A sleepy museum porcupine. Photos by Kristin Anderson.

as were Earle Chiles, Craig Moore, Randy Labbee, and many other Oregon philanthropic luminaries. Don was a charismatic speaker, and his passion was as evident as his knowledge, so after rounds of dinner parties and educational events, he finally accumulated sufficient funds to establish his museum. In 1974, the Western Natural History Institute opened its doors; by 1982, it had evolved into the Oregon High Desert Museum and has been expanding and winning awards ever since.

Today, the High Desert Museum provides a thoughtfully curated, in-depth look at central Oregon's human history, its geological past and future, its diverse ecosystems, its industries and resources, and its blockbuster wild-life—their Birds of Prey show is a prime tourist draw. (Its porcupine exhibit is also oddly endearing.) Visitors leave with a more nuanced portrait of central Oregon then and now, with just as much attention paid to the "now" as to its historical and zoological features. One of the museum's most impressive attributes is how much it conveys about contemporary life in central Oregon, including in-depth information about contemporary Native American life and about the region's economic, industrial, and natural resource struggles.

In 1995, while working with a great horned owl, a talon pierced Don's glove and he contracted viral encephalitis, which has left him paralyzed and unable to speak. But although Don is no longer the museum's director, his imprint is clear throughout it. Today, the High Desert Museum's visitors hail from every corner of the state and leave with a fuller understanding of the strengths, needs, and challenges facing central Oregon's people and environment. As an educational institution that seeks to give voice and power to the local community, the museum has fulfilled Don's vision.

STATEWIDE INNOVATORS

Rural activists and donors are essential to Oregon's wider philanthropic landscape: they highlight local needs and put communities on the statewide philanthropic map. However, the bridge over the urban-rural divide must be built from both sides of the canyon. The enthusiasm, knowledge, and elbow grease of those working at a statewide level to bring Oregon's diverse communities together are just as needed.

DON FRISBEE AND THE OREGON CHAPTER
OF THE AMERICAN LEADERSHIP FORUM

One of these individuals is Portlander Don Frisbee, a nonagenarian who hasn't slowed down much at all. When we spoke to him, he was just about to embark on a sixty-day cruise of the world with Betty Perkins, a neighbor whom he met in 2008 and with whom he celebrated a commitment ceremony in the summer of 2012, when he was eighty-eight and she was eighty-seven (he jokes that he is robbing the cradle). The former president of PacifiCorp, Don has worked his whole life to unite Oregonians from disparate parts of the state. His foremost contribution was to open the Oregon Chapter of the American Leadership Forum (ALF), an organization that selects current and potential leaders from across urban and rural Oregon and brings them together for a wilderness retreat and a year-long series of trainings and workshops. As Don describes it, ALF is "a statewide program to build networks and to develop strong leaders in each community."

Don Frisbee and Betty Perkins at Housecall Providers' 2009 Pearls of Promise dinner. Photo by J. Thomas Shrewsbury. Courtesy Housecall Providers.

Oregon ALF's goal is to link urban and rural citizens from diverse backgrounds in order to foster dialogue and establish shared interests, in turn helping to rejuvenate Oregon's urban/rural interdependence—that shared sense of "one Oregon." The unifying potential of the program was, Don says, "one of the key factors that drove a few of us to make sure the idea was implemented. Our thought was that if we could develop leaders across the state we could have a better understanding of one another's problems and bond people who were destined for leadership so that they could work together more effectively." Oregon ALF took great care to make "sure that each year's group was quite diversified in the sense of where they were from, their economic status, their educational background, and their gender."

For Don, ALF's philosophy of bringing leaders together for local and statewide benefit closely matched his own philosophy as the director of a large company. A stronger rural identity meant a stronger rural economy,

Photo by Kristin Anderson.

he believes, which in turn would develop Oregon's identity and economy as a whole. "Our idea of social and economic improvement was one which benefited the communities we served and benefited us in terms of ensuring a more vital, healthier economic picture—*it just made sense*," he says fervently.

This idea of mutual benefit is not uncommon among Oregon's business leaders: not only are you doing good for the state, you're creating a more diversified, robust economic market that in the long run helps businesses, too. For Don, the boomerang effect was a benefit, but it wasn't his primary motivation. He had been a mentor to several local youth organizations, and a program like Oregon ALF helped to develop these young people into the next generation of leaders. It was the logical next step, he says, a holistic approach to community development that increases Oregonians' unity.

Don also wanted to set an example for his employees. Being an active philanthropist and public servant is part of being a responsible member of the community, he believes. "My community activities were motivated by the fact that as a service company it was important to get employees involved in community work. . . . I think you need to motivate others by example and by leading in the things you really believe in." To Don, the American Leadership Forum represented the very best way of securing Oregon's future and ensuring, in particular, that rural Oregonians would always have a strong voice in statewide affairs. "Caring," Don says, "is really the most important adjective."

BILL THORNDIKE OF MEDFORD AND
THE NORTHWEST AREA FOUNDATION

One beneficiary of the ALF-Oregon program was Bill Thorndike, who in turn has made quite an impact himself. The president of Medford Fabrication, which manufactures heavy-duty steel equipment, Bill is jovial and thoughtful and, like Bob Chandler, is one of those rare people who defines community as the entire state and is as comfortable having a pinot noir in Portland as a beer in Butte Falls. An inexhaustible man, Bill will rise early in Medford, help his wife Angela take care of their horses, and put on a suit and head to work in Medford or in Portland—for him, the distance is inconsequential. He's the kind of person one must catch on the run, and while a Grey Goose martini might lure him into a more relaxed and stationary state, his idea-generating mind never switches off. In the famous noir film *Double Indemnity*, a character from Medford claims that "in Medford, we take our time making up our minds." Bill belies that myth: he works quickly.

Bill's Oregon ALF experience was, in many ways, both typical and extraordinary. Each participant is paired with a buddy at the start of the program. Bill was partnered with Charles Moose, who would become the police chief for Portland. It was a fantastic pairing—a small-town businessman as confidante of Portland's top law enforcer and vice versa. These unconventional relationships are essential to building a more united state, teaching community leaders to look for shared priorities despite disparate backgrounds and politics. "As Oregon has changed during my lifetime," Bill observed recently, "there have been a series of philanthropic initiatives to address the urban-rural divide, a stellar example of which is the American Leadership Forum, which addresses geographical distance and cultural distances."

But there have been other key efforts too, some spurred on by Bill himself, who is an enthusiastic philanthropist and dedicated volunteer. Bill sits on the board of the Northwest Area Foundation (NWAF), a regional grantmaker that develops economic sustainability and focuses on getting people out of poverty, and is a vocal champion of their work. Like many effective philanthropic organizations, one of NWAF's chief attributes is an ability to differentiate between types of need. Bill notes that the types of poverty across the eight states to which NWAF distributes are very different: plains agrarian, migrant worker, inner-urban, high desert, mountain, native—all these groups have very specific needs, he says. One of the philanthropic community's greatest virtues, he notes, is that "we're moving toward being more responsive and sensitive to these communities so that

Bill Thorndike. Courtesy Bill Thorndike.

we can provide them with the types of opportunities they most require." The NWAF uses a model designed to encourage state- and region-wide organizations to work in partnership with local leaders to provide rural communities with the precise mix of services they need: it is a top-down approach firmly grounded in a bottom-up knowledge.

As Bill says, "I try to bring to philanthropy the realization that I'm part of a very complex system of people whose special knowledge and experience we can apply." Anyone can bring something to the system, he suggests, and the more diverse the goals and the deeper the local knowledge, the stronger our state will become. As a society, he says, what we should "pay attention to is richness, in this case the richness which runs from the environment to the economy to education to the arts and culture. . . . That richness is so valuable, and there are so many opportunities to enhance it, from meeting basic needs to procuring artistic opportunities or educational attainment. These are not either/or investments," he adds.

Bill has devoted much of his time, energy, creativity, and corporate and personal resources into strengthening dialogue between urban and rural communities, and into tailoring philanthropic efforts to suit individual communities' needs. Taking inspiration from his parents' charitable work, Bill sees the effect they had on him as he grew up. They "added fuel to the fire of wanting to broaden [my own] impact across as many different areas as possible. I wanted to do my share."

JONATHAN NICHOLAS, JIM BEAVER, AND CYCLE OREGON

One of the most prominent and popular examples of a statewide philanthropic success is the Cycle Oregon project, spearheaded by Jim Beaver and Jonathan Nicholas. Jim Beaver, an Ashland innkeeper, came up with the idea of a sister-city coastal cycle ride from Astoria to Ashland in 1987 and contacted Jonathan Nicholas, an *Oregonian* columnist, who thought it was a great idea. Nicholas' background made him a great candidate to give Beaver's idea wheels: as a journalist, a world traveler, and a Brit who had enthusiastically moved to Oregon about a decade earlier, Jonathan had grown to know Oregon with the depth of a native and the zeal of a convert.

Growing up in Merthyr Tydfil, a coal-mining village in Wales, Jonathan was surrounded by "one of the most ravaged landscapes perhaps in the world, a birthplace of the industrial revolution." The infamous Aberfan disaster happened just four miles down the road from his home: after strong rains, a colliery spoils heap slid down into the village, killing 28 adults and 116 young students at an elementary school. Well aware, then, of the effect that human industry can have on the environment, Nicholas sought out the opposite of that ravaged landscape by taking a job with the British Council and the United Nations Development Programme to help establish the first national park in the Himalayas, Nepal's Rara National Park. While he was there, the decision was made to resettle the three villages within the park, so he saw, on the one hand, an environment desecrated to preserve human economies, and on the other, lives disrupted to preserve a pristine wilderness. "There had been enormous social costs in both," he says, "and my sense was that there had to be some midpoint, a working landscape in which humans could live and work sustainably and sensitively, and I found the possibility of that in Oregon. . . . If you've travelled widely, you'll understand in a very different way the gift that Oregon is, and how enormous our responsibility is to maintain this balance and to *get this right*."

There were plenty of places in the state, however, where Jonathan saw things going wrong. He knew that not only was there an urban-rural divide in Oregon, but that it was worsening year by year as rural natural resource-based economies dwindled and as power and money settled in the I-5 corridor. "Having grown up in a coal-mining town, I saw what happened when the mines dried up: the miners were out of work, divorce rates started to soar . . . all of the social disruption that starts when the economic foundation of a place is taken away," Jonathan explains. "You can see that this threat is present in the small towns of rural Oregon: so much of their economies were based on dwindling timber and natural resource production." But from Portland and the valley, he continues, all we saw was "a loud fight between loggers and environmentalists." The human element, and a more nuanced understanding of the issues, livelihoods, and landscapes at stake, weren't really visible. Part of this disconnect, he assumed, was because urban people didn't have sufficient connections with rural Oregon to understand or appreciate it fully. Part of it, he also knew, was because there were deep inequalities in service provision and economic vitality between urban and rural communities that exacerbated the gulf between them. And so he, Jim Beaver, and Cycle Oregon biked forth to bridge that gap.

Mike Palmgren, Bill Blount, Jonathan Nicholas, and Greg Chaillé after a long day's ride. Courtesy Greg Chaillé.

Elgin main street, as visited by Cycle Oregon. Photo by Kristin Anderson.

After writing a column describing the point of the ride (getting to know other parts of the state is "not a complex idea," he notes) and asking for participants, "we really thought that maybe 50 people would want to do it. Instead we had 1,006 people sign up." The Oregon Department of Tourism helped coordinate the ride, Nike chipped in some T-shirts, Weyerhaeuser donated $10,000 for seed money, and during the six-day cycle from Salem to Brookings, riders bought food from the towns and villages through which they passed, camped in backyards, and swapped stories with locals. "By the time we got to the finish line," Nicholas explains, "we were so exhilarated that everyone decided that we needed to do it again." That was in 1988. Now, 2,200 cyclists participate annually (the spots fill in minutes), and the roughly 350-mile ride has passed through every corner of the state, with different routes each year.

Cycle Oregon's philosophy is two-pronged. First, the ride is explicitly philanthropic, and has been since the beginning. "We knew that we owed much to the communities we'd passed through," explains Jonathan, "and so, in a parking lot in Brookings, we passed the hat around." The first ride generated over $360,000 for participating communities, and now the organization has disbursed over $1.4 million in grants and has brought millions more in economic boosts to local communities.[11] Cycle Oregon invests all of its proceeds into the Cycle Oregon Fund, which distributes grants to the communities through which it passes as well as to other small communities in need. With over $2 million in the Cycle Oregon Fund, it can disburse al-most $100,000 in grants each year. These grants are earmarked to fund local projects across Oregon that will make a qualitative, substantial difference to these local communities.

The ambitions for these grants started small, as Nicholas describes: "buying the Elk Club a dishwasher, fixing the local grange's roof, building a restroom for the ball field." But now the fund issues bigger checks as well, which have been used to restock Diamond Lake with trout, to help pre-serve Wallowa Lake's glacial moraine, to help the community of Halfway repurchase its rodeo and fairgrounds, and to install comprehensive lighting for a football field in Dufur, among many other projects. Cycle Oregon has also helped develop a network of State Scenic Bikeways that will continue year-round the ride's mandate to showcase beautiful, off-the-beaten-path Oregon communities and to unite further urban and rural Oregonians. "These projects," Jonathan adds, "felt like legacies to us and have been very rewarding."

While bringing statewide money and philanthropy to these rural communities is a seminal goal of Cycle Oregon's program, notes Nicholas, "the even greater gift to Oregon and to Oregonians is in taking urbanites out into Oregon in a way that they have never done before. Everyone has driven through central Oregon at some point," he explains, "but the way you experience a place at seven miles an hour is very different than the way you experience it at seventy. You smell it, you feel it, you stop regularly and talk to people, and find that the people who live there are committed to the land on which they live in so many ways that people in urban areas aren't . . ."

It is, he observes, an invaluable process in its own right, and it usually results in leaving the riders with more empathy for and understanding of rural Oregonians, and in leaving rural Oregonians with a more positive impression of the ride's mostly urban participants. And in addition to bringing economic benefits to small towns, it also, he thinks, increases civic pride and self-worth in participating communities by putting the local community back onto a wider map. In short, it builds bridges and engenders a more interdependent understanding of Oregon. "I think that part of the harvest of that is that when you're back in your office in Portland as a lawyer or a plumber and you read that story in the *Oregonian* about some environmental fight or timber crisis in Burns, for instance, you have some understanding and empathy and critical faculty, you think, hang on, I was just there, it didn't feel that way to me," Jonathan explains. "People can start to think of themselves again as Oregonians rather than as Portlanders or urbanites."

On many rides, Nicholas is at the heart of this bridge-building, act-ing as tour guide and philosopher, striding around with a wide and slightly impish smile to teach the riders about where they have traveled that day, describing what it means for the communities through which they have passed, and transforming what could be merely a long-distance bike ride into an empathy-building odyssey. Nicholas is deeply proud of the organization: "I think we have helped knit the state back together in a way that felt really threatened twenty-five years ago," he says. Cycle Oregon is a great success, an example of what a couple of people with a visionary idea can do. Because of the vision of Jim Beaver and Jonathan Nicholas, Cycle Oregon has become a philanthropic institution that has traveled many thousands of miles—literally—to bring Oregonians together.

A UNITED OREGON

These diverse people and projects—from the Americana Project to Don Kerr to the Oregon Trail Interpretive Center—have a shared goal: the unification of Oregon through dialogue and the distribution of knowledge and resources. The urban-rural divide may be deepening, but countless people are working with passion and energy to reverse that trend. Their kind of philanthropy includes volunteerism at its core: healing urban-rural disparities takes time and energy as well as money.

Of course, there are many other excellent organizations and programs helping to close the distance between town and country. Oregon Public Broadcasting works hard to bring rural voices into its programming, and through series like *Oregon Field Guide, Oregon Experience, Art Beat,* and *Our Town,* presents in-depth coverage of rural issues to a statewide audience. Oregon State University's network of extension services helps make higher education more accessible to those living in rural areas and boasts the largest volunteer force (numbering 14,000) in the state; the Nature Conservancy is preserving and stewarding vast tracts of land across Oregon; and Oregon Humanities brings cultural programing, educational opportunities, and public discussions to small towns as well as to metropolitan audiences.

Philanthropic foundations are also pointedly targeting resources at rural areas to help redress the tendency to keep urban wealth in urban areas. The Ford Family Foundation, for example, has established scholarships and grants specifically for rural students and communities in order to help solve economic, educational and social inequity. The Oregon Community Foundation's network of regional leadership councils relies on local expertise in directing philanthropic contributions to small projects and organizations that otherwise would go unnoticed. And the Oregon Cultural Trust gives grants to help develop local and regional arts initiatives from across the state in the expectation that vibrant arts communities leads to healthier communities overall.

Portland rainbow. Photo by Kristin Anderson.

One of many exciting new start-ups working toward the same goals is Slamboo, an innovative poetry slam project started by teacher Charles Sanderson of St. Helen's Middle School, located in a small town between Portland and Astoria. Charles paired up with teachers at Lane, Five Oaks, and Da Vinci middle schools across the greater Portland area. Four times a year, students from these four middle schools—two rural, one suburban, and one deeply urban—come together to perform and workshop poetry, share a meal, and most importantly, learn about each others' problems and experiences. One student, Jodelle Marx, thinks of Slamboo as "a safe place: an amazing community built through writing." Donovan Jacob, a St. Helen's Middle School student, says that the program has already "changed my life for the better. In Slam[boo], we bridged the boundaries between us and them and came together as poets and as friends. Through poetry, my eyes widened and burst with new insight as people I had stereotyped got on stage and told me that my view of them was wrong."

That, says Charles, is exactly what they were hoping for. "The kids in my class can't access the opportunities that exist in terms of arts and culture in Portland for a variety of reasons—geographic, cultural, bureaucratic. So I wanted to find a way to provide them with the cultural capacity to meet other people, to interact, to problem-solve with others who have had a different background. It's exciting for our kids to realize all that they have in common with urban and suburban kids while also celebrating what makes them unique as a rural community." Driven forward by teachers like Charles who volunteer their time and often donate their own money, Slamboo is a scrappy little project, with a hand-to-mouth budget covering an anthology, bus rides, the meals ("we think breaking bread is important," says Charles), and if they're lucky, T-shirts for the kids. But the innovative thinking behind it is clearly making a huge difference in the lives of these students and is ripe with potential for expansion.

This kind of innovation is precisely what is required in the fight against Oregon's many geographic and socioeconomic divisions. At the root of these innovations are exceptional people who are dedicating their lives and resources to improving dialogue and to correcting the many inequalities between urban and rural Oregon. They have fought to tell the story of rural people, to highlight interests and benefits shared between diverse populations, to expose rural needs and urban oversights, to facilitate cultural exchanges in order to further dialogue, and to advocate for qualitative as well as quantitative investment across the state to create sustainable and lasting bonds between metropolitan and rural Oregon. A renewed urban-rural interdependence is their goal.

They've made a good start, but much more still needs to be done. As Jonathan Nicholas says of Cycle Oregon's efforts, "there's no doubt that in many ways the needs in those really small communities are just as great and just as pressing as they were when the ride started. For every Sisters or Joseph (rural towns that have made a successful transition), there are tiny little places that haven't been able to make that transition." There is always the need for more philanthropic investment, for more volunteer hours, for more visionaries, more innovators, and more passionate spokespeople from communities whose voices are not yet fully audible.

Albina Head Start, Portland. Photo by Naim Hasan. Courtesy Albina Head Start.

2
Back to School: Erasing Education Inequity, Closing the Achievement Gap

"Let us in education dream of an aristocracy of achievement arising out of a democracy of opportunity."
—Thomas Jefferson

"This creates tension. But it is necessary tension, the type of positive tension that often precedes meaningful progress."
—Edwin Peterson, former Chief Justice of Oregon's Supreme Court, on his work with the Salem-Keizer Coalition for Equality

In his 1954 decision in the landmark Brown v. Board of Education desegregation case, United States Supreme Court Chief Justice Earl Warren observed that "these days, it is doubtful that any child may reasonably be expected to succeed in life if he is denied the opportunity of an education." His comments, unfortunately, still resonate now. While we Oregonians are familiar with news reports on slipping test scores or ballot measures altering education funding, most of us are less aware of one of the biggest challenges facing

Oregon's education system: ensuring that all students can *equally* access a quality education.

In general, Oregon's schools rate at about average, or a bit below average, nationally (internationally, American education ranks near the bottom of the world's thirty richest countries). But while most of the nation's schools are improving, Oregon's schools remain stagnant or are worsening against the national averages, particularly in their provision for minority, low-income, and additional-needs students. This chapter will discuss one of the biggest challenges facing our state—the widespread disparities in our K-12 education system—and look at some ways in which Oregon donors and volunteers, and the activists, educators, government agencies, and nonprofits with whom they work, are finding innovative solutions to benefit Oregon's children and to help shape the national conversation about education reform.

A SOMBER TRUTH

Oregon is one of five states where the overall achievement gap between white middle-income students and low-income and/or minority students widened between 2003 and 2011. Our test results in math and reading at both fourth- and eighth-grade levels indicate significantly different achievements between white and black students, between white and Hispanic students, between white and Native American students, between students who are ineligible and eligible for subsidized or free lunches, and between students who do not and who do have additional needs (such as English language requirements).

A 2010 national report labels Oregon "worrisome" because low-income students are losing ground compared to higher-income peers, and low-income students in Oregon now rank among the lowest performing in the nation. Race matters, too: in 2011–2012, white students graduated from high school 74.5 percent of the time, compared with 64.9 percent of Hispanic students, 55.7 percent of Native Americans, and 60.4 percent of African Americans.[1] English language learners (ELLs) also face a challenge in Oregon: in 2009, ELLs were 24 percent less likely than average to graduate from high school and are currently performing between 30–50 percent below state averages. Two recent studies have found that those who are behind in reading by third grade fall further behind in all subjects thereafter and that middle-to-upper income white students consistently outperform non-white or low-income students on early reading tests, which suggests that the achievement gap that haunts these students throughout their education begins in their early years. To make matters worse, schools with the highest number of low-income, ELL, and minority students have higher numbers of inexperienced teachers and are losing teachers at a faster rate, therefore ensuring that the professionals who could best help these students have less exposure to them.

Teachers fall out of the system for similar reasons students do. In an age of education cutbacks, swelling class sizes, and shifting student demographics, many established teachers feel undersupported, undervalued, undertrained, and overworked. And many new teachers may not have had sufficient classroom and context-specific training to land on their feet in their first jobs, particularly if those jobs are in schools with a high proportion of at-risk or additional-needs students. Under these circumstances, closing the achievement gap between white, middle-income students and minority, low-income, non-English speaking, or special needs students must seem a Sisyphean task to educators.

Nor is there light at the end of the tunnel. As widespread as these inequities are now, in the coming years, they will affect even greater numbers of Oregon's students. The percentage of Oregon's minority students has increased from 16.3 percent in 1997 to 34.7 percent in 2011–2012, and the percentage of low-income students has increased from 30 percent in 1997 to almost half of all students today.[2] In kindergartens now, one in five children is an English language learner, compared to the 7 percent currently in high school. Oregon's population is diversifying rapidly, and we are just as rapidly falling behind in our provision for those students who need our help the most. According to *Education Week*'s 2013 "Quality Counts" report, Oregon ranks forty-second in K-12 education and receives a C- grade for education equity, scores both unacceptable and demoralizing for those who are working so hard to improve Oregon's schools.[3]

Education inequity is a problem that affects all Oregonians. From a purely pragmatic perspective, there is a stark economic need to eradicate the achievement gap: a 2010 study by ECONorthwest and the Chalkboard Project estimated that, had Oregon eliminated the achievement gap in 1998, Oregon's economy would be between $1.1 and $2.8 billion wealthier in 2008 because of the additional human capital. (Oregon's entire wood products sector represents $2 billion by comparison.)[4] And this estimation does not take into account the increased healthcare, social services, welfare, and policing costs that often go hand-in-hand with education deficiencies. Nor does it place monetary value on the moral satisfaction that comes from knowing all of our state's children are given equal opportunities for success.

For all the teachers, organizers, parents, principals, activists, and donors profiled in this chapter, it is explicitly that *moral* drive, that altruism, that compels them to fight. It is also what unites them: because education inequity is such a comprehensive problem, lone innovators and impassioned philanthropists often work hand-in-hand with nonprofit and community organizations—the need for collaborative efforts in this area is substantial. There is one core message bridging the diverse people and groups working

on this issue: that it really does take a village, a community, to promote education reform and to help advance new generations of Oregon schoolchildren.

A DEFIANT, TIRELESS ADVOCATE:
RON HERNDON AND ALBINA HEAD START

In the needs-driven world of education provision, there are teachers and donors and activists—but many in the sector fill all three roles. Ron Herndon
is one. A rebel, a disrupter, and an ardent defender of kids' rights to a decent
education, his contributions to Portland's black community span decades
and have earned him national recognition and influence. Then as now, Ron
was one of Portland's principal advocates for low-income children, as well
as an educator and a co-founder of the Black United Front. He is a fearsome
critic of both public and private failures to fix systemic social inequities. He is
also a genial, soft-spoken man whose deep civic commitment and experience
as an educator have helped many Oregonians understand how we can do a
better job educating our children and creating equal opportunities for them
in the future.

When Ron was growing up in Coffeyville, Kansas, in the 1950s, the
community's approach to education for its racial minorities mirrored the rest
of the nation's: African Americans attended segregated, poorly provisioned

schools. Yet despite these inequities, Coffeyville's black
community was united in its celebration of its children's
academic accomplishments precisely because the community recognized that quality educations could secure
their children a better future. Ron brought this same spirit
of achievement to Oregon when he moved here in the late
sixties.

"In my all-black school, our first grade teacher talked
to us about college," recalls Ron. Tall, with grey-flecked hair
and a face that loses none of its kindness when he grows
indignant, Ron warms immediately to talking about his
past. "My parents and grandparents pushed us toward edu-

Ron Herndon. Photo by Julie Antiniou.
Courtesy Albina Head Start.

cational achievement, and the whole community did too.
If you got on the honor roll in high school you received as
much attention as a star athlete—they celebrated you in church," he continues. "Despite the odds, it was expected for black kids to either go to college
or join the military: the idea of educational attainment wasn't foreign to me
because both my family, my peers, and all of the community's adults encouraged us to get an education. I'm a product of that environment." This strong
community emphasis on education is, Ron suggests, what has driven him to
be an advocate for educational equality in the state of Oregon. Over the last

Albina Head Start students. Photos by Michael McDermott (left) and Naim Hasan (right). Courtesy Albina Head Start.

forty years, Ron has been an indefatigable campaigner for social justice, fighting on behalf of minority and low-income kids' right to excellent educations. And even now—arguably now more than ever—there is plenty for Ron to be up-in-arms about.

"When I hear reasons for the achievement gap in Oregon's public schools other than lack of educational opportunity, it's insulting to me," he declares. He sees that same community support in Portland's minority and low-income neighborhoods that he saw in Coffeyville's black community—but what he also sees is an educational infrastructure that is failing in its duty to provide equal care to all students. "It's not that there are so many pathologies in our minority and low-income communities that children can't achieve from within them," he declares with frustration, "it's that there are still inequalities in education provision."

Ron's dedication to social justice goes back at least to the mid-sixties. He cut his teeth as a VISTA program worker from 1965 to 1968 fighting against poverty first in New Jersey and then in Harlem. He moved to Portland in 1968 to study political science at Reed, and when he graduated, he went on to found a Northeast Portland school so that kids "in the black community could talk about history and culture as well as academics." They converted a derelict house into the Black Educational Center, which accommodated 130 kids, and he and his friends became de facto teachers. After three years, it grew into a full-time K-5 independent school, and that was when Ron was asked to get involved with the Albina Head Start program, a local office of the nationally run education nonprofit. He became president of Albina's Head Start and has remained there ever since.

Head Start's mission is to provide services to minority and low-income children from birth through age five, and to their families. Its programs range from full- and half-day preschools (with a dedicated emphasis on teaching kids to start reading) to pre-natal, nutritional, parenting, job skills, and adult literacy classes. Its primary innovations are twofold: first, it corrects education inequities by giving low-income kids access to preschool education, which is normally reserved for those who can pay for it but, as survey after survey says, which is crucial to forming strong young students. "In Montessori, they teach kids to do math and read," Ron says, "and we do too. The parents love it." And the parents love for it hits on the second key strength of Head Start: it emphasizes community and parental involvement. Albina Head Start hires mostly from within the community and takes great care to ensure that parents play a key role in shaping their children's education. About 40 percent of their employees are former Head Start parents, Ron says, and "if you're hired here, you went through a parent committee, as does our curriculum and budget—everything is approved by the parents."

Because the program comes from within the community, educators and mentors can address specific needs that might be missed by outsiders. A key problem in Oregon's education system, Ron says, is that there's no requirement for new or established teachers to have had experience or success with low-income or minority students in order to teach them. "You're placed with a mentor—no guarantee that it's a good mentor—for three months in a classroom, and then hell, you're a teacher," he says, outraged. "Kids get blamed for the education training system's failure. None of us would get on a plane where the pilots were trained as poorly as our teachers."

In Head Start, however, most teachers are community members with experience working within the community, who are then trained to be teachers. Unlike state-standard models of teacher training, this strategy has excellent retention rates: over half Albina Head Start's staff have stayed for five years or more, and many have been there for twenty, thirty, or even forty years.

Since becoming the director of Albina Head Start in 1975, Ron has attracted numerous federal grants for major building projects and the development of parent and staff programs in Portland and nearby communities. Despite having a new state-of-the-art Head Start facility up the road, however, Ron's Albina headquarters remain at an old converted bungalow with security bars across the narrow front door, meeting rooms stacked high with papers, and walls decorated with photographs of preschool children sporting oversized sweatshirts from Harvard and Dartmouth.

He has remained an unstoppable campaigner for educational equity outside of his role at Head Start, making headlines as a vocal opponent to Portland Public Schools' controversial busing program and as a media campaigner to raise awareness of the enduring achievement gap in Oregon's minority and low-income communities. "The only time change occurs is when you organize and keep the pressure on," Ron asserts.[5]

Head Start is funded both through the national government (under the Administration for Children and Families in the Department of Health and Human Services) and through required local matches from foundations, companies, and the small donations of individuals. But what really supports Head Start across the nation is the generosity of local communities. "Head Start makes a lie out of the myth that low-income people are incapable of handling their own affairs," says Ron. "When I hear that low-income people don't have the same expectations about education as middle-income people, it's repulsive to me, it goes against everything I ever heard growing up."

Possibly on the strength of such convictions, Ron was elected to chair the National Head Start Association's board in 1993, a position he still holds. Part of his role is to advocate against education inequity at a national level, a role particularly relevant in the wake of the federal "sequestration," which cut $406 million from Head Start's national budget and kicked seventy thousand children out of the program. On Chris Matthews' MSNBC show *Hardball*, Herndon eloquently lamented the effects these federal funding cuts will have both on Albina Head Start and the national program: it will mean ending the program two weeks early, beginning it two weeks late, serving fewer hot meals, and stripping back key program elements such as speech therapy.[6]

Ron Herndon speaking at the national convention of the Head Start Association. Photo by Julie Antiniou. Courtesy Albina Head Start.

Head Start and other early-childhood programs are essential, he explained, because they help right a longstanding inequity in education. "Being poor does not mean one is limited in his or her capacity to learn," he testified to the US House of Representatives Committee on Education in 2001. "Education, particularly when it comes to young children from disadvantaged backgrounds, involves a wide array of complementary inputs that must create a rich environment in which a child acquires basic skills and a parent can become their child's first and best teacher."[7] Albina Head Start has—with the help of a united community effort, small philanthropic acts, and the fiery leadership of Ron Herndon—provided precisely that kind of rich environment.

KEN LEWIS AND THE "I HAVE A DREAM" FOUNDATION

Ken Lewis is a genial, gregarious man who believes in the power of individuals and communities to come together to help each other. At a candlelit table at the Brasserie Montmartre restaurant in Portland, Lewis pulls his wallet out of his back pocket. On a crumpled piece of paper he slips out of the wallet are two quotations, which, he says, provide continual inspiration. The first are the words etched on Jackie Robinson's tombstone: "A life is not important except in the impact it has on other lives." The second is from another baseball great, Roberto Clemente, the right fielder and humanitarian fieldworker who died in a plane crash en route to Nicaragua while on a post-earthquake aid mission. It reads: "Anytime you have an opportunity to make things better and you don't, then you are wasting your time on this earth."

These tandem mottos have driven Ken, a lawyer and business executive, to be one of the most devoted donors in Oregon. The Oregon Ballet Theatre, the Oregon Shakespeare Festival, the World Affairs Council, and many other organizations have benefited from his time and largesse, but his favorite cause is helping children get the education they deserve. "We are falling so far behind in education spending compared with other developed countries," Ken says. "I've always thought that what Roosevelt did with the GI Bill changed America—it democratized education. I saw the opportunities available to those who could finally get a good education, and I saw America start to become more meritocratic," Ken recalls. "But for many reasons—tax, economy, attitude—I think we're regressing now: the divide between the rich and poor is widening, and that includes access to quality education." Providing our kids with outstanding educations is, as Ken says, an integral part of good citizenship—and that's why he helped bring the "I Have a Dream" Foundation to Oregon.

"I started being concerned about the quality of education in high school," Ken says, "in part because teachers are the most unappreciated sector of society, and in part because I saw all of these kids who weren't being given the same chances at success that I was lucky enough to benefit from." Ken was born in Brooklyn to parents who were "barely middle-class" but who knew the value of education and accordingly moved their family from Long Island to a one-bedroom in Manhattan so that Ken and his brother could attend a better school. "They made huge sacrifices for us," he says, sacrifices that led him first to a Princeton scholarship and then to Harvard Law School—"the same path as Michelle Obama," he notes proudly.

Ken Lewis. Courtesy the Oregon Community Foundation.

Accordingly, while employed first as a Portland lawyer, then as CEO of Lasco Shipping, and later on both federal and local trade commissions, Ken also devoted himself to educational philanthropy and activism. His early attempts to create a financial rewards program for exceptional teachers were met with union resistance. Then Ken heard about Eugene Lang and brought him to Portland to speak at Temple Beth Israel synagogue. Lang founded the national "I Have a Dream" Foundation in 1981 in order to counter the rising dropout rate among low-income and minority students in New York. Based on the IHAD Foundation's success in New York and other states, Ken immediately knew that the "I Have a Dream" model could help make a difference to Oregon's struggling schools. Ken partnered with Pamela Jacklin and Leonard Girard, a husband-and-wife team who had also heard of the organization, and after some intensive fundraising and organizing, they started the Oregon chapter of the "I Have a Dream" Foundation.

The IHAD Foundation's model is extraordinary, Ken says, because it targets young at-risk students and provides a support network to them all the way through to high school graduation and beyond. In 1990, the Oregon chapter's first year, the organization "adopted" fifth graders at King Elementary School in Northeast Portland, a school with a high student turnover rate and many low-income and minority students. IHAD Foundation followed these children through their schooling, giving them emotional support, teaching them life skills, providing them with college and career counseling, and even offering tuition support for extracurricular programs and for college. Choosing from the neediest of local schools, the organization has adopted a class every second year since 1990 and, as with King Elementary's students, mentors them all the way through high school.

To succeed, Ken says, the program needs a sympathetic school principal, teachers willing to collaborate, the permission of all parents, and most of all, an effective program coordinator. As Ken notes, the on-site coordinator is perhaps *the* key figure in the program, a person whose role is pastoral, motivational, and educational, and who works with the same kids for eight full years to provide stability and support. One of the IHAD Foundation's attributes is that it relies upon the interest and concern of caring citizens in order to operate. "It actually does take a village," Ken says with a grin.

What it also takes is someone with the determination and vision to instigate such a program. Ken has a strong sense of fairness and sets punishing standards for himself and for others: when talking about social justice, and particularly education equity, his full-court-press is difficult to block. This determination and integrity is what eventually pushed him to become the "I Have a Dream" Foundation's national president. His philanthropy and volunteerism have changed many students' lives for the better, but the effect has been mutual: Ken is clearly warmed by these students, and his affection, when combined with his fierce sense of justice and gratitude for his own successes, is why he is such an effective advocate for education equity.

The Oregon chapter of the "I Have a Dream" Foundation has adopted nearly nine hundred "Dreamers" in seven schools in Portland and three schools in Forest Grove/Cornelius. For these students, it has provided

Graduating class of Dreamers. Courtesy the Oregon "I Have A Dream" Foundation.

long-term relationships with caring mentors, academic and social support services, and career and college training to schools and families. In 2011, 84 percent of Oregon's Dreamers graduated from high school on time, well above the statewide average and nearly three times the average rate for students with their backgrounds.

As of 2011, the Oregon IHAD Foundation also launched the first all-Dreamer School at Alder Elementary, a school where 94 percent of students are eligible for free or reduced lunches and 12.8 percent of students have experienced homelessness. It is a project that will require great generosity from Oregon's philanthropic community, but it should have a tremendous effect on these children's futures and provide a successful model to Oregon's public schools. As Ken says, "philanthropy and government need to work hand-in-hand: philanthropy can provide successful models, which should then influence government policy. The endpoint of this work should be systematic change along these models. I knew that I had the opportunities I had because of my education," Ken declares. "I think it's our obligation as citizens to make sure everyone has those same opportunities."

SMART AND ASPIRE: TWO VOLUNTEER-DRIVEN SUCCESSES

The sheer number and geographic spread of children in need of educational help can make providing for them a logistical challenge. Two organizations in particular have found ways to mobilize local community volunteers in great numbers and to great effect. Start Making a Reader Today (SMART) catches kids when they are young, in the early years when learning to read—or failing to—can make or break a child's educational future. Not only does SMART provide books for children to keep and use in their homes, but it also has recruited over five thousand volunteers across Oregon to provide one-on-one reading support for at-risk young children who might not have a parent at home helping to guide their path into literacy. An independent evaluation of SMART found that fifth graders who participated in SMART in earlier grades are 60 percent more likely to reach state reading standards than students who did not. SMART's reach is impressive—the organization works with over nine thousand at-risk youth per year—and in recognition of its successes, SMART was awarded the $50,000 Library of Congress Literacy Award in 2014.

Another volunteer-driven project catches kids when they are older. ASPIRE (Access to Student Assistance Programs In Reach of Everyone) targets high school students, providing community mentors that give students the skills, knowledge, and resources they need to apply for, find funding for, and meet the standards required of higher education after high school.

The idea behind ASPIRE is straightforward: high school students' decisions about college are often made without adequate advice—few have sufficient access to college counselors. As a result, for trivial (for example, moving away from a girlfriend) or not-so-trivial (assuming that it will be unaffordable) reasons, many students feel discouraged from attending. ASPIRE provides these students access to the guidance they need to make an informed decision about their next steps. It relies on a broad network of volunteer mentors—over 1,500 in total—in each target community, which keeps its operational budget to a minimum. Because of its reliance on community volunteers, ASPIRE has been able to expand into high schools and community sites in Waldport, Ontario, North Bend, Klamath, Umatilla, and 140 other locations spanning the breadth of Oregon, opening the door to higher education for a huge number of students.[8]

ASPIRE was started through a partnership between the Oregon Community Foundation and the Oregon Student Assistance Commission (OSAC), and although it is now funded by several private foundations and federal grants, the service it provides leans heavily on community philanthropy, and particularly on the volunteerism of locals who care about disadvantaged students' education. An innovative example of how much can be accomplished with a lean budget, ASPIRE provides mentor training, coordination, and resource bases to all of its site schools, and it works with these schools to develop a local network of entirely volunteer mentors who provide career guidance, admissions and scholarship application tips, study skills help, referrals to social services, and extracurricular programs or tutoring—almost anything a student might need to make college a more palatable and realistic prospect. As one volunteer humorously deemed it, ASPIRE is partly a "naggers' program" to encourage kids to pursue higher learning and to ensure they're on track in their applications. Oregon has a wealth of local volunteers who care about education, and ASPIRE has been an innovator in recruiting, training, and deploying them efficiently throughout Oregon's communities. In 2011, over ninety-two thousand students attended ASPIRE events, and over seven thousand students were paired with one-on-one mentors who catered to each student's unique and evolving set of needs. That kind of individual attention is difficult to find in Oregon's often-overcrowded schools.

ASPIRE is groundbreaking in its simplicity, providing a network of straightforward, on-the-ground, local programs that fill a small but crucial gap in students' educational experiences. Talking to a young person about college is something that many of us can do, and, acknowledging that fact, ASPIRE has leveraged local volunteers to great effect. Each community benefits from better-educated children, and through ASPIRE, each community can help to better educate their children. A simple model . . . and a brilliant one.

DAVE HATCH AND SALMON CAMP: MENTORING NATIVE YOUTH

Dave Hatch, a Portland engineer and Siletz tribal leader, realized that an umbrella program like ASPIRE sometimes requires additional interventions by more grassroots, targeted initiatives to get students to the point where college can even be considered.

Soft-spoken and laconic, Dave comments that as both a college student and, later, as a STEM (science, technology, engineering, mathematics) sector professional, "no matter where I'm at, there are no other Indians around."

That, to him, is a big problem, because education and engineering were cornerstones of his own upbringing—both his father and grandfather were engineers, and his father was, Dave thinks, the first American Indian to graduate from West Point. A member of the Confederated Tribes of Siletz, Dave earned a master's degree in engineering from OSU and has long been a practicing engineer for the City of Portland. Based on his own education and professional life, Dave knew that there wasn't a big American Indian presence in the science and engineering community, a problem confirmed while he sat on Siletz's tribal council first in the early 1980s and then again in the 1990s. As someone who had benefited from an advanced education, and who had seen American Indian students struggling because of a

Dave Hatch. Courtesy Dave Hatch.

variety of entrenched systemic obstacles, Dave had long had an interest in education reform: not only had he already founded the American Indian Science and Engineering Society at Portland State University, but he had started working with Portland Public Schools to mentor budding young American Indian scientists working on baseline research projects.

When Howard Vollum, the co-founder of Tectronix and a prominent Oregon philanthropist, realized the rarity of Native Americans in his engineering and technology corps, he introduced a scholarship program specifically earmarked to attract young Native Americans into science, math, and engineering degrees and recruited Dave Hatch to sit on the selection committee. But although the scholarship program was generous, it simply wasn't getting enough applicants to fill the places. That was when Dave knew he needed to get involved at a more grassroots level. He and Jeffry Gottfried, then vice president of programs at the Oregon Museum of Science and Industry (OMSI), began writing grant applications for what would become Salmon Camp. Fritz Miller from the Warm Springs tribal association and Joseph Jones, who was operating the OMSI-run Hancock Field Station near Fossil in Wheeler County, also donated time and expertise. With additional contributions of resources and facilities from OMSI and from the Siletz and Warm Springs tribes, Salmon Camp's holistic approach to the education of young Native American scientists was soon proving effective.

Salmon Camp offers free residential science education and mentoring programs for American Indian middle- and high-school students, tackling the achievement gap head-on by mentoring students to improve their academic performance and by encouraging them to pursue higher education and careers in disciplines in which Native Americans are traditionally underrepresented. Just as importantly, it does so in a way that's engaging and entertaining for the students, valuable to the scientific community, and reaffirming of tribal cultures, traditions, and histories.

The inclusivity and sector-specific nature of Salmon Camp's model contributes to its effectiveness. Several times a summer, it assembles American Indian middle- and high school students from across Oregon, Washington, California, and occasionally Alaska for a free week-to-ten-day's worth of residential summer camp and educational programming, including some very high-tech training and lectures by eminent American Indian professionals from various STEM fields.

Typically, camp sessions begin with a tribal culture and history orientation on the Warm Springs reservation, where students are also introduced to fragile salmon spawning beds and learn about key concepts in conservation biology, ecology, engineering, and sustainable development. Following the life cycle of the salmon down the Deschutes, along the Columbia, and then down the coast to the Siletz reservation, Salmon Camp's program is tailored to pique students' interests in scientific topics, to involve them in actual conservation research, and to reinforce the importance of being a contributing member both to tribal communities and to the wider world. But the experience doesn't end there: as with ASPIRE and the IHAD Foundation, long-term mentorship is key to the program's success. Once camp has finished, each camper meets monthly with a mentor. After a year of mentoring and discussion about scientific issues the program culminates with a science fair with prizes, scholarships for university-level science and math classes, and direction on applying for full-scholarship opportunities to college. Salmon Camp has expanded since its beginnings and now provides STEM-sector internship placements, support for increasing parental involvement, online content and guidance, and a partnership with Portland's Native American Youth and Family Center (NAYA—profiled in Chapter Five) to build up community support and resources and to provide students with hands-on experience in real conservation research projects.

As an effective model for combatting education inequities and as an educational cornerstone for its students, Salmon Camp responded with efficiency, creativity, and pedagogical best-practice to a real, on-the-ground gap in education: too few American Indian youth were applying for science and engineering degrees. Salmon Camp provided prospective students with the skills and enthusiasm they needed, and it caught the students at a formative age. "Salmon Camp had to start at middle-school level, that was the age where we *had* to catch the kids in order for it to work," Dave explains. Also innovative was Salmon Camp's foundation on and origin within the needs and traditions of a specific demographic group. "It is really an Indian-run program," Dave Hatch notes, "that's what made it work so well. We were taking kids in residential summer camp, some of whom were really tough kids," but, he says, Salmon Camp knew how to direct them to be both productive tribal community members and productive young scientists.

Its innovative and affirming strategies had tangible, impressive results on the lives of young Native Americans. "The success rate of our scholarship program, our retention rate, is fantastic," Dave says. Part of the reason for that is that Salmon Camp mentors these students well into their college experience. Even at the scholarship interview, Dave says, the tribal panelists in charge of awarding the scholarships give students "advice about how to survive at college and make sure they know that they're important to us as a community." Because such emphasis has been placed on mentoring these students, "about 85–90 percent finish their degrees, a rate which is higher than OSU's average," Dave notes proudly.

While Dave is clearly proud of the success of Salmon Camp's graduates, he takes little credit. He celebrates his co-founders, and also the financial generosity of Howard Vollum's widow Jean in supporting the program ("her heart was so amazing—she just loved everybody," Dave said). When asked about his own contributions, Dave demurs and changes the subject, suggesting that he and his co-founders' actions were ultimately pragmatic: collectively, they identified a problem and figured out a solution. "We needed to improve our students' scores, get them outside, hook them up with Indian professionals, and show them what they could do," he says. Like many donors and volunteers, Dave is both stoical in his philosophy and self-deprecating about his contributions. "It doesn't seem like you have any choice," he concludes, "it just seems like it's what you're supposed to do. You have things that you can do to help people and you're supposed to do that."

A COMMUNITY EFFORT: SELF ENHANCEMENT, INC.

Another organization developed to fulfill the needs of a specific student population is Portland's Self Enhancement, Inc. (SEI), which focuses on ensuring that Portland's young minority and low-income children are supported all the way through high school, college, and beyond. Driving its creation was Tony Hopson, a man whose institution has become as substantial as he is.

Broad-shouldered, tall, and wearing a long, loose suit that accommodates his ex-basketball-player frame, Tony's presence fills his large office. Grey autumn light filters through the blinds as he talks. Tony says that he has known since he was twelve or thirteen years old that he wanted to be an educator and mentor. "I had two strong parents, both of whom worked two or three jobs just to provide for us. That was motivation for me: I saw how hard they worked and recognized that I didn't want to have to work three different jobs just to scrape by. I thought there had to be a better way." After

Tony Hopson and SEI students. Courtesy Self Enhancement, Inc.

all, he explains, "I grew up recognizing that there are major issues and that you're either part of the problem or part of the solution. I figured I could do something that would make life better for kids who looked like me."

As an adult, his professional life confirmed that mission. "I'd been working in the Portland Public Schools for ten years as a teacher and counselor, and I got a chance to see the good, the bad, and the ugly," he begins.

> What I recognized was that there were a lot of gaps in the school system that schools and teachers just can't fill. Things go on in a school beyond just academics: race, economics . . . there are poor black kids and poor white kids, and there are a lot of other gaps that affect a kid's ability to show up at school better prepared to learn, to be on time, to not have behavioral issues, to complete their schooling on time, or at all. . . . There's a great need for services that traditional schooling can't provide, and there are a lot of kids who are falling through the cracks because they're not being provided with it.

That need for wraparound services is how Self Enhancement, Inc. emerged. It began in the early eighties as a summertime basketball camp that had a strong mentoring and disciplinary agenda. In 1988, Tony Hopson partnered with Ray Leary, one of his co-organizers at the camp, and moved SEI into a full-year, full-time effort to cater to the area's most severely at-risk youth. Working in partnership with teachers and school administrators to identify those children who are most at risk (often because of exposure to poverty, abuse, neglect, gangs, substance abuse, absentee parents, and hunger), SEI invites these high-risk students to participate in its services, which range from after-school, weekend, summer, and mentorship programs to full enrollment at its academy. SEI teaches and mentors kids ranging from elementary through high school and guides graduates well into adulthood, too, helping them navigate college or job hunts, and mentoring them on parenting and community spirit.

"All of this comes back to our desire to make sure that all kids have an equal opportunity to get a solid, thorough education," Tony says. "We want our kids to become PCCs, positive contributing citizens. We want them to either go to college, get vocational training, or get a family-friendly job and be successful in it." SEI sticks with them through all of this, and, as a result of this long-term intensive mentoring, it has taken kids from demographics that normally fall well short of average test scores and graduation rates and has ensured not only that they pass their tests, but that they graduate on time, too.

SEI's employees—expert teachers, counselors, housing advisors, and other additional-needs staff, many of whom have that same local community background so essential to Albina Head Start—are crucial to its mission. But SEI relies much more heavily on private and corporate philanthropy than Albina Head Start: it has no national organization or federal grants to help support it. Nike has donated generously to SEI's programs, as have the Meyer Memorial Trust, the Collins Foundation, and others. SEI has also has many individual contributors, including Ellison "Eli" C. Morgan, a private philanthropist and the founder of Portland's 2030 Investors LLC, who has been one of SEI's greatest friends and benefactors.

SEI students. Courtesy Self Enhancement, Inc.

"Much of the success of SEI today I attribute to Eli," Tony says. It was through Eli that SEI finished the construction of its full-time academy, and Eli and his friends have subsequently helped to fund each year's classes and services. "It's the most phenomenal thing to have someone of the magnitude of Eli Morgan involved, both because of his own resources and wisdom and because of the network of philanthropists he brings with him. We have a real close partnership with Eli, much more than that of just a donor: he's a very close friend of mine, and we've been so grateful for his efforts," Tony says.

Though Eli Morgan is retiring when discussing his philanthropic ideology, he admits that when he heard about SEI, it struck a chord with him. Growing up, he had seen friends experience racial discrimination and had witnessed the unfairness of the system. He says, "I was raised to help disadvantaged kids, and there's certainly a need for it. I wanted to help out, and I'm now financially more able to do so." Through his own contributions and his fundraising efforts, Eli's raised tens of millions of dollars for SEI and has also helped negotiate more than $8 million of scholarship money earmarked for SEI graduates to attend the University of Oregon, Oregon State, and Portland State University.

"Eli's done so much for us," Tony continues, "and never wins any of the big philanthropy awards. If this town believes that SEI has made a difference, then Portland needs to know that a large amount of that is owing to Eli Morgan. We're graduating kids at a 98 percent clip, and 85 percent of them head to college or vocational training." With the help of Eli and other generous philanthropists, SEI has been able to help transform the lives of thousands of at-risk, impoverished urban schoolchildren.[9] There is an urgency to their work: as all of the organizations profiled in this chapter attest, education inequity is a looming catastrophe for America's kids and for American society. "I don't think it could be any clearer," Tony says bluntly. "America is browning at a quick pace, and if we can't educate our children of color, America's in deep trouble."

THE CHALKBOARD PROJECT:
HELPING TEACHERS TO HELP STUDENTS

Tony's comments are pointed, and correctly allude to a wider systemic failure. Some of the individuals and organizations profiled above work to correct this at a grassroots level; others work at a systemic level, collaborating with legislators, government officials, school systems, and educators. The Chalkboard Project is an excellent example of an organization working at the systemic level. It has an unusual backstory: in 2004, five of Oregon's leading philanthropic foundations joined forces to decide upon, and then tackle, what they thought to be the most pressing issue facing Oregonians. The coalition convened a series of community councils in which citizens across the state were asked to identify the most pressing challenge facing Oregon: education was almost universally selected. As a result, these five foundations—together called Foundations for a Better Oregon—founded a single nonprofit education advocacy organization, the Chalkboard Project.[10] Today, Chalkboard is funded by six main foundations, with support from over twenty-three foundations and charitable funds: this kind of philanthropic consensus underscores the importance of their work and helps them bring disparate voices to the table.[11]

The Chalkboard Project's mission is both broad and precise: to research, pilot, and advocate for best-practice education reforms. Based in Portland but active statewide—currently the organization works with school districts serving almost 40 percent of Oregon's students—the Chalkboard Project also works with teacher certification institutions, unions, and other stakeholders to improve teacher training and classroom support.

Academic and education reformer Dr. Daniel Fallon writes that a teacher's influence on student achievement in the classroom is a full twenty times greater than that from any other variable, including class size and socioeconomic status.[12] One of Chalkboard's primary goals is to help reform the experience of teachers within the education system: they feel that well-prepared and well-supported educators are key to the eradication of education inequity. There will be at least fifteen thousand openings for teachers in Oregon by 2020, when Oregon will be more socioeconomically and racially diverse than ever. With this many new teachers entering the system, the opportunity to elevate the quality of teaching—and the level of student achievement—statewide is phenomenal. However, it will take concerted effort, careful research, and an ability to leverage systemic change.

Driven by the vision of Sue Hildick, Chalkboard's impassioned president, and with the backing of its key funders, Chalkboard is working hard to effect that change. For Sue, the mission to improve teacher support and therefore student achievement is an unquestionably personal one. "My family's

(Left) The board and affiliate members hearing from members of the Distinguished Educators' Council. (Right) Members of the Distinguished Educators' Council presenting a report. Photos by Aaron Rogosin. Courtesy the Chalkboard Project.

business is early childhood education. I'm a fourth generation Oregonian; my grandmother founded a daycare center and my mother later founded a Montessori school. . . . So I love kids, but I also have a passion for policy." She worked in various nonprofit fields, but ultimately ended up back in education. A leadership training program brought her into Portland Public Schools and led her to realize that it "was really children and their future that connected me—my passion was for education." She adds, "I have a daughter now, a beautiful little five-year-old who makes my passion ooze out of every pore: I hope to send her to public schools, and that's also why I do the work I do."

Since its founding, the Chalkboard Project has been working to improve Oregon's struggling public schools by successfully piloting evidence-based, community-tailored, best-practice programs in Oregon's classrooms and by advocating for expansive legislative and structural education reforms based on those pilot programs. Chalkboard has already helped win several legislative victories, including the passage in 2007 of a bill to revive the Oregon Beginning Teacher and Administrator Mentor Program and a bill in 2011 that revamped educator performance evaluation systems to align with new standards.

One of its most significant accomplishments is the CLASS (Creative Leadership Achieves Student Success) Project, which works to professionalize and reward teaching as a career path by providing teachers with career development opportunities, mentoring and coaching, and recognition for strong performance. Resources are available to established teachers seeking to improve their skills, and a Distinguished Educators' Council has been established to direct and debate policy and pilot programs. CLASS Project's reach is extensive. Trial school districts and school district coalitions extend across Oregon, from the south coast to eastern Oregon and the Willamette Valley. These teaching reforms have had the desired effects on students: between 2008 and 2011, CLASS districts saw an improvement in graduation rates that ranged from between 3.8 percent to 5 percent, compared with a statewide average of 0.9 percent.

CLASS reforms have been particularly effective in improving the achievement of traditionally underperforming populations. In the Tillamook School District, for example, the Hispanic graduation rate improved by 8 percentage points between 2009 and 2012; during the same period, the graduation rate of low-income students (over two-thirds of their students) skyrocketed a full 10 percentage points to 72.7 percent. Because over half (53.2 percent) of Oregon's students fall into the low-income category, and because low-income students have traditionally underperformed by a wide margin, this is very heartening news, not just for Tillamook's students, but for Oregon's as a whole. In fact, students in CLASS districts have consistently shown greater success in state assessments than other Oregon students, and CLASS districts appear to be successfully closing several achievement gaps.[13]

The CLASS Project's long-term support for established teachers is now paired with a newer program called TeachOregon, which creates partnerships between school districts and teacher-training universities, so that schools can give curricular input to universities based on their real-world teaching needs and deficiencies. TeachOregon also helps universities place student teachers with mentors and in classrooms within the schools and communities where they will likely be employed. Ultimately, Chalkboard's TeachOregon is intended to complement the CLASS Project by providing a reformed model that guides prospective teachers from their recruitment and student teaching through their own classroom experience and up the career ladder.

At the outset, Chalkboard's goals were to acquire public support and funding, to make Oregon's K-12 system one of the top ten systems in America, and to provide successful models for national education reform. They are certainly winning plaudits for their work: Chalkboard won national recognition in 2010 when the federal government awarded a $24.4 million Teacher Incentive Fund grant to seven Oregon school districts in order to deepen their CLASS Project work. The US Secretary of Education, Arne Duncan, called the CLASS Project "a tremendous example of the successful work that should be taken to scale, because students benefit when teachers work together to share best practices and learn from one another."

Through all of these innovations, Sue Hildick has been quietly driving Chalkboard forward. Her tenacity and clear-eyed strategy have helped Chalkboard's efficacy. "It doesn't matter where in Oregon you live or what your politics are—we all want our kids surrounded by great teachers so they learn to be successful at whatever comes next." When teachers who are participating in a Chalkboard program give feedback to the Project, they are overwhelmingly positive and grateful to Chalkboard for providing them with encouragement and opportunities. They clearly hunger for mentorship and for a supportive work environment, for a workplace that gives them opportunities to demonstrate what anyone who's had an inspiring teacher knows to be true: good teachers love to teach, and love to teach *well*. As a result of Chalkboard's strategic vision and strong community mandate, teachers across Oregon are feeling more empowered, optimistic, knowledgeable, and fulfilled, and students are reaping the benefits.

SALEM-KEIZER COALITION FOR EQUALITY: A GRASSROOTS ADVOCATE FOR SYSTEMIC CHANGE

Chalkboard's statewide pilot programs and legislative reforms bode very well for Oregon's students and teachers, but there is still a battle to be fought on the ground. Many organizations are advocating for systemic change from the front lines, ensuring that reforms are driven by the local knowledge needed for bottom-up *and* top-down change. Salem hosts the Oregon Department of Education, but it also houses many of the at-risk students that Oregon government, nonprofits, and private citizens are working to help. There, a group of local parents, activists, and educators have joined together to advocate for systemic change across the Salem-Keizer School District and the state as a whole.

The Salem-Keizer Coalition for Equality's (SKCE) headquarters is in a drab office block in north Salem. The corridors, lit with dim fluorescence, are covered in *noticias* and posters filled with lists of employment rights, aid organizations, community events, immigration guidance, and rallying cries of *Sí se puede*, Dolores Huerta's and Cesar Chavéz's motto (which roughly translates to "yes, we can"). Past these, and past study centers, conference rooms, a meeting hall, and a couple of curious children wandering around, is the office of co-founders Eduardo Angulo and Annalivia Palazzo-Angulo.

When we visited, every surface was draped in paper. Tables towered with it, stacks crawled up the walls, reams and folders were buttressed against printers. "Oregon has some of the best minds to write proposals," Eduardo explained in half-joking apology, "and the reason that the office is filled with paper is because these great minds write beautiful education reform proposals with these beautiful mission statements that are, in practice, 90 percent *crap*, and I mean *crap*. How many meetings have we gone to in ten years?" he asked. "*Five thousand* meetings, no exaggeration."

He apologized again, and explained that SKCE had just received some new statistics that suggested that the achievement gap in some areas was widening. Angry and impassioned, he interpreted this news in italics and in bold. "But this is the part where we have to be *courageous*. We must all insist from the governor down that this is *unacceptable* and *has to stop*. We need *accountability*.

Leyendo Avanzamos at Cesar Chavez Elementary. Courtesy Salem-Keizer Coalition for Equality.

We need school districts to take the money they're supposed to be using for English language learners [ELL] and use them for ELL programs. Here's the road map! This same problem is happening across the nation—ELLs, students of color, poor whites—everyone's in the same predicament, badly educated, disempowered... people have been talking about it, crying about it, speaking up, but *no one's listening!* All of these ideas and initiatives, all the *smart Oregonians* get together and then we don't get to first base because we don't make the courageous decisions, we don't say, '*Enough!*'"

His passion and anger come from personal experience. Eduardo and wife Annalivia share similar stories, if not backgrounds. Both grew up poor and disadvantaged, Eduardo in Puerto Rico and Annalivia in Salem. Eduardo moved to New York in his teens and progressed from working in a textile factory to mentoring former gang members in Los Angeles. LA's gang culture finally dispirited him enough that he asked to transfer to the Oregon program, "and as soon as the plane had landed, the greenness of the land, and the Willamette Valley, was just such an incredible, wonderful shift," he recalls. Annalivia, meanwhile, dropped out of high school to marry and have a child, and then, after a divorce at age twenty-eight, opened up a sewing business of her own. Both Annalivia and Eduardo realized that an education would open doors, and they both returned to school, where they met and fell in love.

"I finished my college degree at Chemeketa as valedictorian, then went to Linfield and did a double major in poli-sci and Spanish literature," Eduardo said. Just after he graduated, "Oregon's voters passed Measure 11 [a mandatory minimum sentencing law]—one strike and you're out, the most draconian anti-gang measure in the nation." Oregon's gang population, Eduardo knew, was not nearly as entrenched as LA's, and he thought, "OK, this is doable here—there is hope." He immediately started volunteering with local families to warn them of the one-strike-you're-out policy and of the dire consequences for their children: one fight in the playground can sentence a fifteen-year-old to almost six years in an adult prison. "It has taken a toll on the youth of color in Oregon," Eduardo states, "and it's pushing our kids out of school and away from the opportunities that they need." To combat this injustice, Eduardo started asking questions, talking with the NAACP, Latino leaders, police, principals, and superintendents about how to remedy the situation. "In June of 1999, African American kids represented 1 percent of Salem-Keizer's student body and 49 percent of the disciplinary cases. There's something broken in the system. As a researcher, I knew that bureaucracies exist to perpetuate themselves, they wear you out, so we got people together in order to advocate systematically and *organize.* Let's *sandblast* these bureaucracies, but let's also be part of a *process*," Eduardo says emphatically. "I wanted to challenge people at the decision-making table, because I don't think that anything will happen otherwise."

In response, Eduardo and Annalivia formed the Salem-Keizer Coalition for Equality in 1999. For the first three years, they worked unpaid, funding the organization out of their quickly dwindling savings. "We said to ourselves, if we're going to do anything in life, this is it," Eduardo says. "You can't hold anyone accountable if you can't hold yourself accountable. You can't just ask people to do things without showing them that you're committed to bringing about change." Eduardo and Annalivia's own philanthropic contributions were huge, but in order for the organization to survive, they needed additional support.

That's when Eduardo met Dick Withnell, a prominent Salem philanthropist and the owner of a chain of car dealerships, who was working on a committee with Oregon's chief justice to find an alternative to Measure 11. At their first meeting, Dick immediately asked Eduardo, "You like to stir things up, don't you? So, are you part of the problem or part of the solution?" Dick, an established conservative who dislikes entitlement programs and tax raises, was no doubt surprised when Eduardo responded with the same question back, but as soon as it became apparent that they were both Linfield College graduates, the tension eased—"well, that makes us brothers," both agreed.

"Eduardo's a soldier on the ground," Dick says. "I like seeing the underdog succeed, and I believe in giving back to the community." Dick pledged his support to SKCE, albeit with caveats: "I give with strings attached—I want to see improvements, I want a game plan." Eduardo was able to point to several

(Left) Dick and Gayle Withnell, at SKCE's "Raising the Bar" Gala, 2013. (Right) At the podium: Moises Mendoza, North Salem High School student and SKCE mock trial champion, with Eduardo Angulo. Courtesy SKCE.

ways in which SKCE had already improved students' lives, which, Dick says, was great. "It's so important to see a return on your investment." Investing in education is particularly appealing, he adds, because it benefits the whole community by making a more productive, more successful society. He repeats this mantra several times: "Education is the high tide that raises all boats."

With the support of Dick Withnell and other philanthropists and foundations, Eduardo, Annalivia, and the Salem-Keizer Coalition for Equality have significantly raised awareness of Oregon's education inequities and have improved the prospects of many students of color within Salem-Keizer school district and well beyond it. SKCE's defining principle is, as Eduardo summarizes, "if you start behind, if you're left behind from the beginning, you'll finish behind. The achievement gap isn't caused by a lack of hard work or care on the part of parents and educators: it's a result of being unable to start at the same place." Persistence—and cunning—is needed to get that voice at the table. As Eduardo describes, "I used to go to the gym near the courthouse at five in the morning because I knew Kitzhaber would go and use the treadmill. He'd be running and I'd get onto the treadmill next to him. I got no shame, you know? 'Morning, Governor!' I'd say, and then I'd bring him info and ask for his counsel."

Eduardo's rough-and-ready approach informs SKCE's strategies as a whole. Locally, SKCE is on the ground trying to improve students' learning experiences. They have improved support networks for Latino kids, and both in the field and through their cultural center have consolidated a great deal of information and advice about education, Latino heritage, employment rights, skill acquisition, and community building for parents and children alike. They have commissioned school-by-school studies to see where the problems are and have confronted and partnered with local school and district officials accordingly.

SKCE sponsors robotics teams, mock trial teams, and other complementary curricula programs at schools and in areas that traditionally haven't had resources for such skill- and confidence-building extracurriculars. Such programs have relied on the support of a committed network of volunteer experts, including two former chief justices of the Oregon Supreme Court, Paul De Muniz (Oregon's first Hispanic chief justice) and Edwin Peterson. Chief Justice Peterson explains that he works "with the Latino high school mock trial program to assist, in some small way, with their becoming included in our society, . . . to assist them in speaking up without fear of retribution; in getting a better education; in increasing their personal level of performance; and in increasing their self-confidence." Oregon's minority families, Chief Justice Peterson continues, "want the same opportunities that are available to white people like me. They want to own their home, have a good job, and possibly have a business. They want love, peace and tranquility. . . . I support SKCE because it serves a segment of our society that otherwise would not be served: this area's Hispanic families, particularly those who are fairly recent arrivals in the United States." Moises Mendoza, an SKCE student, describes his experience in their mock trial program as transformative. "I used to be afraid of the police, the courts, judges, and the law. Through Mock Trial, I realized that I have a voice, and I can use the law to help others."

Former chief justice of the Supreme Court of Oregon Paul De Muniz working with SKCE's mock trial team. Photo courtesy SKCE.

Beyond eminent educators, scientists, and legal professionals, SKCE has had huge success in mobilizing the Latino community itself, forming a coalition of concerned parents to participate vocally in their children's education and to help promote systemic change. "The way I see it," Annalivia says, "is that we work from the top down and the bottom up to change the educational outcomes of our Latino and other minority children." They do that, she says, by working with parents to help them advocate on their children's behalf. These parents, many of whom come from central America, often lack much formal education themselves: some of them left school at age eight, speak little English, read Spanish poorly, and know little about the American educational system. "Their kids have access to a comprehensive education system here, but they don't have complete equity in the system: they have to fight for their opportunities," Annalivia says. "We were worried that we were going to lose a generation of students who simply couldn't access the opportunities they had in front of them. We have thousands of kids that need help, and we feel that if you really want social change, you need to make parents the central focus. So we embrace parents as their first teachers and as the best advocates for our children."

SKCE's Leyendo Avanzamos program builds Spanish literacy skills in low-income Spanish-speaking parents so that they can help their children learn to read at grade level from a young age. In the flagship Educate and Inspire (Educa y Inspira) program, parents attend in-depth bilingual and bicultural workshops that teach them why their children's education matters and how to guide their children to maximum benefit. SKCE also runs training-of-trainers sessions, so that community members can take the lessons onward, and they partner with other school districts and education and minority advocacy organizations to ensure their programs are widely disseminated.

The Salem-Keizer Coalition for Equality also advises similar organizations in other communities, including Jackson County's Una Voz (One Voice) group, which also advocates for improved educational opportunities for minority students. And SKCE has helped found the Oregon Alliance for Education Equity (OAEE), which exists "to eliminate racial and ethnic disparities in education, [and] . . . to educate, advocate, and engage with decision-makers to support policy changes." It brings together the most diverse and comprehensive coalition of minority community groups and advocates the state has ever seen, including Latinos, Asians, Pacific islanders, African Americans, unions, teachers, advocates, policy makers, and social workers—over thirty-five prominent organizations ranging from the Oregon ACLU to all nine Native American tribal governments. "Having this alliance is key: we have never been as organized as we are now, and the advocacy of people with color in Oregon has never been this unified or coherent," Eduardo declares proudly.

SKCE's successes have meant many personal sacrifices for Annalivia and Eduardo. With any nonprofit, burnout is a risk, and Eduardo's tireless activism and punishing schedule pushed him to the edge. In the early hours of August 25, 2013, Eduardo was driving in Portland when he crashed into another car, paralyzing its driver from the waist down. In February 2014, he was sentenced to fifty-four months in prison for driving under the influence. Although the accident was hugely tragic both for its victim and for the communities Eduardo worked so extensively with, Annalivia stepped into the directorship, and the Salem-Keizer Coalition for Equality is benefiting from her clarity of purpose.

Annalivia had always been SKCE's pragmatist and administrator, establishing the protocols and underlying structure that kept the organization moving forward. Eduardo was its public face and motivator, busy articulating SKCE's mission, building connections, and creating partnerships. Now, Annalivia finds herself performing both roles.

Although it's been a tough period for SKCE and for her family, Annalivia relishes her new role. "I love being executive director because I love the work we do. The larger picture is that we empower entire families: we give parents the capacity and tools to change the vision of their households, to help them

Children at Leyendo Avanzamos sessions at Four Corners Elementary. Photos courtesy SKCE.

become education advocates with teachers, with the school district, with the legislature, and with their kids at home. If a kid is told often enough that she will get her homework done and will go to college, it will happen. It's about storytelling, not discipline. We want parents to teach their kids about possibilities—that's how you enact systemic change, that's how you lift up a population."

Annalivia and Eduardo's own philanthropy brought them into this work, and their zeal has inspired donors like Dick Withnell to contribute both passion and financial support and volunteers like Paul De Muniz and Edwin Peterson to offer up their expertise and enthusiasm. Because of SKCE's donors and volunteers, because of their army of engaged parents, and because of Eduardo's and Annalivia's shared vision, Oregon's low-income and minority schoolchildren could face a brighter future. But there is much work yet to be done, Annalivia and Eduardo both agree: these reforms, and these programs, have not come easily. "You know," said Eduardo, "this thing is *hard*, the bureaucracy is *hard*. This is a labor of love. We need to be included in the conversation and have our ideas heard. This is not a partisan cause, it's an American cause, a national cause! The British philosopher J. S. Mill said that human beings are intrinsically good, and I believe that fighting for the greater good is the greatest thing any being can do."

HOPE FOR THE FUTURE

In fact, there are many things going right for Oregon's education system, thanks to tireless campaigners, educators, and donors, only a handful of whom we could profile in *State of Giving.* Local innovators across the state are making a difference for Oregon's children, offering after-school sports or other extra-curricular activities, heritage education programs, outdoor schools, and many other life-altering experiences that many low-income or otherwise marginal-ized students would never have access to otherwise. Others are working to reform the system as a whole, ensuring that students, parents, and teachers are supported with equity and efficacy. That both Chalkboard and ASPIRE have been celebrated nationally, and that Ken Lewis and Ron Herndon have served as long-term national presidents for their respective organizations, suggests that Oregon's educators and reformers must be doing something right.

Although it is frustrating that these efforts remain necessary, it is heartening to see citizens and experts from across the state coming together to enact real and substantive improvements to our children's futures. It demonstrates the central role that, for better or worse, donors, nonprofits, and volunteers must play in eradicating the achievement gap and leveling the educational playing field. Through private contributions of money, expertise, and time, the problems in Oregon's education system are being chipped away at by people and organizations who can work in creative, flexible, and community-appropriate ways to solve problems on the ground as well as in the legislature and in the textbooks. With policy experts working top-down, and indefatigable fighters scaling from the bottom up, we have a shot at eradicating the endemic and intractable problem of education inequity in Oregon. But it will require strategic and multifaceted action, more time, more resources, and more passion; it will take a more concerted effort from all of us, perhaps with a whisper of *sí, se puede* on our lips.

3
Urgent Needs:
Hunger and Homelessness

"Heroes are not giant statues framed against a red sky. They are people who say: this is my community, and it's my responsibility to make it better."
—Governor Tom McCall

"If a free society cannot help the many who are poor, it cannot save the few who are rich."
—John F. Kennedy

Many of Oregon's homeless people don't appear particularly homeless. They are not mentally ill or drug dependent; they are physically fit, active, and friendly. They are also *young*. More kids than you might think show up at school in the morning without a home to go to at night. They and their parents are part of a population that, based on the number of people using aid services on one designated night, places Oregon's 2012 homeless population at 15,828. In reality, the number is likely to be much larger,[1] as many adults and children experiencing homelessness are off the radar and not using aid services. The Oregon Department of Education's tally of homeless children found that 20,370[2] children were homeless for at least part of the 2011–2012 school year and that 79 percent of Oregon's school districts had homeless students enrolled. The reasons for this large homeless population are as diverse as the individuals and families themselves, including unemployment, mental illness, drug and alcohol addiction, and base poverty.

Homelessness is one side of the coin of poverty; the other side is hunger. Statewide, the Oregon Food Bank's food box program increased its distributions by 41 percent between 2008 and 2013. In 2012, the network gave out more than 1 million food boxes, and an average of ninety-two thousand children eat from those boxes each month.[3] In fact, because children have become such a large part of the hunger problem in Oregon, schools have taken on a more active role in delivering food directly to families at the school site. In addition to food boxes, many students receive free or federally subsidized lunches at their schools. In the 1990s, fewer than a third of the state's students received these lunches; now, half of all Oregon's students qualify. Overall, almost half a million Oregonians suffered food insecurity between 2009 and 2011, and 5.9 percent of Oregon's households (equivalent to eleven packed Moda Center arenas) were so deprived that they were forced to skip meals or even go without food for entire days.

These appalling statistics aren't just numbers: they tell the story of real humans, deeply destitute and struggling with basic survival. Janeen Wadsworth, then interim CEO of the Oregon Food Bank, observed in a 2012 report: "Once families lose their jobs, savings, and homes, it can take years to get back on their feet again. Moreover, the high cost of food, gas, utilities, and rent is making it even more difficult to cover basic expenses."[4] These difficulties are compounded by the depth of the recession, low wages, inflation, a paucity of job opportunities, related health and healthcare risks, the depth and duration of the recent recession, and a social and bureaucratic structure that makes it difficult for those who have no fixed address, recent work history, or borrowing power to find work and to put down roots.

The temptation is to assume that there will always be an unfortunate few at the bottom of the heap. But most homelessness is preventable, and most of the problems we face today have their origins not in an age-old economic structure, but in governmental welfare and mental healthcare cuts that began in the 1970s and 1980s and have continued to the present. For instance, the February 2014 passage of the US Farm Bill eliminated $8 billion in funding for SNAP (Supplemental Nutrition Assistance Program, colloquially known as food stamps), which means that the neediest Oregonians will be more reliant than ever on individual and community philanthropy.[5]

Hunger and homelessness are arguably the most urgent and fundamental of Oregon's problems, yet, too often, attempts to broach these topics are met with fatalistic resignation, with heated assertions about whose responsibility the problem is or isn't, or, worst of all, with muttered irritation

(Left) Young clients of Food for Lane County. (Right) Beverlee Hughes. Photos by Denise Wendt. Courtesy Food for Lane County.

directed at those who are in need. Fortunately, however, there are plenty of individuals and organizations in Oregon who are taking action to raise awareness of these issues, change public attitudes, and most importantly, assist their neighbors in need.

FOOD FOR LANE COUNTY AND ITS ANONYMOUS BENEFACTOR

Oregon's second most populous city, Eugene, has more than its fair share of hunger and homelessness. Like many regional cities, it is a hub for nearby rural communities that rely on Eugene's services. But the recession hit Oregon's tech, higher education, manufacturing, forestry, and agricultural sectors hard, and Eugene and its nearby towns are heavily weighted in those demographics. As a result, there is still tremendous poverty in the Eugene area.

"There's a lag time from when the recession first started and the time of starkest need," explains Beverlee Hughes, executive director of Food for Lane County, a nonprofit that distributes food and nutritional advice. "Now, we've bottomed out: people who lost their businesses or their jobs when the recession began have burned through their savings, have exhausted friends' and families' help. . . . They don't come to our door until they've exhausted everything they have. The people we're trying to help have nothing left. Kids are coming to school so hungry they can't learn. We're going to be at this for a long time," she says sadly.

Providing long-term services requires long-term financial support, and since only 35 percent of Food for Lane County's revenue comes from the government, they rely on private donations both of food and money. Fortunately, while Food for Lane County (and other similar organizations) always need more money than they are given, Eugene's citizens have been magnanimous

(Left) A client at Food for Lane County's downtown Eugene restaurant. (Right) A client of Food for Lane County's summer food program. Photos by Denise Wendt. Courtesy Food for Lane County.

in helping the organization provide meals and pantries to ever-widening areas of the region, including a great many nearby rural communities.

Although Food for Lane County has a strong support network of donors, one of its most generous individual contributors is also one of its most mysterious. Whereas many of the donors profiled in this book don't mind having their names shared, this donor prefers to remain anonymous. She is not alone. Though donors have many good reasons to release their names, including a desire to inspire philanthropy in others, there are many good reasons why donors might prefer to go unnamed: a retiring and modest nature, a desire to protect the privacy of friends and family, a wish to avoid a philanthropic reputation (and all of the demands and requests that come with it), a wish for independence in choosing causes, or simply a desire for normalcy.

All these reasons shape the thinking of Food for Lane County's anonymous donor. Tall and soft-spoken, the donor is clearly aware, and somewhat in awe, of the power that comes with wealth. She is also outspoken about the redistribution of it. "My father was an investor and made a lot of money—our system is so skewed toward people with money. The more money you have, the more money you can make," she says. "Having a lot of money has amazing benefits—a good house, plenty of heat, nice clothes, vacations—but there's a responsibility that comes with wealth, and for me it's been a process of learning to take responsibility for that. I've never understood why we have such an issue about the wealthy paying more taxes—of *course* we should, there's no reason *not* to give back."

"I've got kids and I'm an academic," she continues, "and after my father died some years ago, I found myself with a lot of money. What I don't have much of is time." Academia is a demanding profession, and when combined with motherhood, it leaves little energy to spare. "I have always been very focused on furthering my academic career, and my priorities are it and my kids. I already feel pulled in a lot of different directions, and the wealth adds to that stress. I remain anonymous in part because I don't want to add further to that stress—I'm very protective of my free time, and I have enough other interests that I don't really identify myself chiefly as a philanthropist. But I also want to give back in a way that seems true to my values. I'm pretty lucky that I can recognize how important a small contribution can be, and how much impact a big contribution can have."

She pauses, and then continues slowly, "financially, large donations don't mean a sacrifice for me . . ." She pauses again, clearly moved by the thought. "But while it's easy for me to commit tens of thousands of dollars, I know it means SO much to other people. It makes me feel humble to be able to do this and to see successes. . . . It's amazing." Her values, she says, lead her to donate to organizations like Outside In, Shelter Care, Planned Parenthood, and of course Food for Lane County, a charity very near to her heart. "Food is so immediate, so essential, and the statistics on hunger in Oregon are shocking," she declares. "There is so much hunger that we don't see, and I have a very high opinion of Food for Lane County. I even recently found out that one of my grad students uses their services," she adds.

Like other organizations discussed in this chapter, Food for Lane County provides services on multiple levels, and its food distribution reach is huge, encompassing at least twenty different towns in the mid-Willamette Valley. The organization leverages vast community support in order to disperse its services as widely as possible, utilizing several food procurement strategies and 116 partner agencies to help with food distribution.

Food for Lane County's programs also serve diverse needs and populations. Its BellyFull program partners with the Elks, Rotary, and with schools to ensure that kids have snack-packs to take home on the weekends to tide them over until Monday. When schools are out and less available to help with food distribution, Food for Lane County's summer food program distributes food at over 150 stops, and has mobile pantries set up in four locations every month. A Brown Bag program delivers supplies to senior living facilities, and rural areas are served through drop-off delivery programs. In addition, Food for Lane County offers cooking classes, food shopping classes, and recipe guides, as well as a new product line of low-cost, nutritious, grain-based meals. Its two gardens and a farm help generate 165,000 pounds of produce and teach thousands of mostly low-income volunteers how to garden and how to cook fresh homegrown meals. The organization also runs a dining room restaurant in Eugene that feeds up to three hundred mostly homeless people per night, ensuring both a hot and nutritious meal and a welcoming

(Left) Food for Lane County's Youth Farm. (Right) Clients at Food for Lane County's dining room. Photos by Denise Wendt. Courtesy Food for Lane County.

space, with flowers and newspapers on the tables, a piano, and waiters who bring them dessert—a gracious, dignifying moment.

Food for Lane County's scope is already expansive, and "the need for food aid is still increasing," explains Beverlee Hughes. Food pantries across Oregon and southwest Washington distributed over 1 million food boxes in 2011; one in five Oregonians participates in SNAP; and Oregon was rated by the US Department of Agriculture to have the highest childhood hunger rate in the nation, with almost 30 percent of Oregon kids found to be food insecure.[6] (This complements Oregon Department of Education's findings that over 53 percent of Oregon's students now qualify for free or reduced school lunches.) The food stamps cut, Beverlee estimates, will threaten food security for at least eighty-two thousand Eugene-area residents—another worry in an already worrisome time.

Due to increased need, Beverlee says, "our need for community philanthropy is increasing too. Half of our food comes from the local community, and we're the only food bank in the state that's not spending a lot of money to buy food. We have arrangements with grocery stores, hospitals, producers, and wholesalers, and private individuals also provide donations of food, as well as money with which to buy food and to expand our services." Their volunteer corps is both enormous and necessary: in addition to their fifty-seven full-time employees, Food for Lane County received sixty-eight thousand volunteer hours last year, the equivalent of thirty-two full-time employees. "There are a lot of people who want to be part of the solution," she says, "and there are so many opportunities to volunteer with us."

There are plenty of opportunities to donate money as well. Two-fifths of Food for Lane County's funding comes from private individuals, which means that their anonymous donor's grants and food purchases have made a huge difference to the quality and extent of services that Food for Lane County can provide. This donor has issued several sizeable challenge grants[7] to spur on other acts of community philanthropy. As she puts it, "you could throw money at a problem, but if you can encourage others to give some, they get interested and are more likely to give again. . . . It's more logical and more sustainable."

One of her favorite innovations was a matching grant levied through food coupons, to which members of the public could donate through participating grocery stores. It has been responsible for raising over $1 million since the program launched in 1996. "I went to my grocery store a few weeks ago," she recalled, "and asked the clerk what the deal was. He told me, and I said, 'So let me get this straight. I donate $5 and it becomes $10?' The cashier said, 'Yeah, some guy promised a whole bunch of money so that all donations are matched.' 'What makes you think it was some guy?' I asked." She grins.

SISTERS OF THE ROAD, PORTLAND

Portland's street population has long been sizeable and, like Eugene's, has grown further as a result of the recession. In 2011, the number of families experiencing homelessness increased by 29 percent, requests for emergency shelter increased by 15 percent, and a quarter of those who requested shelter were turned away due to lack of beds; people who needed meals were turned away in similar numbers.[8] The working poor represent a significant portion of Portland's hungry and homeless population: in 2011, 32 percent of those requesting food assistance were employed. Portlanders experiencing hunger and homelessness have access to a number of resources, although reaching them can be difficult at times. Many faith-based organizations (churches,

Staff and diners at Sisters Of The Road Café. Courtesy Sisters Of The Road.

synagogues, mosques) host soup kitchens, winter warming shelters, and family support services. Organizations such as Human Solutions do great work in helping homeless and low-income families move out of poverty by assisting with utilities payments, job and financial training, and emergency and longer-term free or affordable housing. Other organizations focus on youth services, job services, and much-needed medical and dental care (for example, Missions of Mercy, which runs free dental clinics). Still others, like Habitat for Humanity, focus exclusively on providing affordable housing.

Meanwhile, Sisters Of The Road Café, a venerable Portland restaurant and community center, has been on the front lines of the war against poverty for over thirty years now. Sisters Of The Road Café was a vanguard in championing the rights and dignity of the impoverished and destitute. Today, it meets many of the urgent needs of downtown Portland's homeless population while also providing job training, counseling, and human rights advocacy. Hot meals and dignity are its specialty—providing homeless Portlanders with a place to buy an inexpensive meal or to work in trade for one—but Sisters Of The Road is also a center of social justice, a secular proponent of Dorothy Day's Catholic Worker–style advocacy for equality, respect, and civil rights for all.

At the warm heart of Sisters Of The Road is its co-founder, Genny Nelson. Slight of build and fair-haired, Genny had a clear vision of the environment she wanted to create for homeless people, a vision that she adhered to in the thirty years she worked for and ran Sisters. Born in Lewiston, Idaho, Genny was an idealistic and enthusiastic junior at Portland State University when she began a work-study project on Portland's Skid Row. By the end of her term project, she knew her vocation: to advocate on behalf of the poor and the homeless, and to serve them. Her work began with women, Genny said. "There was a clear lack of services—really, a plain unwillingness to serve women. The missions didn't allow women because they didn't think women belonged on Skid Row, and there was only one nonprofit shelter for women—it only had about ten beds. At the missions, the food wasn't recognizable and they had a prosthelytizing mandate: you were ineligible for a meal unless you participated in a religious service. So we started talking to women about their needs and issues, and what came out of those conversations was that people wanted a community gathering spot, a place to dine with dignity, and a safe public place that welcomed everyone, especially women and children."

Genny and her friend Sandy Gooch set out to meet those requests, and in 1979, they founded Sisters Of The Road in Old Town Portland, a safe space that served hot meals and that, catering for a community vulnerable to violence, explicitly endorsed principles of nonviolence. "The bedrock for Sisters Of The Road is a resounding *no!* to any kind of violence, including humiliation,

Courtesy Sisters Of The Road.

racism, sexism, homophobia, ageism," Nelson explains.[9] "Second is a commitment to love, to be compassionate, responsible, and accountable. Third is our belief that change is a creative process that depends on relationships."

Sisters Of The Road is best known for its nonprofit café, which is usually packed each day at the lunch hour and which serves over 225 meals a day. A meal includes a main course, dessert, and a drink and costs $1.50, a price that has remained unchanged since the café's inception. Those who do not have cash or food stamps to pay can barter for their meal by serving food at the steam table, taking out the trash, or otherwise helping out; fifteen minutes of work buys you a meal, and thirty minutes of work pays for a friend as well, thus providing Sisters' clients with opportunities for generosity they otherwise may not have. "People *want* to pay for their own way and they want to work. With Sisters, we really understood from the very beginning that you can't do for people what they can do for themselves." As Terry Prather, a Sisters client, said in a recent interview with the *Oregonian*, Sisters "is a safe place for everybody. [I like coming here] because I can keep my dignity. I can go to the mission and eat a meal, but here I can come and do some work."[10]

Sisters Of The Road's commitment to dignity and empowerment has helped shift attitudes toward the less well-off. In some organizations, a free meal comes with a lecture or a sermon, but at Sisters, a person earns their meal and has the right to eat it in safety and peace. In the same *Oregonian* interview, Genny observed that, "soon after we opened word began to get out, people quickly got the fact that something different happens here, that this was not business as usual on the street."

Two friends at Sisters Of The Road. Courtesy Sisters Of The Road.

While the café program is the best-known aspect of Sisters Of The Road, the philosophies of nonviolence, dining with dignity, and systemic change deeply guide the organization, and it is nationally known as a fervent and effective advocate for homeless people's rights. Genny explains that today's high rates of homelessness mark a shift from the past, and that it is societal failures, more than individuals' problems, that lead to destitution. In the last few decades, she says, "[i]t stopped being the political will to build affordable housing. We lost most of it in the 1990s, and we've never replaced it. We at Sisters always say you have to go to the root of the problem, and it's a systemic problem." When Genny received an honorary doctorate from the University of Portland and the inaugural Genevieve Nelson Nonviolence and Economic Human Rights Award, she elaborated: "it's not politicians by themselves who are going to wake up one morning and say, 'Oh, let's end homelessness today!' It's people who are dealing with homelessness, and their housed allies, who have identified the root causes of this national problem. It is by building authentic relationships across class and political lines that homelessness will be eradicated. 'It is when we treat strangers specially that the world is transformed,' said Dorothy Day."[11]

Creating this caring community was not always easy. Genny and her staff have appeased knife-wielding clients and have struggled daily to maintain an environment that upholds principles of nonviolence and that remains safe and welcoming. Those threatening violence are asked to leave, but are welcomed back the next day for a fresh start. New beginnings are key to Sisters' model:

not only does it provide hot meals, warmth, and dignity for homeless Portlanders, but Sisters also helps them find the tools—ranging from self-confidence to job training to nonviolent protest skills—with which to help themselves.

After three decades spent leading Sisters, in 2009 Genny Nelson handed the reins over to new leadership, but she continues to keep in close contact. In an interview with *Street Roots* magazine marking her retirement, Nelson said:

> We have stayed the course: Sisters Of The Road is as passionate now as when we first began about who we are. Sisters is a nonprofit organization grounded in the philosophies of nonviolence and gentle personalism, while operating from a community organizing model, all within a systemic change approach.
>
> We believe if you want to solve homelessness, do more than satiate the immediate, urgent needs of the homeless people: build community and share power with them; create systems that teach self-reliance instead of dependence; and remember, until men and women experiencing the calamities of homelessness and poverty are full participants at the table where public policy on homelessness is being decided, we will never resolve it.[12]

Monica Beemer, executive director of Sisters, says that Genny's legacy is "about building relationships and community and challenging the violence within ourselves and society; it's about seeing each other every day and sharing stories."[13] Sisters strives to remind us that people experiencing homelessness

Chefs hard at work. Courtesy Sisters Of The Road.

are just like the rest of us: they too want safe and dignified living arrangements, desire self-determination, and have thoughtful ideas about how to solve the problem of homelessness. Genny's generosity with her time and energy comes with no strings attached: Sisters' clients are her equals, she treats them accordingly, and she encourages them to find their own voice and power.

That creed seems to resonate widely with Portland's citizenry. Thousands of Portlanders have come together to help support the organization: Sisters Of The Road receives no government funding, and over 65 percent of its $1.43 million annual operating budget comes from private donations of $100 or less—an amazing tally. Sisters Of The Road has shown Oregon, and the nation, a different way of dealing with homelessness and hunger. Under Genny Nelson's leadership, Sisters has "rehumanized" the problems of hunger and homelessness and has demonstrated the strength, the creativity, and the firm ethical foundation necessary to tackle one of America's biggest challenges from the ground up. And yet, Genny cautions, the battle's far from over. "My biggest sadness is that there is worse homelessness now than when I started my work in 1979. Systemic issues requires systemic solutions."

SMALL MULTISERVICE PROVIDERS: THE CORVALLIS HOMELESS SHELTER COALITION, BEND'S FAMILY KITCHEN, AND THE CLACKAMAS SERVICE CENTER

Many outstanding organizations working on issues of hunger and homelessness have emerged as spontaneous community responses, developed quickly by a few empathetic citizens and often growing rapidly in response to urgent need and lack of government support. Volunteers and small donors often drive these efforts, collaborating adaptively to meet their communities' most basic needs. Three excellent examples of this type of initiative are the Corvallis Homeless Shelter Coalition, Bend's Family Kitchen, and the Clackamas Service Center.

The Corvallis Homeless Shelter Coalition (CHSC) was formed in 2006 by community members concerned that homeless people had no place to get out of the weather in the wintertime. After several months of meetings, the group located an unused fraternity house, which they upgraded, with volunteer labor, to meet the local fire code. The shelter opened in December 2006 and stayed open until the following March; now, it operates annually from November through March. Except for $5,000 from the Corvallis police department, it operates completely on donations. In its third year, CHSC moved to the Westside Community Church, where it is still located. This new setting has enabled it to expand: housed in a portion of the building that was once a school, clients can use the school's four showers, ensuring that each shelter resident can bathe twice a week. Supported by seventeen faith-based and community organizations, the shelter's structure is straight-forward—each organization is assigned a week during which it provides volunteers and snacks for the guests. In addition, CHSC continues to receive financial support from the Corvallis Police Department and community donors, and, beginning in 2011, it also received grant funding from the city and from United Way.

As a key partner in Corvallis' community service network, the Corvallis Homeless Shelter Coalition became convinced that new solutions were needed for longer-term, rather than just respite and cold-weather, housing. Through participation in a local ten-year plan to reduce homelessness, the organization became aware of the concept of "housing first," which asserts that stable housing should be the first priority and that additional needs can be met once housing is procured. In order to provide these more permanent housing options, the board began planning and applying for grants and pursuing other fundraising with great enthusiasm. As a result of their work and extensive community support, Partners' Place was constructed in 2011. Residents can stay as long as they abide by their lease and can live peacefully with their neighbors. Once admitted, residents have access to a range of wraparound services and support that would be difficult to provide if they were still on the streets or spread across a range of temporary housing facilities. This makes the facility a superb example of a wider movement to provide both emergency and longer-term, and both basic and more holistic, support for those in need.

Another community-based, volunteer-driven success story is the Family Kitchen in Bend, established in 1986. It is a partnership of churches, nonprofits, and businesses, all of whom commit funds and volunteers to regularly preparing and serving meals to central Oregon's poor. The mission of family kitchen is about as generous as it can be: "to serve anyone who needs a nutritious meal in a safe and caring environment." There is no proselytizing: the Family Kitchen welcomes all. With a small, part-time paid staff and a large volunteer corps, Family Kitchen serves a remarkable forty-nine hundred meals per month and is a perfect example of community philanthropy: people stepping forward to help others.

The organization has continued to operate through very difficult times. In September of 2012, Bend's Community Center and Common Table, which also provided meals to the homeless and impoverished, closed, thus leaving more people in dire need of the Family Kitchen's services. On March 6, 2013, Trinity Episcopal Church, the kitchen's home base, was damaged in one of seven fires set in the area. The next day, its volunteers were back distributing food at another nearby church, and the kitchen reopened properly less than a week later—an impressive testament not only to the community's resilience but also to its charitable spirit and compassion.

Photo by Kristin Anderson.

Perhaps the most comprehensive of these three organizations, and also the scrappiest, is the Clackamas Service Center (CSC), which operates out of a dilapidated 1920s clapboard church (purchased in the early eighties for ten dollars) on an unincorporated bit of land surrounded by strip malls, car dealerships, and RV parks. Despite this humble and much-too-small setting, CSC provides an all-in-one experience for Clackamas' many poor and homeless citizens: their strategy is pointedly wraparound.

Anna Jones and her friends Maggie and Julia founded CSC (then the Kendall Community Center) in 1973. A primary caregiver for her disabled daughter, Anna was looking for something to do beyond the house and realized that there was a visible need in her area for both urgent and more long-term basic services. The three women each cobbled together $1,000 of their own money and bought food and clothing for the area's needy, raising more money by hosting local bingo nights. All three volunteered long hours for decades; Maggie quit when she was ninety-three years old (she is ninety-nine now), and Julia when she was of a similar age. Anna, at a sprightly ninety years old, is still volunteering for the center and has no plans to quit or slow down.

Their dedication to CSC isn't unusual. Andy Catts, its executive director and for a long time its sole employee, figures that the average volunteer works regularly for at least five to ten years, a demonstration of exceptional dedication. With a committed volunteer corps of over two hundred and an annual budget that for decades was $100,000 and now (with the help of a volunteer grant writer) has reached $164,000, almost all of CSC's money goes straight back into services. Its overhead in 2011 was only $18,500, and only recently were two more employees hired to help Andy. They figure that for every dollar donated, CSC provides eight dollars worth of services, a frugality that is necessary particularly as Clackamas' homeless rate has grown by 174 percent in the last two years.

As Catts notes, the types of people they serve are "all over the place": families, youths, children, single parents, single people, whites, blacks, Hispanics, Russians, Vietnamese, homeless, refugees, the unemployed, the working poor. "The people who come here know us and trust us," Catts says. Within CSC's walls, clients can receive a hot meal, emergency winter shelter, food boxes, clothing, bedding, and home goods. In addition, clients can receive regular medical and dental treatment from scheduled stops by Outside In's mobile health clinic, regular mental health counseling through CSC's partnership with Cascadia Behavioral Healthcare, as well as regular showers using mobile shower pods.

CSC offers referral services to agencies where people can procure government aid and other services, as well as job and technology training opportunities. And because CSC partners with the Clackamas community courts and juvenile courts, minor offenders can serve community sentences at the service center, where they can also be directed toward services that will help them pull out of poverty and avoid reoffending. Many who serve out their sentences at CSC stay on as volunteers long after their service requirements have been met. And many of CSC's ex-clients also volunteer. For example Dan, formerly a client, has for the last eight years been running their food box program.

CSC has had astounding success with very few resources: now, on a tiny budget, in tiny premises, it serves over thirteen thousand people. Since 2008, the number of food boxes distributed has doubled, and the number of social services provided has also increased. The organization needs offices, meeting rooms, service centers, treatment rooms, a proper kitchen, a proper food-storage facility, and a storage space for clothes and bedding that isn't moldy and unventilated like their existing outbuilding, along with food, clothes, bedding, chairs, tables, and a refrigerator truck for fresh dairy and meat delivery.

That outbuilding, incidentally, is still Anna's domain: she works twice a week supervising the "shop" where clients can choose clothes and bedding. She takes great pride in the bedding in particular, bringing donated sheets and blankets home to wash them and then returning them folded into beautifully tied and labeled rolls. A petite Italian woman whose home in Naples was bombed during the war, Anna has sympathy with those who have lost everything. She is now CSC's resident matriarch: her passion and her status as a

(Left) Anna Jones, co-founder of and tireless volunteer at the Clackamas Service Center. (Right) Anna, with her beautifully bundled bedding rolls. Photos by Ashley Campion.

founding member gives her a gravitas somehow enhanced by her diminutive stature.

"I love these people," she declares, hands on hips, and adds that she knows that expanding CSC is a community imperative, that it will be community donations, from caring citizens, that will help CSC at last grow to match need. Donations are welcome, she says, because CSC can't in its present circumstances live up to its potential. And contributions toward a new facility are urgently needed. "After all," she proclaims, "nobody chooses to be poor!" As for her own involvement, like so many of CSC's volunteers, she's not going anywhere: "my daughter's retiring, my husband just died, but this is a comfort to me. I will stay until I can't." Ashley Campion—a young philanthropist whose advocacy, fundraising, and contributions to CSC have made her part of the organization's bedrock in her own right—says, "without a doubt [Anna is] one of the most outstanding Oregonian volunteers of our time."

Sustained by people like Anna, these three organizations and others like them survive through volunteerism and sheer tenacity. They provide not just food and blankets but the warmth and love that are essential to feeling human even in the depths of stark poverty. They are places that build a sense of community, that solidify a sense of place, and that articulate the difference between basic welfare provision and literal philanthropy.

THE MASLOW PROJECT

Those who work in the nonprofit sector may be familiar with Maslow's Hierarchy of Needs, usually represented as a pyramid whose base consists of physiological needs (food, water, sleep). The next tier is safety (of body, employment, resources, health, property). Subsequent tiers ascend through love and belonging, to esteem, and finally to the pinnacle, self-actualization (established capacities for morality, creativity, appreciation of fact, lack of prejudice, etc.). There are many examples in *State of Giving* of organizations providing for needs on multiple levels of this hierarchy. Medford's Maslow Project, an organization established to help homeless youth, takes provision at all levels of the hierarchy as its mandate, and its success is largely owed to two passionate people: founder Mary Ferrell and board treasurer and committed patron Roger Stokes.

Jackson County has some of the highest homeless numbers in the state, and in Medford's schools, one in ten children has no fixed place to sleep.[14] These children are Maslow's client demographic; the organization delivers as comprehensive a service as possible. "These kids are thinking about really adult things—they're sleeping in a tent and doing homework by flashlight, they're worried about providing meals for a younger brother, or about who's going to sleep next to them," declares founder and director Ferrell. A petite blonde woman with a sleeves-rolled-up-to-her-elbows, hands-on energy, Mary's philosophy is simple: individuals must have survival needs met before they can accomplish higher goals, and thus the provision of food, clothing, and safety can help stabilize homeless children's basic needs so that they can stay engaged in school and have the support and life skills necessary to make it through the rough patches and on to graduation, employment, and contentment. Working with sixteen hundred homeless newborn-to-twenty-one-year-olds and their families, the small staff at the Maslow Project provides both emergency and longer-term services, ranging from toothpaste, soap, school supplies, sleeping bags, food, and clothes to tutoring, counseling, safety training, funding for extracurricular activities, life-skills coaching, legal advice, and guided applications for social services and for post-secondary academic and vocational programs.

At five years old, the Maslow Project is a relative newcomer to southern Oregon's nonprofit community and, with a no-frills operating budget, it is hardly flashy. Its facility is an old 1920s building opposite Central Medford High School that the school district had abandoned as derelict. On busy days it feels like supplies and people are bursting from the building's venerable seams. Despite Maslow's youth and frugality, however, its effect on Jackson County has been huge: it's become a de facto office and home base for Jackson County's homeless youth.

The Maslow Project is a one-stop shop and an all-in-one resource. Clients can obtain soap or school supplies at the same place where they can fill out applications for birth certificates or college. They can also do their homework, use computers, meet with their social worker, undergo counseling or

 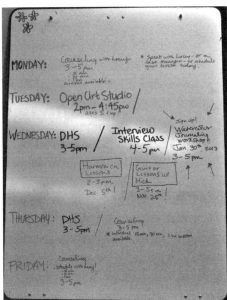

(Left) Mary Ferrell, director of the Maslow Project. (Right) The week's activities at Maslow. Photos by Kristin Anderson.

the Maslow Project's popular new art therapy sessions, shop for free clothes, eat lunch, get referred for medical and dental treatment, and get advice on other needs and goals. And that's not all. As Mary explains, "We also want to give these kids the opportunity to be kids. We fund them for after-school programs and sports and give them the chance to play so that homelessness doesn't become the focus of their existence."

The Maslow Project also provides services that extend beyond its walls. "Here in Medford, kids can come to us, but in the more rural parts of our region, it requires collaborative systems, an underground army," Mary says. That underground army is a key part of their supply chain, and Mary has spent many years building relationships with churches, police, social workers, doctors, businesses, schools, other aid organizations, and private citizens so that, as she puts it, "if a kid in Butte Falls needs a sleeping bag, we find out and can get it to her, and then get her in the system and start helping her move forward."

"The [community] collaboration is so important," adds Roger Stokes, Maslow's treasurer, founding board member, and one of their major donors. A self-effacing guy with a broad smile, Roger prefers to talk more about the organization than his own contributions to it. "It's a different way to provide service," Roger says. Mary pulls out a piece of paper covered with colored bubbles linked to each other in a complicated web. "Within every single bubble," Mary says, "we have a network of humans that we can connect with to help streamline access for these kids and get their needs met quickly and directly. We've identified local partners—media, state police, food pantries, lawyers, therapists, networks of individuals and groups who can help do drives, help provide a friendly face, help provide funds." If Maslow needs to restock its supply of clothing, Mary says, she knows who to call. One church even does a monthly "Undy-Sunday" socks-and-underwear drive for the organization.

"If we find a gap, it guides our growth and helps us expand relationships to fill the need," Mary says. For example, procuring official IDs is difficult for those without one. Maslow acquired a notary and started issuing kids with a government-recognized ID card that also served as a free bus pass ("I called up Nathan at the bus company," Mary says). "I've never had anyone saying, 'no, we don't want to support homeless children,' especially when our approach isn't to list what we need from them but to ask them how they can help, what they can offer, whether it's time, resources, money, or simply encouragement."

This interlocking web of donors, providers, and supporters has helped Maslow "remain nimble so that we can respond quickly and flexibly," Mary notes. "It's a resilient model, and because it's so firmly grounded in community support, it means we have an established group of people who can provide services, alert us to need, and help promote and further our relationships all at once. It really helps keep us mission-focused on the kids, who are at the heart of our organization."

Also at the heart of the Maslow Project are Mary and Roger themselves, both true philanthropists—although both dispute the description. Mary worked for nine years in the school district providing services for homeless youth, but quickly realized that her paid position was inadequate to meet her students' growing needs. In her off-hours, she filled the gap for her students by voluntarily running a parallel service, amassing bedding and toothpaste and taking the kids to food pantries or to social service offices. Based out of a glorified broom closet, as Roger calls it, Mary began building up the network of services, donors, and community members that, after careful consultation and delineation, would form the foundation of the Maslow Project. In 2009, Mary quit her job at the school district and began working full-time as the director of an organization that she had built up from scratch via thousands of unpaid hours and an unwavering dedication to the kids in her care.

Roger became involved with Maslow long before it moved out of the broom closet. "Some communities," Roger notes, "say that they don't need our services, that they don't have any homeless kids. I was like everyone else: you don't see these kids because they're invisible—they're in the shadows, living in cars or tents or couch-surfing without a permanent place to call home. How would you feel if you're six, eight, or ten and don't have a place to spend the night, or have a meal or a wash?"

Roger wears many hats at Maslow: he serves as a consultant, strategist, board member, chief donor, and committed volunteer. He bought them office furniture, helped broker their move to the current facility, helped tear down walls and redecorate once they'd moved, purchased a new industrial freezer after the old one died on a 105-degree day, and, through a managed fund at the Oregon Community Foundation, provides them with regular financial support as well. "Roger's donations were the first unrestricted[15] contributions we received," Mary said, "and they were crucial to our development, a vote of confidence for us." An enthusiastic and youthful grandfather, he says he enjoys working on behalf of all children. "The earlier we can help them, the less time and money society will need to spend on them further down the line," Roger says. "They're all good kids, and they didn't choose to be in these circumstances."

Roger Stokes taking a break in California. Courtesy Roger Stokes.

Together, Mary, Roger, and the Maslow Project's staff members have helped turn around the lives of countless homeless youths. "I've attended five services for clients that we've lost, but I've also attended way more graduations and weddings," Mary says. "This community is tremendously generous if they feel like a cause in just," Roger says, and local generosity has helped build the Maslow Project into a huge success. It has been recognized nationally and internationally for its innovative, grassroots, community-driven structure: the BBC, ABC, and the *New York Times* have all profiled the organization; the Gates Foundation consulted with Maslow staff; Governor Kitzhaber visited Maslow as an example of "what's working in Oregon;" and a Maslow Project has started up in Coos Bay based on the Medford model.

"There's a feeling that we're doing the right thing," Roger adds, "and for every youngster we've helped, that's money that goes back into the schools." With increased philanthropic investment, the Maslow Project should be able to continue developing and expanding its services and range. Mary speaks with pride about what has been achieved. "As a nonprofit we're only five years old, and we've tackled every goal we've put in front of ourselves successfully." They also find a place for everyone who wants to help. "It's not just about writing a check," Mary says, "it's more about finding where you fit in this model, what your piece of the network is, what service you can provide. There's huge heart in this community." When asked why he has devoted so much of his time and money to Maslow, Roger doesn't hesitate:

"It's luck of the draw how you're born, and these kids are bright, interested, capable, no different than anyone else . . . They just need someone to let them know that they care."

THE OLSRUDS AND ACCESS

Across town, in a leafy Medford suburb, Sherm and Wanda Olsrud sit in the living room of their modest midcentury home. They have lived there since 1967, when they moved to Medford from Eugene, and the house probably hasn't changed much since then. It is comfortable, beautifully cared for, and cozy, filled with recliners and overstuffed couches and decorated with bronze horses, paintings, and reminders of their family and their community. The large picture window looks across the adjacent park toward distant Mt. Ashland, and although their view of the peak became somewhat obscured when the city recently planted a few trees, they still enjoy a panoramic vista onto a stunning part of the state.

Long married, Sherm and Wanda are now in their eighties and are moving a bit more slowly than when they first moved to Medford. In Eugene, they ran first a meat shop and then a small grocery store ("we were the first twenty-four-hour market in Eugene," Wanda says, "and our beer sales between eleven and twelve at night were pretty good"). Now, they own and operate three Sherm's Thunderbird Markets and one Sherm's Food4Less. They are used to working twelve- to fourteen-hour days in the stores and office, doing everything from restocking and cashiering to coupon processing, procurement, and investment management. They have recruited their son Steve as a partner in the business, but their interest in the stores and in their community hasn't waned a bit. They know their employees by name, and they recall fondly how employees progressed in their careers.

Sherm and Wanda Olsrud. Courtesy the Olsrud family.

Both have a deep commitment to Oregon in general, and to southern Oregon in particular. Their appreciation for their community has led Sherm and Wanda to become quiet pillars of it, and they have donated much of their profits to local programs and services. Their whole family started up a scholarship fund for students from southern Oregon, and Sherm and Wanda are regular supporters of the local nonprofit Kids Unlimited (whose kids now play and perform in the organization's Olsrud Gymnasium). They donate to the Maslow Project and to the Family Nurturing Center, and are big supporters of 4-H, even buying prize-winning animals from children to sell in their stores. "We donate mostly to things around here," Wanda says, "because these are the people who have supported us and made our work possible."

(Left) Mobility devices for distribution, complete with tennis balls to help slide them along. (Right) Chili on the stove in ACCESS's kitchen at the Olsrud Nutritional Center. Photos by Kristin Anderson.

Of all of the causes the Olsruds support, hunger and poverty relief are closest to their hearts. Both know what poverty feels like. "My parents didn't have anything, we just survived," Wanda says. Because of the Olsruds' close ties to their customers, they have also seen firsthand how endemic poverty is in their community. "Around 33 percent of our sales are from people receiving some kind of government food assistance," Sherm says, and because of the decline in local timber and agriculture, "southern Oregon is all double-digit in unemployment. There's such a need for help."

Recognizing that need is what drew the Olsruds (Sherm, Wanda, and their children) to ACCESS, a local nonprofit that started in the 1970s as a Loaves and Fishes program for the elderly and has slowly become a provider of wraparound services to the homeless and impoverished of all ages. ACCESS delivers both emergency (food boxes and food pantries) and more long-term food assistance. Beyond providing food, ACCESS also provides nutrition counseling, skills tutoring, and energy assistance, including help for heating and weatherization, which, as the Olsruds' son Steve notes, "can cut people's electricity bills by a third or more."

And that's not all. ACCESS also has a growing collection of donated medical equipment that it can lend to those who can't afford it. It also offers advice and referral services on topics ranging from disability to immigration to foreclosure; it has planted and helps run community gardens that supply its pantries; it has established links with local farmers and grocery stores to provide more fresh produce and dairy to its communities; and it advocates for a more integrated ranching and agricultural system that will coordinate local demand and distribution in a collaborative manner. It is an agency licensed by the US Department of Housing and Urban Development to counsel people about housing, and it provides rent and deposit financial assistance as well as eviction prevention support.

Pam Slater, development director of ACCESS, says that their clients include everyone from the unemployed and homeless to those working three jobs who still can't make ends meet. "The need for their services has just exploded in recent years: it's grown enormously. ACCESS does a great job," Sherm says.

Of course, ACCESS wouldn't be able to do as good a job without the help of donors like the Olsruds. "Philanthropy, no matter how big or small, is essential to our programs," Pam Slater says. The Olsruds, Pam continues, "have been amazing: they've been tremendous supporters for a lot of years both financially and in kind." Much of the food ACCESS distributes has been provided by the Olsrud's stores, and the Olsrud Family Nutrition Center (dedicated in 2002) serves as ACCESS's office, education and advice center, and storage and distribution hub for the twenty-four food pantries that it supplies. "We have a good relationship with ACCESS," says Sherm. "We sell food, they give food away," he says, sinking back onto his couch. Wanda leans forward. "This community has really been supportive of us: so many people have shopped with us for years, and we have a lot of employees who've been with us for thirty years. What better to do with our money than to give it back?"

RISING NEEDS, A RISING NEED FOR PARTICIPATION

Throughout Oregon, the need for food and housing services is rising, government assistance has dwindled, and community-based nonprofits are proving that they can react to urgent needs with proven flexibility, sensitivity, and thoroughness. As a result, there is more need than ever for philanthropic and volunteer support of these organizations, and for leadership within the community to create initiatives that recognize and fulfill specific local needs.

Many essential organizations address related issues that we have barely touched upon. Portland's Outside In provides shelter, medical care, and other services to homeless youth, gay youth, and others; Ontario's Project Dove provides shelter for abused women and children; Legal Aid Services of Oregon provides low-income Oregonians with

Sisters Of The Road diner. Courtesy Sisters Of The Road.

legal advice and in-court assistance; P:ear gives homeless Portland youth a chance to express themselves creatively and to relax and rest (a rarity on the streets); and Tillamook's Food Roots plants school and community gardens and grants microloans to help the area's low-income residents have access to home-grown foodstuffs and learn subsistence strategies.

These and many other organizations acknowledge homelessness and hunger to be interrelated problems, the human costs of shifting economies and of an increasingly constricted social welfare system. The root causes of poverty—racism, failed education, inadequate health care, lack of jobs (especially jobs with a living wage)—must be addressed head-on if we are to fulfill our communities' needs in the long run. We can do that at the ballot box, of course, by voting for policies that amend these inequities. But we can also address them on the ground. Oregon is filled with organizations doing just that: mobilizing enterprising, sympathetic, dedicated, open-minded volunteers and donors to provide services to those whose hardships are greatest.

Motivating most of these donors and volunteers is empathy for others and the desire to give back to communities which have supported them and which they call home. "I feel pretty strongly about it," Roger Stokes declares. "I came to Medford not knowing a soul thirty years ago, and the community was so welcoming to me so many ways. I'd like to do what I can to help it in return."

Punchbowl Falls, at Eagle Creek in the Columbia River Gorge. Photo by Kristin Anderson.

4
Sustaining a Balance:
Conserving Oregon's Natural Heritage

*"The most destructive force in the American West is its commanding
views, because they foster the illusion that we command."*
—Richard Manning

"People protect what they love."
—Jacques Cousteau

In 1940, when the authors of the Federal Writers' Project published their
weighty guide to the state, they described Oregon as boasting "an ever-
green beauty as seductive as the lotus of ancient myth" and quoted Claire
Warner Churchill, who wrote that here, "[i]t rains. It snows. It scorches.
It droughts. It suspends itself in celestial moments of sheer clarity that
hearten the soul. Whatever else it may do, it challenges rather than ener-
vates. Rather than complacency, it breeds philosophy."[1]

However romantic these passages may be, they describe what most
Oregonians feel deeply: that there is something unique and sublime about
our geography, something qualitatively remarkable and invigorating about
the landscapes we call home. As Wallace Stegner, the great chronicler of
the modern West, writes, "We simply need that wild country available to

us, even if we never do more than drive to its edge and look in. For it can be a means of reassuring ourselves of our sanity as creatures, a part of the geography of hope."[2]

But we as a species seem incapable of leaving these wild places genuinely untouched: Oregon's natural world is a treasured thing, and a perennially threatened one. In his iconic *A Sand County Almanac*, the conservationist Aldo Leopold suggests that "we abuse land because we view it as a commodity belonging to us. When we see land as a community to which we belong, we may begin to use it with love and respect."[3] Stewarding Oregon's natural resources in accordance with Leopold's principles is one of the preeminent challenges facing our state. Sustainable—or resilient—living is at the heart of this challenge. It represents a way of existing in which human economic and social needs are balanced with environmental ones—an equilibrium known as the "triple bottom line."

Many Oregonians are rising to Leopold's challenge, acknowledging that because so many of us make a living and draw personal value from its lands and waters, our state's economic and social health is bound inextricably to its environmental health. The organizations and individuals profiled in this chapter have been chosen not because they are always successful or beyond controversy, but because they represent a cross section of Oregon's conservation efforts and because their contributions have been altruistic and innovative. Their efforts are diverse in method and goal; what unifies them is a common regard for community—both human and ecological—as essential to their efforts and to their successes.

Gorge with distant windfarms. Photo by Kristin Anderson.

OREGON'S NATURAL WORLD:
CONTROVERSIES, CHALLENGES, AND OPPORTUNITIES

The natural assets that have driven our state's development and economy and that have given us, as Oregonians, a very distinct sense of place have also been sources of conflict at least since the arrival of the first frontiersmen. Anyone who lives in Oregon knows the contentiousness of discussions about how those lands and waters are defined, used, appreciated, distributed, and stewarded. Public awareness of the spotted owl, coal trains, renewable energy, clear-cutting, and wilderness testify to the centrality of environmental concerns within our state and region—there are few other places in the world where water rights and salmon habitat regularly make headlines.

We know, then, that our cherished places are also economically valuable, and that, as a state, our reputation as stewards of the land is mixed. We have a long history of using up our natural resources for economic benefit. But in part because we have relied so heavily on those resources, we have also been forced to confront questions of conservation and sustainability with urgency and innovation.

Despite the often acrimonious tenor of conservation debates, disparate stakeholders have moved toward compromise and consensus, uniting in a kind of ecosystem of good citizenship in which governments, scientists, tribal communities, businesses, consumers, activists, donors, volunteers, and nonprofits have realized they share common sustainability goals. These collaborations have been happening in Oregon across decades, geographies, and industries, and on multiple scales and fronts that range from research initiatives into best-practice stewardship strategies to the creation of vast land and marine reserves to the conservation of individual species, like Owyhee clover or the Oregon spotted frog. This chapter will discuss how Oregon's nonprofits—powered by philanthropists and volunteers—are helping to research, catalyze, and provide ongoing support to conservation and sustainability initiatives as well as foster collaboration and a more civil civic discourse.

Of course, businesses, politicians, and individual citizens also deserve acknowledgment for their efforts. For example, cattle ranchers Doc and Connie Hatfield, who in 1986 founded the Country Natural Beef cooperative, helped launch a premium market for grass-fed, sustainably grazed meat. Since 1980, Eugene's Winter Green Farm, started by Jack Gray and his family, produces vegetables, fruits, and herbs to sell at farmers' markets and through subscription service: their agricultural successes have paved the way for a whole new generation of sustainable farmers and for Oregon's thriving organic, farm-to-table food culture. And the national nonprofit B Lab founded the B Corps certification, which over forty Oregon businesses, including The Joinery and New Seasons Markets, have attained. B Corps certification is part of a wider "benefit corporation" movement: in Oregon, benefit corporations have their own tax status and represent a growing fourth sector of institutions that build social and environmental benefit into their profit models—that is, they formally subscribe to the triple bottom line of "people, planet, and profits."

Oregon conservation and sustainability initiatives have also benefited from strong leadership from multiple generations of politicians and political appointees from both parties. Oswald West, Charles Sprague, Vic Atiyeh, Tom McCall, Barbara Roberts, Neil Goldschmidt, Jackie Dingfelder, Angus Duncan, Kate Brown, Tina Kotek, Hector Macpherson Jr., Bob Straub, Earl Blumenauer, Ron Wyden, and others have laid a legislative foundation for the stewardship of our lands and waters. Tribal governments have also taken the lead: for example, Columbia River Inter-Tribal Fish Commission has recently launched a Pacific lamprey conservation program, and many tribes place an emphasis on sustainable farming, ranching, fishing, hunting, and foraging practices.[4]

And of course, many individual Oregonians are practicing civic leadership at the domestic level by taking actions to live and work more sustainably, by trying to produce less waste in their daily life, and by supporting environmental stewardship initiatives with their voices and their votes. Certainly, one lesson that Oregonians have learned over the years is how interconnected we are. The type of fertilizer you use on your crops affects watershed health. The type of forestry you practice affects wildfire voracity. The kind of fish you eat or the kind of car you drive determines what species are fished or what cars are manufactured. And all of these decisions affect future generations of Oregonians, the future health of ecosystems and economies, and, in no small part, the future health of the global community.

Because of actions taken by civic leaders—whether conservationists, businesses, politicians, or everyday citizens—Oregon is now regarded as one of America's greenest states, with robust land-use laws, decades-old recycling and antipollution initiatives, a burgeoning renewable energy economy, and cutting-edge environmental science research. And cities such as Portland are celebrated for their commitment to sustainable urban development and living.

But while Oregon has shown leadership and great progress in some areas, the overall picture is still far from rosy. Oregon's conservation landscape is changing, but it's not changing everywhere; nor is it changing quickly. Discussions of natural resource stewardship are complicated by the large number of stakeholders; the urban-rural divide resurfaces here, too. In many

Central Oregon forest. Photo by Kristin Anderson.

Southern Oregon coast. Photo by Kristin Anderson.

rural communities, where economies have been particularly dependent on natural resources and many jobs have been lost as resources are depleted or regulations are tightened, tensions surrounding the terms *environmentalism*, *conservation*, *sustainability*, and *clean energy* remain high. Forest products, ranching, agriculture, fishing, and other natural resource–based industries like mining and power-generation are still sectors filled with hostilities, and Oregon has a significant subsection of interest groups on both sides who have, in frustration, moved away from dialogue toward legislation and litigation.

This means that a third-sector approach, anchored neither in government nor in business, can be valuable: nonprofits and their supporters can open pathways for dialogue and community involvement and can provide impartiality in highly partisan conflicts. Accordingly, the impact of donors and volunteers on these nonprofits, and by extension on Oregon's environmental health, can be far-reaching, long-lived, and of profound ecological, economic, and social value.

All the leaders profiled in this chapter—whether donors, businesspeople, volunteers, nonprofit directors, or a mixture of all these roles—are pragmatists, working hard to find sustainable ways of living. Most are romantics, too, finding in Oregon's rugged landscapes something transcendent, something worthy of preservation.

JOHN AND BETTY GRAY AND THE GRAY FAMILY FOUNDATION: AN ENVIRONMENTAL LEGACY

One Oregon philanthropist who believed in the intrinsic value of a healthy natural world was John Gray, a man whose appreciation of Oregon's landscapes motivated him and his family to become some of the most thoughtful environmental philanthropists in Oregon. Geography was John's great love: he traveled the state, fascinated by all corners of its geologies, ecologies, and cultures. While his and his wife Betty's patronage ranged from OMSI to Reed College to Habitat for Humanity (John Russell, a Portland developer, declared that "John Gray has been to Oregon what Lorenzo de' Medici was to Florence"[5]), arguably their most enduring philanthropic legacies have been contributions to projects that raise public respect for Oregon's natural landscapes.

Betty, who died in 2003, was an engaged partner in John's philanthropy, although her own funding priorities focused more on education and human services. John, who died in 2012 at the age of ninety-three, shared her interests, but also cared deeply, and contributed extensively, to conservation and land-use causes. At first glance, John would seem an unlikely conservationist: he began working in saw-chain manufacturing and later became the developer of several prominent Oregon resort communities. But Gray was never your typical property developer. Born in Ontario, Oregon, against a backdrop of high plains, basalt ridges, and big skies, John was raised by his mother in the mid-Willamette valley village of Monroe in a small, rustic house. His rural youth gave him a strong connection to the natural world. John was no pristine wilderness advocate: as his daughter Joan summarizes, "he believed that a land ethic could go hand-in-hand with land use, and that conservation should and could be a part of natural resource extraction."

Nevertheless, he acknowledged that humans were only one species in a wider, richer ecosystem, and he understood that we, as Oregonians, have a deep connection to *place*. This connection, he knew, was reinforced when natural landscapes were *experienced*: experience of a place helps reinforce our desire to preserve it. His developments—first Salishan Lodge, built overlooking a coastal spit jutting out into Siletz Bay near Newport; then Sunriver Resort, tucked into high desert meadowlands outside of Bend;[6] then John's Landing in Portland and Skamania Lodge in the Columbia River Gorge—may not always have brought in profits, but they did help develop regional economies, and, just as importantly, they impressed upon tourists the beauty and import of their surroundings. "John's resorts are like Japanese paintings, with the natural world in the foreground and human lives depicted small within the wider landscape," says Lara Christensen, program officer for the Gray Family Foundation. His careful siting and appreciation for each resort's natural and social context won over many skeptics. As John said, "You want to be sensitive to the landform and environment . . . [to] make it blend in . . . with the local environment and local needs."[7]

This respect for Oregon's natural assets also found its way into Gray's politics. His huge contributions toward the creation and later the defense of Oregon's rigorous land-use planning laws was perhaps a surprising stance for a property developer. He helped found and fund 1000 Friends of Oregon, an advocacy organization that works to ensure the state's land-use laws are maintained and upheld.[8] Moreover, he did not simply give money to defend land-use laws: he also commissioned research to assess their validity and utility, and to develop successful tactics to promote them. "Intelligent land-use planning doesn't curtail development. It chooses where it should go," Gray explained.[9]

John Gray in 2011. Photo Courtesy the Oregon Community Foundation.

John's development projects and political advocacy contributed to Oregon's responsible tourism and land-use policies, and John and Betty's philanthropy extended this commitment. The Gray Family Foundation, housed at OCF, prioritizes not only environmental education programs but also research into the conservation strategies likely to have the greatest effect. "We were the first donor-advised fund at OCF to commission research, to ask, 'What's the data, what are the trends, what are people not doing, where can we have an impact?'" says John's grandson Nicholas Walrod.

The Gray family's philanthropy has been far-sighted and effective. Laura Winter, an OCF vice president who works with the Gray Family Foundation, recalls John as "a passionate life-long learner. He tried to figure out how he could stretch his vision and ensure long-term efficacy—he was thinking out to 3014!" That long-term view has led to land trusts becoming a significant area of family investment: over the years, the Grays have committed millions of dollars to permanently restricting the use of ecologically valuable pieces of land and have commissioned research on how to make land trusts more effective.

The Gray family's most prominent cause, outdoor education, was reached with typical thoughtfulness; they concluded that the most practical way to make certain that the natural world will be appreciated and sustained would be to ensure that every child in Oregon receives some exposure to outdoor experiential education. The family's rationale is straightforward, Nicholas explains. "Higher education is placing strong emphasis on environmental literacy, but younger kids' scientific literacy is falling, and poverty, technology, and education cuts are all impacting young kids' exposure to the natural world. Our funds can change that." Outdoor school gives children "hard science skills: the practical hands-on education experience which is a medium for kids to excel scientifically and to explore jobs, as well as soft skills such as social interaction and experiencing the equanimity of nature," says Nicholas. "The indelible mark that nature makes on kids will be with them for the rest of their life."

Together, three generations of Grays have begun investing in all aspects of outdoor education, from grants to schools and districts for kids' travel and expenses, to contributions to camps for improving and maintaining facilities. "It has been a learning process from a giving perspective," says Nicholas. "We struggle sometimes with how you maximize dollars and amplify the experience. For example, I spoke with a teacher in Harney County who said that 80 percent of her kids had never been to the coast, and having an experience of the coast has a powerful impact on these kids even though the trip would cost more than one to a nearby camp." As the family refines its giving strategies, they never lose sight of John Gray's passion—he was fond of saying that as a society we must "never forget to get kids outside."

The natural stewardship that the Gray family has helped instill in thousands of Oregon children should ensure a brighter future for Oregon's conservation efforts. Their work is about "being a global citizen, whether it's in your town of two hundred or in the wider world," Nicholas says. "It's about how you relate to this sense of and love of place, and how you can help to produce an engaged citizenry and a clear sense of what it means to be an Oregonian." Philanthropically speaking, this is high-impact giving. "I think it's a responsibility and a privilege," Joan says. "It gives us amazing opportunities to learn more about Oregon and about people, and an opportunity to try to empower other people into that partnership of using these resources sustainably."

"GOOD FOR ECOLOGY, GOOD FOR THE SOUL": MALHEUR FIELD STATION

The Gray family's belief in the importance of outdoor education is shared with a diverse group of individuals and institutions. One of the more remote (and perhaps one of the more eccentric and wonderful) examples is the Malheur Field Station, which is positioned in one of the most lovely and

Eastern Oregon storm brewing. Photo by Kristin Anderson.

Adults during an in-the-field lecture on geology by Dr. Michael Cummings during a Road Scholar (Elderhostel) program at MFS. Photo by Lyla R. Messick. Courtesy Malheur Field Station.

least visited sectors of the state, its rustic campus tucked amongst the sage, migratory birds, rangeland, and huge skies of the Great Basin. Winters there are snowy and frigid, summers arid and hot, and the natural world is always *present*, sometimes gentle, sometimes harsh.

The Field Station's buildings are ad hoc, a mixture of dusty green clapboard-sided modular units, a few old sheds and hangars, a dormitory, a cafeteria, and a handful of trailers that serve as extra visitor accommodations. The facility has had a varied history, beginning life as a Job Corps center and then cycling through a number of research and education purposes until it was eventually taken over by the Great Basin Society, a nonprofit established to educate Oregonians about the environmental distinctiveness of the state's last frontier. Three hundred miles away from the I-5 corridor, the Field Station looks like what it is: an outpost of civilization.

The Field Station's existence has been controversial: it is an environmental education and advocacy organization deep within conservative cattle-ranching country. The poverty rate in Malheur County is above 25 percent, and many people regard environmentalist pursuits as challenging what little economic growth (through ranching and agriculture, and even through wind farms[10]) might be on the horizon. The fact that the Field Station remains in existence at all is a result of the doggedness of its leadership, grassroots community support, consensus-building efforts within those communities, and innovative and eclectic programming for both adults and schoolchildren visiting the region.

One of its two directors is Duncan Evered, an Oxford-educated Englishman whose ornithology research first brought him to the area decades ago. He is passionate about the region and speaks warmly about the effect that this very distinctive landscape and ecology has on visiting schoolchildren and adults. "In this high-tech, super-busy world it is very difficult and very important to maintain a place like this," Duncan says. "Where else can 550 kids from the Reynolds School District[11] spend five days in the desert?" Some of the urban students who visit have never seen the stars; others have never gone on a hike. The experience is equally transformative for adults, whether visitors are participating in an astronomy or ornithology weekend, an outdoor painting workshop, or one of their more eclectic offerings, such as the course where participants are sent out into the landscape armed with headphones playing classical music selections chosen to heighten their experience of the geography.

The station also hosts seminars and academic events and houses conservation and scientific research projects, all of which fit into the organization's broad mandate. "We are a conservation group in the sense that what we do here is objective ecology and conservation, be it through Audubon Society groups or through a family from the I-5 corridor," Duncan explains. "These projects also directly or indirectly raise awareness of conservation issues of the Great Basin and the desert. I get it from all over," Duncan says. "Once people visit this place, it's impossible to forget it. These visits are really important and have a huge impact on people."

Certainly, Malheur Field Station instills in visitors a desire to see this landscape protected and conserved. But its survival in both a harsh landscape and a harsh regional economy is always a worry for Duncan and for Lyla Messick, his co-director. Duncan explains, "We're a small organization with a big mission, and we're working from a very difficult starting point. We are in logistical isolation. . . . It's really difficult to get kids out here: travel costs are high; just maintaining the buildings is expensive, and funding from school districts for programs like this has withered. We wouldn't be here without support from donor-advised funds from OCF and without the generosity of the Meyer, Collins, and Murdoch Foundations. But we really need millions to deal with a lot of the deferred maintenance of the buildings and it's hard to get grants for that kind of thing."

Support from the local community hasn't been large financially, but it has been enthusiastic, especially for a small institution located in one of the most sparsely populated quadrants of the state. The Field Station has built up a diverse network of grassroots supporters, including ranchers and farmers, many of whom are not always traditionally aligned with conservation ideals. The organization works hard to build consensus and to show how controversial initiatives can have unexpected benefits. "We join whenever invited to the dialogue out here, whether it's sage grouse or refuse disposal. Change is slow, and common ground shifts slowly, but we have to have honest and empathetic conversations about these things in order to progress," notes

Duncan. "Grazing isn't justified ecologically and we need to remain faithful to scientific evidence, but people also need to be connected to the land and we need to be realistic about what we can accomplish. After all, we'd rather have cattle than dirt bikes."

As a result of this outreach, their grassroots support is impressive. In their annual appeals letter, they get a 12 to 14 percent response, which is, as Duncan says, "three or four times what you could possibly hope for." Their average donation is $100, which indicates that "people are really making an effort to contribute to us, responding every year to the fullest degree that they can. Our supporters are incredibly loyal, and we're getting checks from people with limited income that are proportionately huge to their income."

Slowly and tenaciously, Malheur Field Station is helping to bring the southeast corner of Oregon to statewide visibility, mobilizing cross-sector local support to raise awareness of the conservation challenges and natural wonders of this remote region. Places like the Malheur Field Station, as Duncan knows, are essential both intellectually and emotionally. He says that such places introduce new perspectives and new ways of living, and they build empathy between communities and geographies. Duncan's philosophy is simple: "It's important that people get out of the city and meet themselves in a different context. It's important for people to learn and see Oregon in its fullest state. It's good for Oregon, it's good for ecology, and it's good for the soul."

"SMALL THINGS HAVE A BIG EFFECT": BRING RECYCLING'S BATTLE AGAINST WASTE

Another nonprofit that has benefited from a diverse and grassroots donor base is BRING Recycling in Eugene. Among Oregon's most venerable conservation organizations, BRING was founded in 1971 as an outgrowth of the first Earth Day (1970) and the burgeoning ecology movement. Now in its fifth decade, its mission to "reduce, reuse, recycle, rethink" has only increased in relevance and urgency, and the organization has remained nimble in adapting their services to changing social and environmental needs.

On a frosty winter morning, Executive Director Julie Daniel shared what BRING has accomplished and how it's changed over the years. Daniel, originally from England, is elegant and animated. "We see ourselves as a social change organization," she begins. "There's a social equity angle to the work we do: pollution and climate change have a far greater effect on the poor and disadvantaged in the world. We needed to help people understand that we need to do more with less for reasons of equity, economy, and environment."

How the organization has advanced this message has changed over the decades, Daniels notes. For the first thirty years, BRING was a recycling

BRING's electrical aisle. Photo by Kristin Anderson.

center, processing and reselling recycled materials. "Even though we were a social change organization, we operated like a business, supported by our income," Daniel says. But BRING was a victim of its own success: Lane County grew to have the highest recycling rate in Oregon, and recycling became big and high-tech business across the country.

In the late nineties, BRING decided to refocus. "Recycling is how you manage waste you've already made," Daniel explains. "We realized that in order to achieve our mission, we needed to focus more on waste prevention and reuse. We also needed to rebrand," she adds. "We had this kind of hippie, counterculture image. We wanted our message to go mainstream." They had an ambitious vision of what they wanted: a sleek, modern processing center and an appealing storefront for reusable goods, with educational content, community space, and a strong emphasis on chic design and artistic appeal. "We wanted [to be] a desirable thing rather than a negative message: we didn't want 'the world is going to hell in a handbasket and dolphins are dying'—we wanted something fun and creative and positive."

What they dreamed into existence was the Planet Improvement Center, a complex that incorporates the BRING offices, a lush bioswale garden, a showroom, and several adjacent warehouses and workshops in which reusable goods are repaired, organized, and displayed for resale. The complex also features a courtyard that has hosted several weddings and a yard for storing bigger reclaimed items like lumber, pipes, and railroad ties. Every corner houses creative works of art and architecture, including a life-size rhinoceros lording over the garden: all are constructed out of reused or donated goods.

This attractive new hub allows BRING to not only sell their goods more effectively but also to expand their outreach agenda. They provide conservation education for all Lane County students in grades K-12, both through

An elaborate fence made of reused materials, with the rhinoceros wallowing in the bioswale behind. Photo by Kristin Anderson.

classroom visits and through leading field trips to their own or other waste-handling facilities. They also give talks to service organizations, clubs, and community centers, lead how-to workshops on conservation and reuse at their center, and offer businesses free confidential consulting on how they can cut down on waste and water usage and increase energy efficiency.

But before BRING could do all of this—build the center and expand its outreach—it needed to approach donors and grantmakers in a much more strategic way. The Gray Family Foundation, the Meyer Memorial Trust, and the Murdoch Foundation each awarded the organization six-figure grants to help get off the ground, and the Collins Foundation, Weyerhaeuser, and others gave them additional large grants and gifts. However, much of the $3 million raised came from grassroots supporters and smaller donors, many of whom had been supporting BRING for twenty or thirty years. "We'd do house parties, talk to individuals, ask for anything from $5 to $1000, and then next year, we'd talk to them again and they'd give a little bit more," Julie explains. "We became a lot more accountable: the process of raising funds put us out in the community and raised awareness, but we also learned how to explain ourselves better to the business community, to grantmakers, and even to our long-term supporters; we learned to build up points of intersection," Julie says. "Philanthropy has helped us to grow up. When people start giving you money, it gives you a tremendous sense of responsibility." BRING feels a deep commitment to their volunteers and donors, she says. "We have a strong and committed volunteer board, and we are very dependent upon and grateful for our smaller donors. When someone says to you, 'Here's fifteen dollars; I wish I could give more but I'm on a fixed income,' they're looking to you to do things that they believe in. We want to prove ourselves accountable stewards of each gift."

Julie pauses and then shares an example. "We got a note from an elderly couple, Jeanne and Herb," she tells us, "each of whom contributed $5 and sent it in." BRING sent them a thank-you note, and Julie, touched by the couple's faith in them, describes what happened next. "They sent us a letter back with another $10 and a note that said, 'Your courteous note thanking us for our paltry donation has inspired us to give a little more. Thanks for the work that you do.' It was so moving. . . . We don't take *any* gifts for granted," she asserts fervently.

BRING is the kind of organization that inspires this kind of response across the community. It has a mailing list of over sixty-five hundred households, and the number of its regular donors is not much smaller. One, Ardyth McGrath, has never been to their new facility, but she is a devotee of BRING's mission nonetheless. At eighty-one, Ardyth has been contributing regularly since 2007 and has donated over $350 through donations of $10. "I remember when I first heard about them. They said what they were doing and I thought they needed help," Ardyth explains. "I live alone, and there's not too many ways I can help the environment. I just think that BRING is doing a great job. . . . I can't do very much, but if I give what I can every month, and if a thousand other people do the same, then they're getting a lot of money," she declares. "I feel better if I give. God has been good to me, and it's time for me to give back."

Ardyth's rationale echoes Julie Daniel's precisely. Julie says that if it weren't for BRING's volunteers and corps of small donors, they wouldn't be who they are now: a pillar of Eugene's community and a success both as conservation educators and as a comprehensive source—a treasure trove, really—of reusable materials. When asked about their successes, Julie is proud. "I think we've created a culture: the idea that when you're done with something it doesn't go in the garbage." Their mission dovetails perfectly with their funding model, Julie says. "Philanthropy is a lot like recycling. One piece of paper in the scheme of things is irrelevant; one $5 gift is too, but if you do it regularly, and if ten people do it regularly, then you've got a system that works. There's no difference between your regular $5 and a one-time big check. Small things, done over time, have a big effect."

Another BRING donor, Julie Rogers, whom Julie Daniel calls "Julie II," agrees. Julie Rogers is seventy-three years old and has donated about twenty times, totaling over $300. Julie describes her as "a true believer." Ms. Rogers started off as a volunteer with BRING many years ago and has supported them ever since. "Recycling is a part of me; it's what I've been doing all my life," she says. "I was at the first Earth Day and it just seemed to make so much sense, so I was delighted when I discovered BRING." Ms. Rogers, a retired teacher, says that BRING's accomplishments "take your breath away. They're a wonderful asset to the world, and to the community, and everyone I know uses BRING or gives goods to it. There's a Hebrew phrase, *tikkun olam*, which means 'world repair.' That's exactly what BRING does."

CONSERVATION THROUGH ART: BANDON'S VOLUNTEER-DRIVEN WASHED ASHORE PROJECT

Across the coast range and down Highway 101 from Eugene, a very different "world repair" project is emerging. The south coast town of Bandon may be famous for its golf and its dunes, but to artist and educator Angela Haseltine Pozzi, its beaches were becoming famous for a less appealing feature: trash.

"I'd spent every summer of my childhood poking around in tide pools in Bandon," Angela explains. "And then in 2004, when my husband and I were living in Portland, he had a stroke, was diagnosed with a brain tumor, and died. It stopped my whole world," she says. "I reached a point where I felt like I needed a big change. I escaped back to the ocean, which was my healing place." She spent many hours walking up and down Bandon's beaches, but in those months after the move, she began to notice something. "I started seeing more and more plastic on the beach and I couldn't believe what was happening to an environment I'd always loved. I came to the ocean to heal," she declares, "and found that it needed healing itself. And then I realized I'd found my purpose."

An art teacher and gallery artist for over thirty years, she decided she could work with the skills she already had. She recruited volunteers to help collect pieces of marine debris—soda cans, fishing lines, floats, flip-flops, glass bottles, Styrofoam, tires, milk jugs, and countless other types of detritus. Some clearly had been dumped locally, and other pieces had washed ashore

Bandon's shoreline. Photo by Kristin Anderson.

from Japan, Korea, Thailand, Ecuador, and other far-flung locales. In 2010, Angela got a grant for $500 from the Coos County Cultural Commission. With it, she bought drills, a welder, and wire. As she became more adept at welding, weaving, and layering, her vision for the project grew. With much help from volunteers and a small staff that grew out of her volunteers corps, the Washed Ashore Project was launched.

A fearsome fish at Washed Ashore. Photo by Kristin Anderson.

Its Bandon gallery is a fascinating and memorable place to visit. There are about twenty marine creatures in the room, all made out of the ocean debris that threatens them. Ranging from life-size to enormous, the sculptures are commanding. Their components—bottles, cans, rubber, and other waste—are left apparent, leaving little doubt as to their significance. But step back and the creatures display surprising charisma. Lidia the seal, with her wire whiskers and glass-float eyes, is plaintive and adorable; Henry the fish, with plastic shards for teeth, is ferocious. The whale's ribcage made from plastic jugs and the jellyfish made from plastic cups convey the breadth of marine species threatened by humankind's carelessness. A huge upside-down sea star sits in the corner of the room, with plastic water bottles from the Beijing Olympics and glass bottles of all colors forming the layers of the starfish's arms. A mallet sits nearby: the starfish's bottles and tubs can be played as a musical instrument. "It's tunable to E minor," notes Mary Johnson, the organization's outreach director.

In-depth informational displays explain the size and origins of floating "trash islands," the biological effects of this detritus on specific species, the longevity of many of these discarded items, and the artistic techniques used to make the sculptures. The overall effect of the colors, science, and species is both fun and sobering. Angela describes how she uses the arts to teach conservation:

> Our pieces are both interactive—such as the musical starfish—and kinetic. If you're trying to reach a wide variety of people, you need to involve all of the senses. If you have a kid pounding on a Styrofoam drum set or walking through a whale rib cage, that helps them remember the message and gives them something to talk about, to transmit it. Similarly, we try to connect each sculpture's materials back to the animal threatened by them, so that Lidia the seal has a net wrapped around her neck so that we can discuss the entanglement issues. . . . Each sculpture is the jumping-off point for a lesson.

(Left) Angela Haseltine Pozzi with one of her creatures. Photo by Frank Rocco. Courtesy Washed Ashore Project. (Right) Jennifer Little working on a penguin. Photo courtesy Jennifer Little.

The lessons are working, and The Washed Ashore Project's message is getting out with the help of impressive local support. For instance, Mike Keiser, owner of the Bandon Dunes golf resort, has given generously through his fund at OCF and the Wild Rivers Coastal Alliance, a nonprofit he established to help conserve the south coast. And the organization couldn't do without Kirk and Betty Day, two local philanthropists who donated six months of the rent at the Harbortown Events Center in downtown Bandon where Washed Ashore is housed.

Angela also relies heavily on the support of volunteers to engage the community on several levels. Not only have she and her volunteers cleaned up over seven tons of trash from twenty miles of coastline, but the sculptures she creates are largely constructed by volunteers. School groups visit the workshop often, and adults come too. Recruiting visitors and locals to help construct the sculptures means that not only are the final pieces interactive, but the process of creation is too—a very effective way of encouraging visitors to take ownership of the project, ensuring that volunteers leave Washed Ashore as evangelists of its goals.

Jennifer Little, one of Angela's most committed volunteers, explains why she helps out: "I believe in the project. Local beaches are now clean, and there's an awesome impact in seeing piles of crap picked up and turned into something fun, cute, and full of character. But it's also important because they make you realize that all of this material is from just one small stretch of beach. How much is out there around the world on beaches, and in the ocean?"

Raising awareness of precisely that message—the danger that oceanic litter poses to delicate marine and coastal ecosystems—is the point of Washed Ashore, which is taking the message statewide with tours and residencies at schools, universities, businesses, tourist attractions, and public buildings. Its work has also gone national—Washed Ashore has created pieces for NOAA (the National Oceanic and Atmospheric Administration), shown pieces in museums and institutes on both the east and west coasts, created a display for the Smithsonian, and partnered with Sea World. The organization even has a sister program in Alaska. Through the strength of one woman's creative merging of art and ecology, and through an upwelling of philanthropic support and a huge network of volunteers, the Washed Ashore Project is making waves nationwide.

PRESERVING LAND AND WATER: THE NATURE CONSERVANCY AND THE MCKENZIE RIVER TRUST

Collecting and curtailing marine debris is one aspect of a much wider conservation landscape. Land trusts are another: they are nonprofit organizations that conserve vulnerable ecosystems either by encouraging landowners to accept conservation easements on their property that limit their development and use, or by purchasing property outright and holding them in trust in perpetuity to preserve their ecological value. The Nature Conservancy has long championed land trusts as a means of conservation, and as a result, it is one of the biggest landowners in the world, a steward of a vast and distinctive collection of reserves globally. In Oregon, the Nature Conservancy owns or manages twenty-two properties that the public can visit, including Cascade Head, the Metolius River, and Medford's Table Rocks. Eight more protected areas are closed to public use. These preserves sometimes originate from state- or federally owned lands, but many result from acts of philanthropy, either as donations toward the purchase of a property, donations of property, or easements on a property.

According to Russ Hoeflich, former Oregon state director of the Nature Conservancy, "if I were to identify a champion of the land-use system of the state of Oregon, I would call out Ned Hayes." Ned came from a timber family: his father, Edmund Hayes, was an Oregon forest products businessman who was an early advocate for more sustainable forestry practices. Ned advanced his father's message by giving time and money to help uphold Oregon's land-use laws and help the Nature Conservancy secure a number of properties, including the Zumwalt Prairie and Sycan Marsh preserves. Ned died in 2009, but his wife Sis supports these causes still. "[Ned] had a quiet voice," Russ said, "but he saw the power of investing in the nonprofit sector the venture capital that was needed to achieve conservation, and he also had the vision to choose excellent nonprofit leaders to throw his support behind. . . . [Sis] and Ned really believed in the power of people and the power of inspiration."

Hoeflich also speaks of three Oregon women—Jean Vollum, Patty Wessinger, and Helen Malarkey Thompson—who have had a disproportionately large impact on the creation and stewardship of land trusts and government protected areas in our state. These three women, Russ says, "worked so hard to reach out to friends and colleagues, and to use personal as well as political contacts to advance the cause of conservation. They lived and breathed and cared so deeply about the state. They'd volunteer, they'd give up both their means and their time. . . . [They were] so inspirational, and they knew the state so thoroughly." Through their passion, fundraising prowess, and persuasiveness, not only was Senator Mark Hatfield convinced to protect the Opal Creek Wilderness after a mysterious thirty-minute conference with these women in a stand of old-growth trees, but the Nature Conservancy gained several properties with their help, including thousands of acres of the vast and billowing Zumwalt Prairie on the edge of Hells Canyon.

The Nature Conservancy's main approaches to conservation—warding off environmental degradation and/or aiding environmental recovery by walling off land to development and industry—depends almost exclusively on volunteerism and philanthropy in the acquisition stage as well as in the stewardship stage. In both, the Nature Conservancy has benefited tremendously from the largesse of private donors like Ned and Sis Hayes, Jean Vollum, Helen Malarkey Thompson, and Patty Wessinger.

However, not all land trusts are created or managed by global institutions like the Nature Conservancy. Some, like the McKenzie River Trust, remain determinedly centered around the singular place they attempt to preserve. Halfway up a wooded hill a few miles outside of Eugene is the Bowerman property. Angular and mustachioed, Tom Bowerman has a distance runner's frame; he offers a warm greeting as he opens the door into the home he and his wife Kris built by hand with wood Tom felled and milled up the hill. Inside, an insistent Siamese cat and a wiggling dog jockey for affection. Their house is small, simple, and perfect. Its focal points are the kitchen, anchored by a vast wood-burning stove that heats the house, and the adjacent drawing room, which is lightly furnished so that all attention goes first to the enormous jade plant in the corner and then to the picture window behind them looking out into the forest. The house seems an extension of the trees; cantilevered at canopy level onto a sharply sloping hillside, it is a home rooted in its place.

The McKenzie River Trust was Tom Bowerman's brainchild, and he has been one of its most ardent contributors and leaders. "We have deep roots here: our ancestors were pioneers," he explains. Because of this, he has a strong respect for Oregon's unique places, he says, and for him, the McKenzie River, with some of the purest waters in Oregon, is one of them. "I grew up on the McKenzie, but I'm not a water-baby," he says. "Fly fishermen have a connection to the water in that pastoral, mythological way. I don't have that. My philosophical motivations run in a much more general vein. I see the mountains and the uplands and the river as all part of a larger system. To me, there is significant value in trying to preserve that over an extended period of time."

Tom Bowerman. Photo courtesy the Oregon Community Foundation.

Together he and environmental leader Bob Doppelt committed themselves to protecting the riparian areas that are integral to the river's biodiversity and water quality. They took a long-term approach, gradually raising funds for and purchasing vulnerable properties, negotiating easements on other properties, and building relationships with the Eugene Water and Electric Board (EWEB) and other agencies. Tom is thoughtful as a fundraiser and as a conservationist, and he explains the urgency of the project passionately. "Rivers are like the earth's vascular system. The interface between terrestrial and aquatic is intense: we love our waters and love them to death. . . . Natural systems work best when they're natural systems, not manicured or manipulated."

Tom has contributed his own money and land to the project, and his expertise as well. "I'm a contemporary donor," he says. "I pay attention as a public citizen would. It's that pioneer spirit: you have to dig in deep." The McKenzie River Trust now has eight staff members and a committed board, and Tom has helped them see the trust through a number of potential pitfalls. For example, "we've had some challenges in curtailing invasive species," he says. "They take some management to deal with—we can't leave the river alone entirely." Another challenge facing land trusts is ensuring regulation and longevity: it's a big job to figure out how any land trust will continue to exist in perpetuity. "This means thinking in both the short and the long term," Tom says. "I'm concerned about the proliferation of little land trusts, which are popping up all over the place. Many people don't think about the long-term financial and regulatory framework when they start up. Sometimes, their energy would be better spent working with an existing land trust organization."

The McKenzie River Trust would certainly be a good reference point for those interested in land trusts: it has been, and continues to be, a successful riparian conservation project. It owns almost 2,000 acres; it has negotiated conservation easements on another 1,800; and it has also negotiated "partner assist" agreements with an additional 444 acres. On these sites, all

Photo by Kristin Anderson.

of which are vulnerable and ecologically valuable riparian areas, it has initiated habitat restoration projects, allowed drained sloughs and marshlands and flood plains to return to more natural states, and charted the recovery of several bird, amphibian, fish, reptile, insect, and plant species. The McKenzie River Trust has also exported its model to other watersheds, expanding its properties and easements to include areas on the Siuslaw, Umpqua, Long Tom, Middle Fork of the Willamette, and Upper Willamette rivers, and on coastal streams from Yachats to Reedsport. The Trust has seen a broad-based increase in the ecological health of its conservation areas, including the rediscovery of chubb fish (last seen in the McKenzie in 1899 and considered to be extinct in the area) in a Trust-held backwater, a shining moment for the organization.

These accomplishments have been satisfying for Tom. "To see the successes of the Trust is like seeing a child grow up. It's not a sense of prideful ownership, it's a sense of being pleased with the capacity and individuality of that person." However, he cautions, their work is merely part of a much bigger picture.

Somewhere in my philosophical construct is the acknowledgement that people don't really *own* land, so it's natural that land conservancy has to happen at a collective level. And while we are talking about the McKenzie River Trust and philanthropy, I think there's a bigger picture here, too. There's a huge amount of denial about what we as a species are doing to our larger system. This kind of work is about engaging our culture in a dialogue about what's really important, about how we are choosing to live.

PORT ORFORD OCEAN RESOURCE TEAM:
COMMUNITY-LED SUSTAINABLE FISHING

Less than an hour's drive down Highway 101 from Bandon's Washed Ashore Project is Port Orford, home to a very different type of marine conservation program. Port Orford is a tiny town of about eleven hundred residents, built along the highway and nestled between the coast range to the east, fog-peaked Humbug Mountain to the south, and the Cape Blanco headland to the west. The westernmost town in the lower forty-eight states, Port Orford is also one of the more economically depressed: it is located in Curry County, whose low tax rate affords little safety net or basic services provision, and its economy has been slammed by the shuttering of its timber industry and by the boom and bust cycle of the local fishing industry, upon which the town's livelihoods largely still depend.

Fishing is at the heart of this community. Even though the ocean is not visible from Port Orford's main street, everything in town points toward it, from the Crazy Norwegian Fish n' Chips restaurant to the giant lettering painted on the asphalt of a side road that reads "OCEAN VIEW THIS WAY." On the bluffs just past this directive is the headquarters of Port Orford Ocean Resource Team (POORT), located in a former B&B overlooking the pounding waves and jagged pinnacles of the bay below. Inside POORT's office, the atmosphere is cozy: a pot-bellied stove warms a corner, maps and placards cover the walls, and the household refrigerator is decorated with a bumper sticker that says "We [heart] Mayor Jim." But the informality of the office belies the organization's power and successes. POORT is a regional leader in grassroots marine conservation and community-led sustainable fishing, and with the help of local volunteers and a diverse donor community, it is helping to spur the economic revitalization of Port Orford.

Port Orford's fishery challenges have a long lineage. Generations of overfishing and habitat degradation through practices like bottom trawling, which scrapes the seabed and disrupts much more than the target fish species, threaten marine biodiversity and have led to a decline in fish stocks. The town's fishermen also struggle with the effects of warming and acidifying oceans— the results of global climate change—and with pollution, fish diseases and toxins, and riparian threats to fish spawning and estuarial and marine health, including fertilizer run-off, damming, and low water flow due to irrigation.

To aid threatened fish populations, government, conservation coalitions, and other large institutions have tried to regulate against overfishing by limiting the catch on specific species, creating marine preserves, and banning certain practices. These top-down regulations are broad-reaching in an effort to help counter such a leviathan set of conservation challenges, but many

Aaron Longton, board president, and Leesa Cobb, executive director, POORT, in front of Port Orford Bay with Redfish Rocks in the distance. Photo by Kristin Anderson.

communities feel they aren't nuanced or locally focused enough, and that the voices of the fishermen, whose lives and livelihoods are affected by these policies, are being lost.

The Port Orford Ocean Resource Team aims to develop and deploy a long-term marine stewardship strategy founded on the participation of the town's fisherman, with the goal of creating a sustainable fishing industry for generations to come. Leesa Cobb, POORT's executive director and a fisherman's wife, and Aaron Longton, the board president and a commercial salmon and black cod fisherman, explain how it came to be.

"POORT arose out necessity," Aaron begins. "Our town had lost its timber jobs, and the fishing was hit-or-miss because of overfishing, low salmon runs in the Klamath and Sacramento river systems, and large swathes of ocean closed off as rockfish conservation areas. Everyone knew there'd be change, and that to weather the storms, we'd have to adapt, and in order to do that, we'd have to organize ourselves." Laura Anderson, who owns the legendary Local Ocean restaurant in Newport, grew concerned and contacted Leesa Cobb, who had a background in community organizing. Together, Leesa, Laura, Aaron, and other stakeholders began speaking to others within the local fishing community to try to see what livable solutions they could find. "Everyone on board with POORT had a vision about how things needed to be done locally: they didn't want to complain about top-down policies, they wanted to find local solutions," Leesa observes.

The goal was to marry marine conservation efforts with community engagement to find a triple-bottom-line solution, letting a human economy and society thrive while also letting fish stocks rebound and the ecosystem recover. However, finding community support for sustainable fishing in a town that felt widely victimized by conservation policies was an uphill battle.

Even if it meant ensuring that fishing remained a livelihood for generations to come, people's wallets were thin and long-term solutions seemed both too gradual and too good to be true.

In the early days, Leesa and the fishermen on her board sat down with every Port Orford boat owner, discussing possible conservation strategies and compromises. "It took a few of us with some willingness to battle it out," Aaron said. "Even now, there are still a few on the other end of the spectrum who are digging their heels in, and a few more who take credit when we get it right and shout like hell when we get it wrong." Leesa agrees, and adds, "Not everyone's thrilled with us, but we work really hard to collaborate with everyone." POORT's homegrown origins helped: led by a group of fisherman and run by a fisherman's wife, POORT has credibility because it emerged out of the community it works to assist. In the end, the majority of the community got behind them. This was crucial, because, as Leesa and Aaron say, the whole point of POORT is for it to be *community-led* marine stewardship. "POORT is a branding exercise for our community, too," adds Leesa. "We believed that there was a benefit from long-term conservation, and we believed that it could go hand-in-hand with fishing, but we also wanted to call out Port Orford as a place that's a bit different in a positive light."

Over the years, POORT has developed a multifaceted strategy to help ensure that subsequent generations of fishermen have jobs and that biodiversity and fish stocks are restored. One of its signature projects has been to designate protection for an area called Redfish Rocks (visible from POORT's offices), which the state finally accepted as one of Oregon's first Marine Reserves in 2009. The area is closed to all fishing and has been preserved as a critical habitat and research area, in part because it is home to a lot of what Leesa and Aaron jokingly refer to as BOFFFFs (Big Old Fat Fertile Female Fish). An adjacent area twice as big has limited harvests. Leesa knows that the fishermen will treat the reserve with respect: "People comply because it's of value to them."

Beyond the Redfish Rocks Reserve, POORT has established a much larger community stewardship area, which encourages Port Orford's fishermen to manage the waters they fish in a way that takes into account shifting local fish stocks and locally specific conservation advice. "Once we realized that we wanted to make a positive impact on our marine ecosystem, we wanted to define an area which we could influence—our range, our *place*," explains Leesa. "We got everyone together, got markers out, drew all over maps, and we figured out that our boundaries were 1,320 square miles, which incorporates 935 square miles of ocean habitat, as well as the upland watersheds which connect land with sea."

Within this area, they practice low-impact fishing techniques and partner with Oregon State University to conduct scientific research on fish, seaweed, and other marine organisms. They have lobbied for a stormwater ordinance and have worked with the Surfrider Foundation to participate in Blue Water Task Force, which conducts monthly water quality testing. They also conduct workshops on the land-sea connection and watershed health, and they have launched the Community Fishing Association (CFA), a kind of local co-op designed to keep Port Orford competitive with larger industrial fishing ports and companies. The fishermen of POORT are looking toward the future. "The national policy movement is toward big boats and consolidated companies. That's completely opposite of Port Orford's fishing businesses," Leesa explains. "We wanted to develop a program to ensure Port Orford remains a fishing community. When Aaron and my husband retire, the CFA will mean their permits won't be passed on to the highest bidder but rather will remain within our community of small-boat, independent fishermen."

Photo courtesy Port Orford Ocean
Resource Team.

Perhaps POORT's most visible initiative is the launch of Port Orford Sustainable Seafood, which capitalizes on the town's growing reputation as a conservation hub by selling fish to restaurants, farmers' markets, and shareholders, who receive a half or a whole order of fish by monthly subscription. This program brings in larger returns and not only places monetary value on sustainable fishing practices but also gives Port Orford's fishermen a way to adapt to changing fish stocks and conservation requirements: its subscription service guarantees a market for less well-known fish like rockfish and black cod.

POORT's forward-thinking stewardship of natural resources and their successes in bringing together a diverse group of stakeholders to work for sustainable solutions have won them much deserved recognition, including both the National Oceanic and Atmospheric Administration 2010 Non-Governmental Organization of the Year Award and the Governors' Gold Award for 2012. In 2012, Leesa Cobb prominently advocated for full congressional funding of the National Ocean Policy, which seeks to coordinate federal agencies' work on ocean stewardship and to create a support framework for local initiatives. Even given its work at a national level, arguably POORT's biggest success has been within the Port Orford community, where local fishermen are starting to feel more stable and empowered about their profession, and where political allegiances have often been swept aside in favor of pragmatism and compromise.

POORT's ability to build consensus within Port Orford is reflected in the number of philanthropic partners; it relies heavily on grantmakers and donors for operating expenses as well as for research and program costs. The Surfrider Foundation has worked with them for over ten years—"they're definitely our *partners* in this work," says Leesa—and they've received generous support from the David and Lucille Packard Foundation, the Lazar Foundation, the Coon Family Foundation, Pew Charitable Trusts, Our Oceans (a Pew subsidiary), the Wild Rivers Coast Alliance, the M. J. Murdock Charitable Trust, and many others. Countless individuals have donated too. "We think our funders are pretty terrific," Leesa says. "It's so important to us to help them understand how much of a difference their investment makes, and we're so grateful for their willingness to invest in a small community-based project in a town that no one's invested in in a really long time. Towns like ours are struggling, and I can't begin to say how much of an amazing difference philanthropy has made to projects like ours."

POORT has also benefited from partnerships with state and federal agencies, with other nonprofits like Ecotrust, and with local government. Port Orford Mayor Jim Auburn even volunteered to drive a seafood delivery five hours up the road to Portland. And POORT has collaborated with OSU so effectively that the university is establishing a permanent research field station on its premises.

At the very heart of POORT are the town's fishermen, who are its members, volunteers, collaborators, supporters, and bosses all in one. "We are founded upon and driven by local leadership," says Leesa, "with thousands of hours of volunteer investment from our fishermen, and so much community support and local government time and energy devoted to the project." Leesa's leadership has made a huge difference, too. Susan Allen, director of the Our Ocean project,[12] calls Leesa "the original article, a fourth or fifth generation Oregonian, maverick, smart, and ridiculously humble—she's fabulous." Leesa, in turn, credits their successes to her devoted board. "I work for five commercial fishermen who had a vision about wanting to see a healthy marine ecosystem and a future in fishing for their kids. Their expertise and their commitment to what was working in fishing, to cutting out what wasn't working, and to being innovative and not afraid to fail has been amazing," she says.

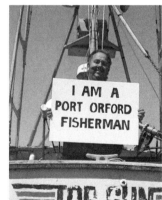

Jeff Miles on his boat. Photo courtesy Port Orford Ocean Resource Team.

Of course, success is a relative thing. Leesa believes that true success for POORT will mean two things. First, the model will spread: "we've set up the boundaries of our conservation area so that they won't overlap with other towns' potential areas. We really *hope* that we'll be replicated somewhere:

Bandon, for instance, or Gold Beach." The second measure of success will be self-sufficiency. POORT's generous donor base supports a kind of teach-a-man-to-fish strategy: the research facility, the education program, and the cooperative ownership of Sustainable Seafood should all grow to be self-sustaining. Until the organization gets to that point, it will have to rely heavily on philanthropic support. Leesa states the situation concisely: "if we can get these stand-alone assets in place, and *if philanthropists can hang in there with us until we do*, then we can give the community a way to survive. The goal is to work ourselves out of a job, and we *love* that goal."

Meanwhile, POORT will be fighting the good fight, Leesa says. "We take our obligations to our community, and to our partner organizations and funders, very seriously," she declares. "I want everyone to be proud that they've helped this scrappy little cutting-edge town raise itself up." Aaron chimes in, "We're stubborn here. We're going to keep fishing, we're going to stay represented, we're going to keep advocating for the community and for the environment." Everyone can contribute to the cause, he says, wherever you're from. "Personally, I always think of it this way: if you want to support change, vote with your fork and with your shopping bag. Buy our sustainable seafood and *eat more black cod*!"

OREGON FORESTRY AND FOREST PRODUCTS INDUSTRIES: CONFLICTS AND OPPORTUNITIES

Out of all of these natural resource-based sectors, forest products—our heritage industry—still comes first in Oregon as a point of contention between and within governments (state, federal, tribal), communities, conservationists, and business.[13] Tensions surrounding the forest products industry are understandable: Oregon's forestry and logging regulations are some of the least restrictive in the West,[14] and forests cover about 48 percent of the state's total landmass. About 60 percent of Oregon's forestlands are owned by the federal government, which means the public has a strong voice in the debates—although its voice is far more powerful in eastern forests, as many western forests are privately owned.[15] Many other forces have come into play, too, and the forest products industry has undergone dramatic changes over the years: tree harvests have declined; old growth has disappeared or been placed off-limits; some regulatory legislations have been enacted; flashpoints like the spotted owl debate have altered public opinion; market demand has fluctuated; and new markets have emerged, such as those for Forest Stewardship Council (FSC) certified lumber, and lumber byproducts for biomass fuel plants. Many forest products companies have closed as the timber industry has declined in Oregon, and many communities' livelihoods have disappeared. As a result, the tensions surrounding forestry stewardship

Coos Bay log yard. Photo by Kristin Anderson.

and sustainability are wholly understandable: as with fisheries, the long-term economic health of many rural communities hangs in the balance.

The forest products industry has been a cornerstone of Oregon philanthropy, particularly in previous decades. But while many of Oregon's forest products families have been generous with their profits, they have not always practiced or valued long-term forest management. The Collins Companies are prominent exceptions: for over eighty years, they have been thinning, replanting, and managing forests, and they are conscientious about concerns like watershed health and biodiversity. They now measure their success by the triple bottom line of sustaining people, planet, and profits. "I feel very strongly about the sustainable management of our forestlands," explains Truman W. Collins Jr., the president of the Collins Foundation.[16] "It's important to make choices that are good for the long-term health of the company, good for the employees, and good for the environment. If that means having to do something over the short-term that's more difficult than we want, then we'll do it."

John Shelk, owner of Ochoco Lumber and Malheur Lumber Company in John Day and, with his wife Linda, also a prominent regional philanthropist, came to a similar conclusion. Shelk has helped lead what is increasingly—at least in eastern forests—becoming a trend of compromise and partnership to work toward sustainable ends. In 2009, faced with the imminent closure of the Malheur mill due to lack of logs, Shelk forged an unlikely alliance with environmentalist Andy Kerr and a handful of conservationists concerned about insect damage and the increasing voracity of fires in unthinned national forests. With support from US Senator Ron Wyden and the US Forest Service, the Malheur Lumber Company has kept its doors open, starting up limited, sustainable logging operations in the Malheur National Forest and thus ensuring both that forests are healthier and that local timber workers remain in work. John says, "We now have a future we can rely on. I'm hopeful that the collaboration done to date will point the way to . . . a more positive and creative way of dealing with disagreement and controversy."

SUSTAINABLE FORESTRY, PASSIONATE PHILOSOPHY: THE HAYES FAMILY AND HYLA WOODS

As with Collins Companies and Malheur Lumber Company, widespread demand for workable solutions means that the forest products industry has benefited from thoughtful and innovative partnerships between nonprofits, philanthropy, business, conservationists, and communities. This is particularly true in eastern forests; west of the Cascades, the higher percentage of privately owned forests means that conservation groups have less traction.[17] But the Hayes family, owners of the experimental forest Hyla Woods, are working hard to find creative and positive solutions to the decades-old timber wars, and to prove that western forest products industries can balance profit and conservation as well.

Hyla Woods' spokesperson and leader is Peter Hayes, the son of Ned and Sis Hayes (whose philanthropy has been so seminal to the Oregon Nature Conservancy); as such, Peter has both the timber industry *and* conservation in the genes. Building on his family's sixteen decades of working with forests and quarter century of investing in Coast Range forests, Hayes is investing his own money to research best-practice forest stewardship and is donating long hours and expertise to help establish new markets for sustainable forest products. He is certainly a jack of all trades: a conservationist, forest products manufacturer, salesman, activist and policy advocate, researcher, educator, natural philosopher, and zealous volunteer all in one.

The Hayes family's business and research base, Hyla Woods, is 1,000 acres of family-run forestland on the northeastern flank of the Coast Range near Gaston. The three properties that make up Hyla have a very typical Oregon history: logged between 1920 and 1950, their ecological value is much lower than what it was pre-logging, but they also have the potential to become biodiverse, richly productive forests once more.[18] Peter arrives at the gate of Hyla Woods' Mt. Richmond forest in a mud-splattered stick-shift Subaru filled with tools and papers. Hyla's mill and office are at the top of the forest's steep slopes in a small clearing that, under previous owners, used to be a surely terrifying little airstrip. Rounding switchback after switchback, Peter knows exactly when to gun the car to get it up steep sections. He describes the forest as he goes, explaining dominant tree types, soil types, undergrowth, logging and replanting history, conservation milestones, and the highly localized thinning and logging tactics they have been experimenting with to help restore the working forest. Halfway up, in a stand of oaks, another car rounds a bend: the driver, one of the craftsmen who buys Hyla's wood, has just picked up a slab of milled oak destined to become a polished bar counter.

At the top of the hill the woods open up into a misty clearing. Two small buildings lurk in silhouette: the larger is Hyla's mill (tiny by mill standards), and the smaller is the one-room cabin that serves as an office and warming station. The cabin is a microcosm of Hyla Woods, built of thirteen different tree species all harvested and milled on the property. Inside, notebooks and diaries are scattered about: Peter and his family keep detailed daily logs of animal and plant sightings and phenotypes. Near the notebooks, a wooden cube rests on the table, with quotations pasted on each facet from Aldo Leopold. The nearest quotation reads, "The American public for many years has been abusing the wasteful lumberman. A public which lives in wooden houses should be careful about throwing stones at lumbermen, even wasteful ones, until it has learned how its own arbitrary demands help cause the waste which it decries. . . . The long and the short of the matter is that forest conservation depends in part on intelligent consumption, as well as intelligent production of lumber."

"Leopold made the case that we have choices in life and that we have a responsibility to the future to make the correct choices," explains Peter. Timber has been the family business for generations, Peter says, but early generations "had greater allegiance to capital than to place," progressing west from Massachusetts over decades and harvesting timber along the way. Like his parents, Ned and Sis, Peter has worked to ensure that disconnection with place is a thing of the past. His family's plan for Hyla Woods is, he explains, to find a way to create a replicable, transferrable model that unites forest stewardship with market demand for sustainable forest products. That means cultivating a healthy, biodiverse, and resilient forest that is also a working forest that will yield multiple products and generate multiple revenue streams. "Hyla's forests are recovering from decades of being used as a single revenue source created out of a single

Peter Hayes. Courtesy the Hayes family.

resource: a forest managed for its trees like an agricultural crop," Peter says. His goal is something more complex and enduring, a model that understands that the economic and social health of a timber community is intrinsically tied to the maintenance of a forest with all natural complexities intact.

The Hayes family's methods attend to both ends of the problem: on the one hand, they try to increase forest health by experimenting with best-practices in silviculture and harvesting; on the other, they are trying to assess community needs, build up partnerships, and develop a marketplace for sustainable forest products. Like many small family forestry operations, the Hayes log selected trees, sell logs to other mills, and mill their own logs as

Hyla Woods' log yard. Photo by Michael Anderson.

well. Their milling operation is low-impact: the hand-built mill's equipment is compact and efficient, and to dry their lumber, they have built an ingenious solar-heated kiln. Hyla Woods is intentionally tiny, with small harvest and low production, and with an emphasis on product quality rather than quantity. They produce boards of varying dimensions and species, as well as artisanal, finely grained slabs, and finished items such as cutting boards and flooring.

But they also offer a product that does not yet have an easily assessed commercial value: their forest's health. The Hayes family harvests trees at a rate that is less than half the forest's annual growth rate, so the forest's volume and age continue to increase. They log carefully, with minimal habitat disruption, and they thin out weaker trees and replant with multiple species to increase ecological complexity. Education is another unquantifiable product Hyla offers: the family invites school and university groups to the area to learn about sustainable forestry and to help conduct research and species population surveys. And then, of course, there are the climate benefits of a healthy forest: Peter estimates that their forest's rate of carbon sequestration (that is, the amount of carbon taken out of the atmosphere and stored within the trees) increases annually and currently stands at roughly fifty times the rate produced by the Hayes family in a year.

With these products, Peter hopes to use Hyla as a testing ground for more sustainable forest-based economies. He and his family are working hard not only to develop and promote robust forest stewardship practices, but also to develop a marketplace that values goods produced to these standards. Peter spends much of his time building relationships: for example, since 2005, he has worked to create a collaboration between sustainable forest products manufacturers, contractors, architects, and craftspeople called the Build Local Alliance. Bridging the urban-rural divide is also one of Hyla's key strategies: to educate urban consumers to appreciate the higher value that local and sustainable products offer. Consumers' ethics are, for the Hayes family, just as crucial as producers' ethics—both of these essential ingredients drive conservation forward. The grower/consumer relationship taps into a core tenet of his beliefs: that the responsibility for conserving our lands lies with each individual. It's up to consumers to make conscientious choices as well as growers to provide them with the opportunity. "Business is a mechanism for making things happen," Peter says.

Hyla Woods is not a nonprofit—it explicitly sets out to provide a model of sustainable business—but it has been operating like one, with a strong educational and research agenda, and with a commercial model wholly founded on the family's conservation ethic. A healthy forest *and* a market for high quality, sustainable forest products are its long-term goals, and ambitious ones given that Peter has a business to run. When asked if Hyla Woods is breaking even yet, Peter laughs. "Yes, we break even and are profitable, but not as profitable as we must become to meet our goal of being a replicable model to others." Moreover, he says, "it also depends on how you define profits: we make choices, and part of the profit we generate goes beyond dollars and cents—storing carbon, providing clean water and safe havens to valuable species, or working with school groups don't have dollar values attached."

The family looks on its investments of time and money as a pragmatic form of impact investing that they believe will provide tangible returns to them and the larger community in years to come. Unlike many nonprofit advocates for sustainability, Peter's research and outreach are less constrained by the need to secure short- and medium-term funding while he works to pilot transferable models for long-term forest resiliency and business self-sufficiency. He resists being called a philanthropist, but the label fits. "Forests have been good to us, and it makes sense for use to try to return the favor," he explains. "We're fortunate to have the latitude to experiment to find out how we can make this a landscape that, in my children's and my great-grandchildren's times, can flow back into the community in a way that rebuilds its natural integrity."

Although their forests are only 1,000 acres, the Hayes family's idealism is a beacon for Oregon's rural economies. Russ Hoeflich, Oregon director of the Nature Conservancy, calls Peter "a powerful voice for conservation: he's learned from the best, and he's a highly principled visionary—a real leader among leaders." Aldo Leopold writes that "when the land does well for its owner, and the owner does well by his land; when both ends up better by reason of their partnership, we have conservation. When one or the other grows poorer, we do not." Peter and his family are working hard to prove that this elusive balance is possible.

PLACE-BASED, PEOPLE-BASED CONSERVATION: SUSTAINABLE NORTHWEST, LAKE COUNTY RESOURCES INITIATIVE, AND WALLOWA RESOURCES

As with many of these initiatives, effective conservation and sustainable development often depend on grassroots collaboration. Portland-based nonprofit Sustainable Northwest helps cultivate partnerships, and has itself partnered both with Hyla Woods and with Malheur Lumber Company to help build sustainable forestry initiatives, as well as with communities statewide to create a number of energy, rangeland, and water sustainability initiatives.

Sustainable Northwest was founded and for many years led by Martin Goebel, who cut his teeth as Mexico director of the World Wildlife Fund and held similar positions with the Nature Conservancy and Conservation International. For Martin, these experiences cemented the idea that conservation starts at a local and personal level. "People who think that you can do conservation and related economic development without community participation are 100 percent incorrect," he declares.

Created in 1994, Sustainable Northwest works to prove that assertion, providing support to local communities by facilitating conversations and collaboration around conservation issues. Over the last few decades, rural communities in Oregon found themselves at the center of rancorous standoffs between environmentalists and natural-resource industries, then the lifeblood of many small towns. Sustainable Northwest has worked with these communities to support local leaders as they find ways to restore ecosystems, create living-wage jobs, and build relationships within and between communities. Some communities find it helpful to have outside perspective, both for mediation in discussions and as a resource on working solutions. In those roles, Sustainable Northwest has helped to build lasting collaborations between often-disparate interest groups, including state, federal, and tribal government, ranchers, farmers, lumbermen, businesses, and environmentalists; it has also helped fund the resulting projects.

Martin Goebel, next to the Wallowa River. Photo by Kristin Anderson.

The organization's projects are diverse and tailored. In eastern Oregon, it has partnered with local stakeholders to restore forests and jobs in the so-called Dry Forest Zone. In the Klamath basin, Sustainable Northwest helped to enable negotiations on water rights between tribes, ranchers, farmers, and downstream fishermen. Across the Northwest, it has helped rural communities leverage renewable energy options like micro-hydropower, wind, geothermal, and biomass; it operates leadership, national advocacy, and capacity-building forums to help rural leaders be heard more widely; and it offers an FSC-certification process for wood products companies to help create and fulfill demand for sustainably produced forest products.

To several of Oregon's rural communities, Sustainable Northwest is best known as a supporter of local consensus-building initiatives and as an incubator of locally run nonprofits that meet that community's specific needs and context. One of the nonprofit organizations it helped launch is Lake County Resources Initiatives (LCRI), led by Jim Walls, a man whose maverick boldness has paired perfectly with both organizations' ambitious hopes for the project. Lake County has suffered from two decades of economic contraction and has lost five of the six timber mills that used to sustain its economy. LCRI's work has, by all measures, been a huge success: 20 percent unemployment has turned into 10 percent; $3.5 million has been invested into new timber projects and has led to the building of a new sawmill by Collins Companies; and renewable energy—solar, hydropower, and geothermal—is becoming a mainstay of the local economy. Remarkably, Lake County is set to become the first carbon neutral county in America.

Jim Walls attributes LCRI's successes in large part to the philanthropic funding they've received, much of it initially directed through or obtained with the support of Sustainable Northwest. "To me, philanthropy's done two things," Jim explains. "It's allowed for agreements to keep our last sawmill here. It was going to close, and now I don't think there are too many people who would disagree with how our forests are managed. But it's also changed our whole economy: we are a renewable energy learning and innovation center now, and all of the renewables we have will really make long-term change from the depressed last two decades to a really positive future."

Philanthropic grants have also brought the community together and empowered it, Jim adds. "Lumbermen are rallying around forest stewardship practices, everyday citizens are embracing renewable energy as the means to communal survival, and LCRI is now an equal partner to Sustainable Northwest—we are an independent organization and its collaborator." As in Port Orford, donors and foundations were key to kickstarting these community conservation initiatives. "Philanthropy started it all, and sustains organizations like ours still," Martin Goebel says. "Conflict has given way to cooperation. This is the kind of long-term visionary philanthropy that conservation projects demand. Change takes time, and so does working with communities to build that change from the bottom up."

Before Sustainable Northwest began partnering with Lake County residents, it worked with communities in Wallowa County, where the organization got its start. It was the mid-nineties, at the height of the timber wars. Environmentalists were litigating furiously against the US Forest Service to delay or cancel altogether new timber sales on public land. In response, one Wallowa County town burned two prominent environmentalists in effigy. At the invitation of Ben Boswell, chair of the Wallowa County Board of Commissioners, and with the support of a handful of state politicians eager to find consensus, Martin Goebel began travelling to Joseph and Enterprise as a listener, joining a series of community meetings in which residents responded to changes in public land management and local economies.

"By this time in Wallowa County, all three sawmills were closing or closed, and they had 23 percent unemployment," says Martin. At the beginning of each new meeting, the attendees would go over the ecological, economic, and policy opinions which had been hotly debated at the previous meeting, and try to push forward a step or two. It was a tense and dispiriting period for the county, and these conversations often ended in stalemates and frustration. Arriving back in Portland after a particularly disheartening round of meetings, Martin found an envelope on his desk with a check in it for $10,000 and a note from one of the meetings' regulars, Doug McDaniel. It said something along the lines of "don't give up on us."

Doug's contribution was a huge vote of confidence for Sustainable Northwest, and after a while, the meetings started moving toward points of agreement rather than dissent. "For instance, Wallowa County was the first county in all of Oregon to institute a salmon habitat recovery plan that was codified in county regulation," Martin recalls. "Who doesn't want to save the salmon? We all fish and hunt and eat . . . we all share similar values that aren't that far off from sustainable visions." Often, the community found, changing terminology helped the process along. In a room with a sizeable population of ranchers, farmers, loggers, and mill owners, the word *environmentalist* had a hugely negative connotation: it was avoided as a matter of course. Then County Judge Ben Boswell pushed a little further, asking, "Could we not use the words *sustainable* or *sustainability* at meetings?" Martin chuckles: this was quite a challenge, given Sustainable Northwest's name. But he agreed.

Out of these meetings, good ideas began to emerge. The county had a surplus of small diameter timber that needed harvesting and a broad range of restoration needs. To guide this work, the nonprofit Wallowa Resources was founded in 1996 as Sustainable Northwest's first partner organization, and limited watershed restoration and logging operations began anew in the Wallowa Valley Ranger District north of Enterprise.

As Wallowa Resources developed its strategies and support network, its current executive director Nils Christoffersen rose up through its ranks. Nils, with a background in sustainable forestry in Africa and a master's degree from the University of Oxford, brought an extensive knowledge base to Enterprise, as well as a respect for place and a sense of belonging. His expertise, geniality, and listening skills have served Wallowa Resources well: during his first year at the organization, he helped them earn a five-year $750,000 grant from the Ford Foundation which, Nils says, "provided a continuity of funding and tremendous flexibility; . . . it meant we could experiment and try different tactics." Because the Ford Foundation grant provided relatively sustained funding, it helped Wallowa Resources to develop, with Wallowa County's Natural Resource Advisory, their own watershed assessments, so that they could evaluate and accomplish a full suite of restoration projects. Nils recounts that "we've seen $370,000 spent on watershed assessment generated over $6 million of economic benefit to the county."

Wallowa Resources now has a strong educational agenda as well, running summer camps and teaching college interns and volunteers. The organization hosts educational programs at nearby schools (which the superintendent has

Nils Christoffersen. Photo by Kristin Anderson.

suggested may be responsible for rising test scores in scientific literacy), and it has picked up projects that the Forest Service has been forced to cut, including river restoration, trail clearing projects, and the maintenance of over 100 campsites in the Wallowa Whitman National Forest. The organization has also launched a number of consultancy projects and spin-off revenue streams, most recently and perhaps impressively, the Integrated Biomass Energy Campus (IBEC). The IBEC is a diversified facility that processes small-diameter logs (in this context, a sustainable material) into a number of products: posts and poles, firewood, wood chips, and biomass fuel that will generate heat and electricity. The Biomass Campus has created a local small log market and has currently created twenty-eight jobs: log purchases and payroll alone will contribute over $2 million annually into the community.

These projects are all triumphs, Nils says, but the biggest triumph is in bringing so many disparate parties together in the same room, working extensively with the Forest Service and with the Bureau of Land Management; contracting for and consulting with the county; and balancing the concerns of ranchers and lumbermen with the concerns of conservationists to their mutual satisfaction. Of course, Nils says, "there are always pockets of skeptics. Any time you try to offer win-win solutions, people think you have a hidden agenda. But we've brought new jobs and new revenue streams into the community, and more science is being incorporated into policy and practice." Of course, Nils adds, there is "a need for humility: no one can say with certainty that what we're doing is right, but we are doing the best thing we can right now, which is continuing to learn and actively experiment. . . . Working in a nonprofit is not always easy, but we've been able to develop strong relationships, be innovative, take risks, collaborate . . . we've been able to do the things that keep us and our community motivated."

Its accomplishments are a direct result of Wallowa Resources' strong local donor base, but it's quite possible that its successes would have taken much longer to materialize without Doug McDaniel's $10,000 check to Sustainable

Wallowa Resources' Integrated Biomass Energy Campus. Photo by Kristin Anderson.

Northwest. That check was just his first contribution, Nils explains. "Doug has been a quiet but very important supporter of Wallowa Resources." A visit to Doug at his ranch, built halfway up a bluff overlooking pastureland and a meandering stretch of the Wallowa River near the town of Lostine, yields insight into his philanthropic motivations. A rancher, former engineer, and road-builder who contracted for the Forest Service,[19] Doug is weathered and laconic but extends a warm welcome. With the first autumnal snow dusting the Wallowas, Doug is out in his open-air workshop debarking poles for a teepee he intends to erect on his property, work that comes easily to him though he's nearly eighty.

Doug McDaniel and friend Jake on a bridge Doug built by hand over the section of restored Wallowa River. Photo by Kristin Anderson.

Doug is reticent about his philanthropy but is happy to talk about how he grew interested in conservation issues and became a founding supporter of Wallowa Resources. "I've lived in Wallowa County all my life, and three of the first five families in the county were great-great-uncles," Doug says. "But too many good jobs are gone from around here, and the dollar becomes the most important thing. This community just had too much at stake and we were just desperately looking for a way out." That's why he latched on to Wallowa Resources, he says: it provided some hope of rejuvenated economies. "I was of the belief that we had to have lines of communication with the environmental community: they controlled the vote, it wasn't people who were on the land. . . . What we needed was someone to help us communicate with the other side, and we needed someone to keep the Forest Service moving too, and that's one of Wallowa Resources biggest accomplishments: we have open communication with these two entities."

When Wallowa Resources was getting off the ground, it needed a project to prove its conservation credentials. Doug offered one of his own longtime challenges. "When I was a boy, this river was meandering all over the place, with logjams, cottonwood trees, you name it: you could catch some big fish in this river. After World War II, though, they came in and straightened the whole river from start to finish." The straightening steepened its gradient and soon all of the fish spawning areas had been washed away. "When I got this property," Doug notes, "I could see where the river had been, so I thought, well, I could move it back to where it was and get a few fishing holes in." After trying to get permits for over a decade, Doug asked Wallowa Resources to help. Nils and his team made it happen, with grants and additional funding from Doug. Now, Doug says, "it's amazing. . . . It looks pretty old and natural." Fish had returned within six months of its restoration, and although Doug had planted

Wallowa Lake. Photo by Kristin Anderson.

about 450 cottonwood trees, after a year or two of seasonal flooding, "Mother Nature came in and planted 2,000 . . . she humbles you pretty rapidly."

That humility is something that Doug, as a longtime supporter of Wallowa Resources, carries with him constantly. When complimented for his generosity to the organization, he unfailingly changes the subject to someone else's good works. But when asked why he gives, he responds slowly and passionately: "When you live someplace, and you love something, and you think you kind of understand a little about what's going on, and you think you should have the ability to make a change but you doubt your ability to do so, that's why I try to support people I think have that ability. Nils Christoffersen has that ability; so does Martin Goebel."

Doug's philanthropy, then, is personal: he has invested in the people and organizations he regards as having the capacity to help catalyze positive change. In a 2011 letter to the *Wallowa County Chieftain*, Doug explains further reasons for his support. "While 20 percent of the US population lives in rural areas, less than 10 percent of the total charitable dollars go to rural causes. When I understood this disparity, . . . I became an even stronger advocate for Wallowa Resources and other nonprofits here. . . . For every private dollar donated to Wallowa Resources in 2009, we were able to get nineteen grant dollars. That's a great return on investment in our community."[20]

Like their partners Sustainable Northwest and Lake County Resources Initiative, Wallowa Resources has responded to local needs with local solutions. Wallowa Resources is the product of a vast collaborative effort between grassroots stakeholders, a process that lies at the heart of Sustainable Northwest's methodology. Although Martin Goebel has now retired from Sustainable Northwest after nineteen years at its helm, his passion for the work remains unabated. "What drives me is what we can get done if we all work together more effectively. I have a huge confidence in people's goodness, and magical things can happen when people collaborate."

Back in Lostine, Doug McDaniel agrees. The pace of change can be frustrating, Doug owns, but "things are happening, and although it's just terrible tough for us to suffer the slowness of it sometimes, we have an asset in Wallowa County that's beautiful and that's very worthy of taking care of. There's no reason we can't do it economically and sustainably: we can increase the health of that asset and by doing so we can create a lot of good family-wage jobs and more sustainable natural resources." With the aid of long-term philanthropic investment, visionary nonprofit strategies, and grassroots community support, that's precisely what Wallowa Resources, Lake County Resource Initiative, and Sustainable Northwest are doing.

TAKING RISKS, INVESTING IN THE LONG GAME

> *"Nature is not a place to visit. It is home."*
> —Gary Snyder

The organizations and individuals profiled in this chapter make up only a tiny fraction of Oregon's conservation community. More aggressive organizations like the Western Environmental Law Center and Water Watch help push the debate along, litigating for urgent protections for vulnerable ecosystems and giving leverage to consensus-building organizations like Sustainable Northwest and POORT. Watchdog organizations like the Friends of the Columbia River Gorge and 1000 Friends of Oregon make sure that land-use and other conservation initiatives are implemented and upheld. Others, like Renewable Northwest, work across the region to provide policy guidance and advocacy for cleaner, greener energy initiatives. Many organizations focus on the conservation of certain species and habitats: for instance, the

Wind turbine. Photo by Michael O'Brien.

international but Oregon-based Xerces Society directs its resources toward invertebrate conservation, and the Oregon Flora Project (based at OSU, and funded by grants and small donations) invaluably catalogues and conserves Oregon's vascular plant populations. And Portland, a famously green city, is home to a number of great projects, ranging from Free Geek, which recycles and repurposes electronics and computers, to Neighbors for Clean Air, a group that campaigns to improve Oregon's air quality.

Motivating many of these projects, directly or indirectly, is the increasingly tangible phenomenon of climate change and our need to mitigate and adapt to global climactic shifts. According to Tom Bowerman, "climate change isn't the problem; it's the symptom. It's about how we choose to live, and we're at a tipping point." Making this kind of change takes commitment—through informed, sustainable consumption and through personal and public philanthropy. It also takes patience. "It's a long-term change proposition," according to Martin Goebel. "Most philanthropists or grantmakers think that after a five-year grant or donation the problem is solved. But in natural resources, it takes far-sighted vision: trees grow slowly, coral reefs grow slowly, rivers repair slowly, and communities learn slowly."

In 2011, Oregonians contributed about $81 million to environmental nonprofits, compared with $493 million to education nonprofits, $196 million to human services, $134 million to health nonprofits, and $86 million to arts organizations.[21] This low number is probably because environmental problems can appear less urgent than immediate human needs, and the results of conservation work are gradual rather than immediate, thus more difficult to measure, promote, and celebrate. Yet the work these organizations do will, in the long-run, tangibly affect most aspects of human life, as well as protect the Oregon landscapes that are so essential to our concepts of place, of self, and of home.

In order for sustainable communities to exist and thrive, and for Stegner's "geography of hope" to endure, environmental nonprofits need more money and volunteers than they are receiving, and they need contributors willing to take risks and to stick around for the long haul. Jim Martin, conservation director of the Berkley Conservation Institute, articulates why: "Philanthropy is the heart of maintaining the nonprofit structure we have, and the nonprofit structure is what is constantly nudging the body politic toward addressing conservation issues. Nonprofits' constant advocacy helps us move the needle on public opinion." Martin Goebel agrees: "Nonprofits are what take scientific conservation research and push the public conversation toward evidence-based policy changes; philanthropy is required to fund that change." As Julie Daniel, from BRING Recycling, says, "the message needs to be repeated over and over again. Philanthropy has been vital: without it, none of what we've done would have happened."

Courtesy the Center for Intercultural Organizing.

5
Toward a Common Cause:
Supporting Inclusion and Equality

*"We will never have true civilization until we have
learned to recognize the rights of others."*
—Will Rogers

When Thomas Jefferson drafted the most famous lines of the Declaration of Independence—"that all men are created equal, that they are endowed by their Creator with certain unalienable Rights, that among these are Life, Liberty, and the Pursuit of Happiness"—America was a profoundly unequal place: these rights didn't really apply to women, Native Americans, or African Americans. And although America is more equal now than it was at its founding, glaring inequities still remain.

Like the rest of the nation, Oregon's history of systemic discrimination means that current inequities have deep roots. As early as 1843, the Oregon territory passed exclusion laws banning African Americans from settling here. In the 1900s, Oregon introduced "sundown" laws to ban minorities from remaining in towns after sunset. Women's suffrage failed five times in the state legislature before being passed in 1912 on its sixth attempt; Oregon was the last state in the West to grant these rights. In 1923, the Oregon legislature (populated largely by Ku Klux Klansmen) banned many Japanese Americans from owning or leasing land. Two decades later, Japanese Americans were forcibly interned in camps during World War II. In 1935, Oregon law mandated that Latinos attend segregated schools. In 1954, sixty-one tribes west of the Cascades were "terminated," a process in which what little land, assets, and subsidies remained to them were withdrawn. In 1988, Mulugeta Seraw, an Ethiopian student and father, was beaten to death with a baseball bat in Portland by white-supremacist skinheads. In that same year, Measure 8 repealed Governor Goldschmidt's executive order against discrimination based on sexual orientation and enacted a statute to deny employment rights to Oregon's LGBTQ (lesbian, gay, bisexual, transgender, queer) community.

Largely as a result of persistent nonprofit and philanthropic advocacy, equity laws have now been enacted to protect most rights for most citizens. Nevertheless, they are not always upheld or interpreted fairly, and institutional and structural racism, sexism, homophobia, and discriminations and stigmas are still commonplace. Oregon women earn seventy-nine cents for every dollar earned by men.[1] Only 16 percent of Oregonians with disabilities graduate from college and only 8 percent have a significant other.[2] And people of color are two to three times as likely as their white counterparts to have no health insurance[3] and earn half the income of white Oregonians.[4]

With tenacity and ardor, nonprofits have been chipping away at these inequities, and individual donors, volunteers, and foundations have helped expand and protect the rights of marginalized groups with their support for initiatives and programs. However, Oregon philanthropy contains its own inequities. Communities of color make up a little more than a fifth of Oregon's population, but organizations that support them receive only 5.6 percent of foundation grant dollars.[5] Elderly citizens get 1.8 percent of Oregon grant dollars while 22.2 percent go to youth. LGBTQ organizations receive 0.3 percent of grant dollars, and immigrants and refugees just 0.2 percent.[6] Urban-rural inequities also persist, as do education inequities. As one grant-maker summarized, "Philanthropy is often perceived and perpetuated as an elitist field. [These numbers] remind us that . . . there are real needs in the community and that communities are more diverse than the field of philanthropy itself. We must be intentional[ly] and overtly committed to principles of diversity and inclusion."[7] That dictate applies to both foundations and individuals, who in their giving and volunteering often overlook communities outside of their day-to-day experience and often fail to acknowledge and confront societal and personal prejudices.

Oregon's demographics are changing. Almost 20 percent of kindergarteners are English language learners, and over a third of our K-12 students are non-white.[8] More people are finding the courage to acknowledge disabilities

Urban League in Salem. Photo by Ethan Bloom. Courtesy Urban League.

and to be open about their sexual orientation. As we welcome a more diverse population, we must ensure that all Oregonians have equal opportunities and protections: the status quo simply is not good enough. Some of the nonprofits serving this cause work by celebrating a specific culture, heritage or identity—examples of this also appear in the chapter on arts, culture, and heritage. Others support leaders and activists from marginalized populations or help to increase "cultural competency" within communities. Some engage in direct civil action and advocacy in order to bring visibility to a cause and to seek legal or legislative redress. Others provide services to populations suffering from discrimination or marginalization. These organizations and their supporters share the same goal: making Oregon equitable, inclusive, and united.

HARRIET DENISON AND THE CAPACES LEADERSHIP INSTITUTE

Portlander Harriet Denison is a superb example of a citizen working with marginalized communities to elevate their visibility and voice. A self-described introvert whose passion is bird watching, Harriet has nevertheless been an effective and determined proponent of strategic, well-researched, and tightly managed philanthropic activism. Her privacy is legendary—"You'll have to work hard to get to her," warned one friend—but her philanthropy is at once deeply personal and deeply social.

Just returned from an ornithology excursion to South America, Harriet begins by mentioning that her family has long roots in America. "One of my ancestors funded the Mayflower, and then they came over shortly thereafter—an early example of a venture capital start-up," she says with a wry smile. For Harriet, a longtime donor to progressive causes, philanthropy is entwined with her deep roots here. Her family's foundation, the Ralph L.

Smith Foundation, was passed down from her grandfather. It has always had a strong focus on advocating for social justice: Harriet's grandfather awarded scholarships to African and African American medical students, and Harriet's mother funded domestic violence shelters long before they became mainstream.

When it was Harriet's turn to become a trustee, she followed in her mother's footsteps, prioritizing organizations advocating for equity and minority rights in Oregon. "As a former Peace Corps volunteer, I knew I couldn't change the world," she said, "but I did think I could help a bit." True to her training overseas, Harriet decided that a proactive approach to philanthropy would make it more effective: on-the-ground, real-time research was key. She describes how Andrew Carnegie visited many of the sites where his libraries were built. Getting out into communities like that is important, Harriet says. "If you give money well, you learn a lot from the process. You meet people, you get a chance to hear their own stories. That's what appeals to me."

Harriet Denison on Hamilton Mountain. Courtesy Harriet Denison.

She started by attending workshops for people with wealth held by the MacKenzie River Gathering (MRG) Foundation, a progressive organization that vets and distributes money to grassroots nonprofits advocating for social change. She also became involved with other social justice–driven organizations including the Western States Center and A Territory Resource (now Social Justice Fund NW). Through the latter, she met Larry Kleinman, a long-ago Chicago transplant who came out west in the 1970s as a VISTA volunteer and became active in the civil rights movements.

Larry took Harriet on a site visit to PCUN (Piñeros y Campesinos Unidos del Noroeste), a farm and timber workers union for Latino immigrants that he helped found. Based in Woodburn (a town with a majority Latino population of just over 50 percent), PCUN has been organizing workers for almost three decades now, pushing for an enforceable minimum wage, health care, job safety, better living conditions (migrant workers often are housed in ghettoized camps), and access to other basic rights and benefits. Under the leadership of Jaime Arredondo, PCUN operates two nonprofits: some programs fall under the wing of their educational and service nonprofit (a 501(c)3), and some fall under their political arm (a 501(c)4).[9]

During Harriet's visit to PCUN's communities, she witnessed the squalid living quarters in which farmworkers were housed, an experience that catalyzed her immediate support of PCUN. She also took a leadership role in funding the CAPACES Leadership Institute (CLI), which brings together the leaders of nine mid-Willamette Valley Latino social change organizations. CAPACES (which translates to "able" or "capable") started in 2003 as a sister program to PCUN. In 2008, the organization began a three-year process to raise funds for and build the CAPACES Leadership Institute, an independent nonprofit that has now become a gathering place, strategic center, and ideas generator for Hispanic social change leaders. CLI focuses its efforts primarily on serving the staff and boards of the nine Latino service organizations: CAUSA (immigrants' rights), Farmworker Housing Development Corporation, Latinos Unidos Siempre (youth leadership), Mano a Mano Family Center (social services), Mujeres Luchadoras Progresistas (women's economic development), Oregon Farmworker Ministry (faith-based solidarity), Salem-Keizer Coalition for Equality (education reform, discussed in Chapter Two), Voz Hispana Causa Chavista (voter organizing and civic engagement), and PCUN. All of the CLI member organizations provide services to the local community deliberately from *within* the local community. Through these nine organizations, CLI estimates that it has assisted six thousand immigrants to gain legal status and provided thousands with important information through Radio Movimiento, PCUN's non-commercial FM radio station.

Their work is timely and necessary. About 80 percent of those served by the CLI and its members are Latino immigrants or from Latino immigrant families; more than half are under thirty-five years old; 60 percent are women; and many have had little formal education in the United States or in their home country. Currently making up 12 percent of Oregon's population, Hispanic Oregonians tend to be among the poorest and most marginalized of our demographic groups. According to the 2010 US Census, Oregon's Hispanic population grew five times as fast as the state's total population in the past decade. Hispanic residents make up an even larger segment of our younger generations, and non-Latino white Oregonians are expected to become a minority at some point between 2042 and 2050.

At the CLI, Executive Director Laura Isiordia and her staff work with community leaders to conduct classes on social change history, organize seminars about education about legal rights and economic structures, and hold strategy symposia, among many other programs. One of CLI's most exciting initiatives is TURNO, a program that identifies talented youths and helps prepare them to become movement leaders for the current and future generations. The program gives them many different experiences of leadership: for example, recently former Governor Barbara Roberts sat down with them to speak about her path to the governorship. The CAPACES building itself—the first commercial or office structure in the United States constructed to "Passive House" standards—is a metaphor for the organization's progressive and unifying mandate. It is covered in vibrant murals, painted by local volunteers, which celebrate the Hispanic community's strength and centrality to Oregon's economic and social structures.

CAPACES' successes have been significantly aided by Harriet Denison's strong interest in the organization's work. With over twenty years of experience in working with CLI, PCUN and their partners, founders, and supporters, Harriet has absolute trust in their judgment. Recently, she provided a $500,000 grant with no strings attached to CAPACES, who used it as a challenge grant to raise the rest of the money needed to complete their beautiful new headquarters. With the endorsement that an unrestricted grant of that size brings to an organization, CLI brought in a remarkable 140 new donors and raised a total of $750,000, an enormous amount for a grassroots community organization. This cornerstone gift, however, was the result of much Smith family strategy. After Harriet spoke with her fellow trustees about the trust's future, they decided that subsequent generations did not share their interests or philanthropic passion. They decided to spend down its assets instead of continuing it indefinitely. "It's very clear that all of the nonprofits we had been funding were existing and thinking in terms of scarcity. I thought about what good they could do if they had a large amount of money, so we gave CAPACES half a million," explains Harriet. The trustees divided the rest between the Western States Center and the McKenzie River Gathering Foundation.

Harriet is particularly proud of the support she was able to direct toward CAPACES, not least because their goals so closely reflect her own beliefs and experience. She needs a wake-up call sometimes, she says: much of her philanthropy is driven by lessons she learned through travelling around meeting people. "For instance, I was at a workshop on 'Undoing Classism' one time," Harriet recalls, "and a woman named Maria came up to me and said, 'I'm a short, fat, Latino lesbian who was raised poor, and I think you need to get to know me.' She was absolutely right: becoming friends with her gives me perspective on social classism and on other inequities." That kind of experience, says Harriet, means that not only is her philanthropy more targeted but that she also advances her own development as a citizen and as a person. "Seriously, I think that a lot of my philanthropy has to do with my own personal growth: having the foundation meant that I opened myself up to a lot of experiences that I wouldn't have been able to otherwise," she says. "And I loved thinking about what smaller organizations could do with such resources. We targeted organizations that were fairly stable but lacked the next level of lobbying or advocacy ability. Conservative philanthropy and big foundations usually focus on delivering services, but as a small private foundation, we could support nonprofits that advocate for systemic

(Left) PCUN's Risberg Hall during a mayoral visit. (Right) Young community members at CAPACES. Photos courtesy PCUN.

changes; we could look further into the distance and take a risk." Rising Latino leaders will certainly benefit from her strategy.

COMMUNITY SUPPORT: THE NATIVE AMERICAN YOUTH AND FAMILY CENTER (NAYA)

Columbia Boulevard in Northeast Portland is the opposite of scenic. Cars and trucks speed down it en route to the airport, to the Gorge, to Vancouver, or to one of the many industrial complexes and freight businesses that line it. Those who live nearby are those who cannot afford to move away, and its crime rates, as well as its accident rates, are high. But among the trucks and warehouses is a low-lying building with sprawling wings and outbuildings: it is home to the Native American Youth and Family Center (NAYA), an institution that provides a wide variety of services and a sense of community to Portland's Native American population.

NAYA's work supports a population often in dire need. In the 2010 Census, the Portland Metropolitan area contained almost fifteen thousand Native Americans, many of whom are among the poorest residents of the Metro area. About a half of NAYA's clients live in deep poverty. Portland's Native American community suffers the highest rates unemployment and homelessness of any demographic, and it also endures severe health crises, including high rates of depression, addiction, and diabetes.[10] High school graduation rates for Native youth were hovering at around 50 percent in 2012,[11] and Native children make up nearly a quarter of all those in foster care in Multnomah County. In these rates of inequalities and challenges, NAYA's community of urban Native Americans parallels tribal communities (those still living on or near tribal lands or reservations). However, NAYA's community faces added difficulties. Hailing from over 380 different tribes, many of Portland's American Indians were uprooted from tribal life because of tribal termination and forced relocation or, for younger generations, because of weak economies that drove their families to Portland in search of work. Portland's scattered and often seemingly invisible urban Indian population

Young children dancing at NAYA's Neerchokikoo Powwow, 2012. Courtesy NAYA.

can feel both disconnected from their respective tribal cultures and unable to access community-based, culturally sensitive help.

NAYA's constituents, then, are more diverse than tribal communities. Twenty-one different tribes are represented in Washington County alone, and NAYA serves three other counties besides, as well as clients who come to Portland from more distant tribal communities. Matt Morton, from the Squaxin Island tribe in the southern Puget Sound, is NAYA's executive director and has worked in Oregon for a long while. Matt says that NAYA is well placed to help these groups because they are working from within the Native community rather from outside of or above it. "We are effective because we are culturally specific; we're working with knowledge given by the community," he says. "The first group we consult is our Elders Council, but we have an extensive . . . network of board, staff, funders, community members, native and non-native organizations, elected officials, and others. As executive director I feel incredibly empowered to know that we're working to give the community what they need. Everything we do has this foundation of community voice."

NAYA's mission is broad, Matt explains, providing wraparound services and advocacy. "We work with our partners to improve the lives of the community in three clear areas. The first is youth and education services, which include afterschool programs like tutoring, sports, and tribal culture and arts classes; college counseling; spring break and summer camps focused variously on science, math, language, cultural knowledge, and leadership; our Early College Academy, which is a fully functioning college preparatory high school; and our team of youth advocates, which is based in seventy-nine different schools and does case management and gang prevention and homeless youth work. . . . Gangs and homelessness are big problems with our kids," Matt adds.

Family services—including Head Start and playgroup programs, domestic violence counseling, elder services (exercise classes, weekday lunches, outings, and help accessing other services and information), and working with foster families and youth as well as with the state to intervene before Native children are removed from their parents unnecessarily—form the second broad area of NAYA's offerings. Helping mend a broken foster care system is urgent work, Matt says. "The 1978 Indian Child Welfare Act removed about 25 percent of children from their tribal communities and placed them into non-native families; a pretty aggressive and effective way to kill a culture is to remove its children," he says bluntly. "Unfortunately, Native children still constitute almost a quarter of all children living in foster care, so in addition to fighting to lower these numbers, we do a lot of work with foster families so these children can still interact with tribal communities and elders."

NAYA's third area of work is in community empowerment and economic development. It offers leadership development programs and strong and vocal advocacy against discriminatory policies, social biases, and inaccurate government and social assessments of their communities. Economic services are also prominent, including workforce training and development, job search assistance, emergency rental and housing assistance, and home ownership assistance—"we've placed 120 families in homes in the Portland area during a time wherein it's been difficult to get credit," Matt mentions proudly. They also offer emergency energy relief, a food pantry, and other goods to those in urgent need, and they are working on a microlending program to provide start-up assistance for new businesses. NAYA also houses two in-house income generating businesses—a catering company and a construction company—both of which provide earnings for the organization as well as employment training and income for their workers.

Across all of these programs, they try to retain cultural relevance, taking great care to link services and assistance to tribal traditions. For example, elk antler purses, which some coastal cultures used to carry dentalium shell currency, form the prop for a discussion about savings accounts and other personal banking. And at their Early College Academy, NAYA's students start off the week by gathering in a circle to engage in a cleansing ritual. It has been so popular that they have asked to do it on Fridays, too, to wipe away the week's baggage before beginning the weekend. "I think there's something about this place that centers you and allows for a little more of the unknown to enter you," Matt suggests.

That NAYA can feel so welcoming and culturally specific while also providing so many diverse services is a testament to NAYA's committed and talented staff and to its wide-ranging network of sympathetic organizations, ranging from NARA (the Native American Rehabilitation Association of the Northwest) to a women's roller-derby team that practices on their grounds.

Philanthropy, too, has played a seminal role. "We've been really generously supported by foundations," Matt says. "To be able to find partners who are generous with their resources but also committed to a level of partnership and service to your community means that you move away from a transaction and more toward a relationship with your donors and supporters, which is wonderful." The Northwest Area Foundation has been a long-term and constant partner, he says, along with the Meyer Memorial Trust and many other funders.

Joe Finkbonner and his wife at NAYA's annual gala. Courtesy the Finkbonner family.

Individuals like Joe Finkbonner, of the Lummi tribe, also contribute their expertise and resources. Joe is executive director of the Northwest Portland Area Indian Health Board (NPAIHB), and his background dovetails neatly with NAYA's mission. An expert on issues of Native American disease prevention and health, for a number of years he was also his tribe's general manager. He thus knows that the health of a community is defined broadly, meaning everything from well-lit roads to a well-educated population. There is a tangible link between social and economic inequities and medical prognoses, he says:

> With that expanded view of public health, it led me to believe that in order to make a difference in my tribe's population, we needed the best school system, the best public works, the best law enforcement, and everything else. We believe that you judge a tribe by how well it treats its kids and its elderly: if you are generous and caring to both of those vulnerable populations, it will raise, it will lift up the whole community. NAYA is helping our most vulnerable people, and I feel good that I can help them out with cash when I can. It's the gift I get, knowing that it's going to an organization like NAYA.

Contributions from community donors like Joe are a pillar of NAYA's support, says Matt Morton: "the grassroots community giving that takes place is the most consistent river that flows through the organization."

Elders showing off their talents. Courtesy NAYA.

Volunteer support is perhaps the largest tributary of this river, he adds. "The only thing a lot of our people have to offer is their time, their presence, and their emotional support, and that's invaluable. The fact that we have community volunteers coming here almost every night of the week to provide tutoring, to greet at the door, to provide cultural programming or weekend staffing . . . if it weren't for that, we'd have to either add another hundred staff members or cut many different programs."

NAYA's strong volunteer tradition in some ways reflects the practice of potlatch,[12] Matt says, "where the demonstration of your wealth is in giving it away, and where the community comes together to welcome other communities and to work as a team." It is a cultural honor, a recognition of leadership, to give freely of your resources and your time, Matt suggests. "That's the challenge of working in the Native community: if someone says they need you somewhere, you have to go! You do it, not begrudgingly—that's how we support each other."

Portland's Native community still needs all of the support they can get, Matt adds. "There's a degree of invisibility we still need to overcome. We've been told there are no homelessness or gang issues in our population. Eight years ago, when we started doing our housing-to-homeownership program we were told there wasn't an interest in ownership within the Native community," he says, frustrated. "We still have a significant number of community members who are in need of stability, whether that's housing, employment, education, or other issues." The variety and depth of NAYA's programming is, by any measure, astounding, as is its huge corps of volunteers and grassroots donors. Matt says that NAYA's mission, ultimately, is straightforward. "We

Dancers at NAYA Neerchokikoo's Powwow 2012. Courtesy NAYA.

want to be a growing, healthy, and proud community where we have culturally relevant access to safe housing, education, health care, community-owned businesses, and we want our region to realize that in order for all of us as a society to thrive, the Native community needs to thrive."

THE URBAN LEAGUE OF PORTLAND:
EIGHT DECADES OF SERVICE AND ACTIVISM

Like many minority communities, Oregon's African Americans have lived under overtly racist policies until recently. The state's ban on interracial marriages was enforced until 1955; in the 1920s, Oregon's Ku Klux Klan was the strongest in the West; and Jim Crow laws kept the black community segregated for years. Now, the laws have been repealed, but institutional racism and private prejudices still remain. This is borne out by the facts: black incarceration rates are six times those for whites in Oregon, and only 37 percent of black households own their own homes compared with 68 percent of white households. As of 2012, the unemployment rate for African Americans was 18.4 percent compared to a rate of 8.7 percent for whites, and African Americans are still overrepresented in service occupations and underrepresented in managerial and professional positions.[13]

The Urban League, one of Oregon's most established advocacy organizations, is working at a feverish pace to fix this. Its home is a beige brick building near the Broadway Bridge in Portland. Its neighborhood used to be predominantly black; now, its residents are more diverse, and the area is gentrifying quickly. The Urban League has a broad mandate, like many service and advocacy organizations: they fight for social change and justice and provide services to those who have been victimized by inequities. The building's façade proudly proclaims the Urban League's mission, its sage trim adorned by portraits of many leaders who have fought against racial and socioeconomic inequities, blending national and international figures such as Rosa Parks and Nelson Mandela with local heroes like Dr. DeNorval Unthank (Dr. Walt Reynolds' mentor); Margaret Carter and Avel Gordly (state legislators representing northeast and north Portland); and Gretchen Kafoury (former Portland City Commissioner who pushed for inner Portland urban renewal and against predatory lenders).

"I think that the Urban League's work is as urgent now as it was when it was founded here in 1945," says Midge Purcell, the Urban League's director of Advocacy and Public Policy and the force behind 2009's seminal *State of Black Oregon* report, a landmark publication that helped reinvigorate discussions about racial inequality at the political and local levels. Midge continues:

> For decades, African Americans have been aware of the disparities in education, employment, health outcomes, and criminal justice, but this report assessed some important factors that are not usually documented in standard survey data. In education, for instance, people start at the achievement gap, but teachers' lower expectations of African American students and lack of cultural competency contributes to the gap. These pieces are harder

Portland's Urban League staff and headquarters. Courtesy the Urban League of Portland.

to document in terms of quantitative data, but they are such an important part of the story.

The Urban League embraces this depth of research, which is needed in order to tackle our most entrenched social inequities. In addition to an extensive research agenda, however, the League provides broad-based services to its community as well as advocating for greater equity between communities. "The purpose of the Urban League has always been to provide intervention to increase opportunity for the African American community either through direct services or advocacy, and we do both," Midge says. "We know that if nothing is done to address those disparities and inequities, they're not static: they get worse."

Eighty percent of Oregon's black population lives within the three counties (Multnomah, Washington, and Clackamas) of the Portland Metro area, and because of gentrification, these communities are becoming increasingly dispersed. Nevertheless, the League's services reach many community members. For instance, for the last forty years, they have run a comprehensive senior program—the only program targeted to African American seniors in the state—which serves over six hundred seniors a year. "It provides support to our elders, those who have experienced the worst circumstances and ravages of racism in their lives," Midge explains. "The fact that they're able to be supported and cared for by people who look like them, who love them, who can keep them active and healthy and in their homes . . . it's wonderful work and it provides them not only with activities, care, and case management, but it gives them a built-in community."

The League's new community health worker (CHW) training program also pushes for tailored, community-centered approaches to health care, as well as aiding with community employment. To date, the Urban League has trained over fifty new CHWs. And its general workforce development program also has had great success, although it has been difficult to keep it fully funded. The Urban League provides guidance and job leads year round, but their training programs, which have proven particularly effective in securing long-term employment opportunities, are resource-intensive and funders are always needed to underwrite them. Midge knows that the need is urgent. "Considering that youth unemployment is at 45 percent, we need to be doing a lot more of this. People associate the Urban League as a place to get a job, and they trust us to provide competent training and advice—when we have the resources to do it, that is!"

One of the League's most successful programs has been its annual Social Justice and Civic Leadership Program, which trains twenty-five community members in civic engagement and organizing. One of the 2012 graduates,

(Left) Seniors at the Urban League's Multicultural Senior Center. Photo by Kelly Johnson. (Right) Participants in a workforce training program. Photo by Harold Hutchinson Photography. Courtesy the Urban League.

Amber Starks, was the spark behind the passing of the hair-care bill (HB 3409) in the Oregon legislature. She wanted to volunteer to do the hair of African American kids who were in foster care—many foster parents are not familiar with braiding and other black hair-care techniques. Amber was told she could not do it without a cosmetologist's license (which requires seventeen hundred hours of training and typically costs $10,000–$20,000). Amber felt this was overregulation, at once restrictive and discriminatory. She campaigned for a change in the law, and it passed with strong bipartisan support. "In our training, we talked about how you move legislation . . . and then she went and did it!" Midge says. "The Urban League's mission is empowerment and that was a great example of empowerment, giving people the skills and support they need to make change in their communities." Amber agrees: "support from the Urban League empowered me to lead bravely, and boldly."[14]

Amber's success in moving legislation mirrors the Urban League's own legislative strategies. Midge says, "we've firmly put health and racial equity on the agenda, including the social determinants of health." And since the publication of the *State of Black Oregon* report, many of its recommendations have been enacted, including a cultural competency bill, regulations to prevent disproportionate disciplining of black pupils in the schools, and a requirement for schools to develop equity plans. A similarly impressive set of accomplishments have been enacted by the city government, too. And many more policy recommendations are in the works, both at local and statewide levels.

"Those are some things we can point to as progress," Midge says. "It's not enough, and a lot of it is . . . not quite structural, because the structures that create inequities are still there. . . . We've made some headway, it's just not nearly enough." They are working on a new *State of Black Oregon* (check its website: www.stateofblackoregon.org), which Midge hopes will propel the cause forward and catalyze an even broader range of policy changes. The report will be even more wide-angled this time, she says. The issues are intersectional and cannot be put into silos—education outcomes influence employment, housing influences education outcomes, housing and employment influence health. The report's demographics will be far more inclusive and statewide, too: "we left out key pieces of the black community in Oregon—older adults, new and growing African immigrants, the LGBT community, and the rural black community . . . each of those groups face similar challenges, but also their own unique challenges. This report will reinforce the fact that black Oregonians live everywhere in Oregon. Policy makers need to know that the problems facing black Oregonians aren't just Portland problems. The report will be as holistic as possible."

The Urban League has been consistently and generously funded by the Northwest Health Foundation, who, Midge says, "have been amazing: we couldn't have done what we've done without them." They have also received funding for various programs from government and city agencies. But they do all of their advocacy work, policy work, and extensive service provision on a budget that's only a little over $1 million a year. The lack of resources is frustrating for Midge. "I feel the lack of funding and resources really keenly because our aspirations and our needs are so great. We have expertise that has made a huge contribution, and we just need more resources to do more. For instance, we've been developing a high-profile campaign to address issues of black unemployment and yet I have *no* money to launch it," she says with frustration.

When asked what they could do with a big gift, Midge replies without hesitation: "Two things. If we got a big gift, we could really develop our workforce development program and significantly make an impact in our community's ability to gain and retain employment—it responds to such incredible need in the community, and it's a really robust service. I would also replicate my staff: they've done such an extraordinary job, and they've made such incredible sacrifices to work here. They work here for passion, definitely not for money."

She pauses, then adds, "But if we even had enough for just one more staff person, we could make such a bigger impact on Oregon. Black Oregonians contribute a great deal to this state, and we could contribute more if society didn't marginalize our communities socially and economically. It's a net waste to the state of Oregon to keep the status quo. Think about all of the creativity and innovation we can offer."

Immigrants and refugees from around the world proudly display their traditional attire at IRCO's 35th Anniversary event. Photo by Katie Anderson Photography. Courtesy IRCO.

IMMIGRANT AND REFUGEE COMMUNITY ORGANIZATION (IRCO): A MULTIETHNIC COMMUNITY WITH MULTIFACETED NEEDS

Even though Oregon has a troubled legacy of ethnic and racial discrimination, it is worth remembering that some people see our state as a refuge: they come to find freedom, safety, or prosperity. However, the transition to American life is seldom easy for them: not only do immigrants and refugees often find themselves victims of the same prejudices experienced by domestic communities of color and other marginalized populations, but they have the added stress of learning to survive in a society and culture that are completely foreign to them.

Sokhom Tauch is one such individual. He fled Cambodia in 1975 in order to escape the Khmer Rouge. He eventually landed in Portland as a refugee, then a city unused to foreigners and unprepared to accommodate even refugees' most basic needs. He tells of taking a bus to Chinatown to buy rice, and then not being allowed back on the bus to return to his lodging. Heaving the rice onto his shoulders, he walked ten miles across the Steel Bridge and up I-84 to where he was staying, following the bus route up the freeway so that he could not get lost. This type of unnecessary hardship, exacerbated by his lack of a guide to both local geographies and customs, was not uncommon, he believes.

Over the following years, as refugees from Southeast Asia were joined by refugees from Russia, eastern Europe, various African countries, Central Asia, and many other regions, it eventually became apparent to Tauch that there was a sizeable refugee community in Portland with many needs that were not being met. Not long after he arrived in Oregon, the International Refugee Center of Oregon (IRCO) was launched, and a few years after that, Tauch became its director. He says, "we felt that regardless of where you came from, we're going to try to build a common agenda. We encouraged people to form their own ethnic organizations to preserve their culture and language, but when refugees come together there is much they share in common and many needs they also share." In the mid-1990s, Tauch notes, immigrants began coming to IRCO and asked why they only served refugees. "Fortunately," he says, smiling, "we didn't have to change our acronym: we renamed ourselves the Immigrant and Refugee Community Organization, and started serving everyone we could."

IRCO's facilities and programming grew slowly over time with government and foundation funding. Djimet Dogo, director of their Africa House program, explains how great the demand for their services became. "Not many Americans understand our federal policy: the government only gives eight months for new refugees and legal immigrants to establish themselves before withdrawing their support. If you're a refugee, you're dropped here not by design but by default and you're seeking sanctuary and safety. Eight months is a very challenging, very brief period for people new to the language, to the markets, to the technologies, and to the bureaucracies of America to find self-sufficiency in." IRCO's main goal is to get their clients established and self-sufficient as quickly as possible. For those who need more than eight months to adjust and integrate, IRCO provides sustained support and community.

"The philosophy and the value behind it is cradle-to-grave," explains Lee Po Cha, IRCO's associate director and the director of IRCO's Asian Family Center. "We have early childhood all the way to senior services; we have academic programming; we help people work toward citizenship or a green card, and we are pretty much a one-stop shop for this population." Lee, who came to Portland as a Hmong refugee from Laos, adds that "the greatest issues facing our community are employment, job skills, and health care, all of which we can help with, but another challenge is that a person may come from a country without freedom and, once here, can find freedom and choices very confusing. Being uprooted from recognized social structures is also difficult, and families sometimes fall apart as traditional values seem more distant."

In total, IRCO has served almost 150,000 people from all over the state (but mostly in greater Portland), offering over a hundred specific services ranging from childcare and English language classes to domestic violence counseling to Loaves and Fishes meals, activities, and exercise classes for seniors. ("It can be a bizarre and wonderful sight," Lee says, "to watch Burmese and Rwandan seniors dancing with Iraqis and Afghans to Russian music.")

(Left) Pacific Islander clients perform at IRCO Asian Family Center's cultural night. Photo by Sabrina Biffer. (Right) An Eastern European couple attends the weekly meal for immigrant and refugee elders held in IRCO's Community Center. Photo by Katherine Kimball. Courtesy IRCO.

IRCO has a pro bono immigration lawyer on call; it can help guide clients' business plans and licensing; it runs summer schools and tutoring programs for struggling students; and it also engages mainstream Portlanders through internships, volunteer work, and a variety of tours and workshops. Its goal is to create a more harmonious, inclusive, and integrated multiethnic community. IRCO has even managed to defuse ethnic tensions between refugees from warring tribes, nations, or religions.

IRCO also has a comparatively high rate of success with its individual interventions, placing over eight hundred individuals in jobs each year, with 99 percent of those placed in those jobs still working in the same jobs after three months. The placement process can be frustrating for some clients, Djimet admits. Refugees tend to have higher levels of education than most Oregonians, but unfortunately, because certain credentials are required for working in some fields in America, their foreign degrees are not accepted and they end up working in lower-skilled jobs. Even so, it is a first step, and IRCO can help them advance up the ladder, too. Tauch says that employment is their number-one priority because it is the key to self-sufficiency.

IRCO's approach to solving difficult problems has not gone unnoticed: its creative, flexible, and responsive model of programming has been very successful, and sister organizations modeled on IRCOs have been established in Texas and Florida. "We're addressing the social challenges, the economic disparities, and all of the other difficulties that come with a growing multiculturalism," explains Lee. "We try to be everything and to work on multiple levels. Many states have service structures wherein each small community provides services to their own; here, we can link experiences and needs and provide services more efficiently but also with greater adaptability and experience. I think that's why IRCO has become a national exportable model."

Despite its successes, however, IRCO is still struggling to attract funding from Oregon's individual donors and foundation community. A few years ago, IRCO moved into a converted lumberyard east of I-205 in Portland (an area that has a high population of refugee and otherwise socioeconomically deprived populations). While it did receive foundation support to purchase and convert the facility, it also went door to door collecting from former and current clients, asking for anything that could be spared toward the cause. Almost all gave a few dollars happily and gratefully. Regular financial support from its clients is necessarily small, however, and rates of giving to communities of color by foundations is lower than it should be. In IRCO's case, funding is further complicated because the organization works broadly and does not target a culturally specific community. Djimet explains: "We're not where we want to be yet in terms of our relationships with foundations. Not too many grantmakers know about issues in the refugee community, and if they don't know the communities, they struggle to help them," Djimet explains.

What is unique about IRCO is that it employs staff from over thirty distinct ethnic groups who speak over fifty languages, which means that those

Five Burmese refugee youth pose after performing a traditional dance at an IRCO celebration. Photo by Sabrina Biffer. Courtesy IRCO.

receiving help are often receiving it from within their community. IRCO's services are adaptable and tailored precisely because of this—which also means that the organization has a nuanced knowledge of how best to direct a funder's aid. "We can help link donors to those who most need help," Djimet says. "IRCO's population is among Oregon's most vulnerable, but we have a lot of hope and expertise. Our community's needs are growing, and we need help making our voices heard." Lee agrees, pleading for "more foundations and individual donors to get out of their offices and out into the community." What IRCO is doing makes sense for us all, he adds. "Whether we're looking at immigrants or refugees, I think that as a nation of immigrants, they may be immigrants today but they'll be citizens tomorrow. If we don't address these issues intentionally, then we're just doing it the hard way."

THE CENTER FOR INTERCULTURAL ORGANIZING (CIO): MULTICULTURAL COMMUNITY BUILDING

The Center for Intercultural Organizing (CIO), originally created by immigrants and refugees to counter widespread anti-Muslim sentiment after 9/11, is taking a different approach to similar issues and communities. Kayse Jama, a Somali refugee and the poetic and genial co-founder of CIO, tells the story of the organization's inception. After he fled Somalia and eventually came to Portland, he began working as a youth advocate in a social service agency.

It was an awakening for him: "I realized that the organizations doing peace work here were mainly white and that I was the only person of color in the crowd. It seemed like there was a lack of racial and ethnic collaboration within our city."

But it took two other incidents to trigger CIO's found-ing. "The first was when, in 2002, Portland authorities ar-rested Sheik Mohammed Abdirahman Kariye, a prominent religious leader of Oregon's Somali communities, on a false terrorism charge. To see their spiritual leader arrested shook the Somalian refugee community to its foundation with its unfairness," Kayse says. A second incident oc-curred shortly thereafter. Kayse had been helping African women's groups establish their own community organiza-tions, and during one meeting he asked them what was happening on the streets of Portland. "When I'm in a suit, people can't tell I'm a Muslim," Kayse explains. "But Mus-lim women are much more visible. One woman told a story about how she'd had trash thrown at her out a window and had been called 'Osama.' She was laughing about this, but I was horrified, and I realized that even though I was the

CIO's 2011 Legislative Action Day. Courtesy the Center for Intercultural Organizing.

closest person to them, even *I* didn't know what they were experiencing. Something had to be done."

Kayse decided to organize a public discussion forum, and he contacted Stephanie Stephens, a communications specialist for the City Club, for some messaging and marketing help. They have since married and both of them played central roles in CIO's development. Since its founding, CIO has grown from a community organizing group opposed to the profiling of Muslims to a nonprofit that seeks to build power in immigrant and refugee communities through community education, policy advocacy, intergenera-tional leadership development, and organizing and mobilizing.

Although its constituent communities overlap in both demographics and needs, CIO's model is substantially different from IRCO's, which places a higher priority on the provision of human services. CIO does provide some material services, particularly support for asylum seekers—those who are as yet undocumented, unlike those already granted asylum or refugee status. However, CIO's main focus is on political advocacy and on qualita-tive community-building. "We help them find a sense of home," Stephanie says. "The immigration experience is what brings people together. There are a lot of culturally specific ethnic organizations around that are doing good work and that are much-needed, but there was little movement around cross-cultural organizing and there was no one holding those deep conversations

Mayoral Forum with Portland mayor Charlie Hales. Photo by Jules Garza. Courtesy CIO.

on politics, religion, worldview, etc., which have to happen for a multicultural society to become genuinely tolerant and interactive."

CIO has over a thousand members now, hailing from more than seventy countries. Its members have joined with other coalitions and have helped achieve a number of landmark legislative victories, including tuition equity for all of Oregon's students, ending Section 8 discrimination, and improving cultural competency in health care. CIO has engaged with community members to build the organizing skills needed to mobilize and bring about positive social changes and has led leadership training programs intended to build up lasting relationships between refugee, immigrant, and existing communities of color in Oregon.

All members either pay financial dues to help with operational and salary expenses for CIO's six employees, or they volunteer their time. "Eighty percent of our members choose labor equity, so we have tens of thousands of hours of labor a year—we calculated it at $1.2 million worth of volunteer labor," Stephanie says proudly. The quantity of volunteer support means that CIO's reach extends far beyond the capacity of its six-person staff. "The majority of our actual dollars are from foundations or government," she explains. "We don't really have high donors who are members"—there are less than five people who give over $1,000. "Since most members of our community are stretched thin just trying to eke out a living, the actual hours that people are giving are a huge part of our story." With the strength of its volunteer corps, CIO managed to grow its budget during the recent recession while other nonprofits were struggling to stay afloat, and its large number of members attests to its success.

Out of a disparate and often traumatized group of people, CIO has fostered a sense of community and unity while pushing for progressive changes that will further empower its members. "Multiethnic organizing is how democracy gets renewed, how we incorporate the opinions of all people, ranging from the oldest Native inhabitants to the most recent immigrants," Kayse believes. "If the notion of this young country is about building democracy and good governance for our community, and if we're looking forward to an increasingly multiracial, multicultural future, then we need to find out how to build that infrastructure from the bottom up."

That commitment to tolerance, dialogue, and multiculturalism as a *norm* is what drew Baher Butti, the director of the Iraqi Society of Oregon and CIO's board chair, to the organization. "I came from Iraq as a refugee in 2007," he says. "I was [a psychiatrist and] an activist in Iraq, and when I fled, I needed a place to restart, a place to find myself again. I met Kayse while working with Middle Easterners and Iraqis here, and I liked it that while they supported me in founding an Iraqi group, they were really about the *intercultural* aspect." Many refugee and immigrant communities are too small to be visible or effective on their own, he says. "And if we keep separating between the mainstream and the margins, it's not going to work. America's social structure is changing and it is going to be multicultural. [CIO] is a place that creates a multicultural identity so that you don't have to keep this dichotomy of one or the other, mainstream or margins, American or Iraqi. You can be both: the way to resolve these conflicts is to advocate for a multicultural society."

Bringing people together is CIO's specialty. Its model of intercultural tolerance bodes well for Oregon's future, but it also helps its members in the present to find common ground with others who, like themselves, have been uprooted. The activism is empowering, but so are the moments of intersection. "People come to us for a sense of community, a sense of a new home," Kayse says. "Members tell me that they feel a sense of place and belonging here. It helps them regain what they've lost."

INCIGHT: UNLOCKING THE POTENTIAL OF PEOPLE WITH DISABILITIES

When they were undergraduates at the University of Portland, Vail Horton, Scott Hatley, and Jerry Carleton were inseparable. Scott, who uses a motorized wheelchair, and Jerry, who is able-bodied, used to do a *Titanic* routine, flying around campus with Jerry perched on the back of Scott's wheelchair, arms outstretched, crowing "I'm the king of the world!" One day Vail, who was born without legs and used crutches to get around, was told by his doctor that the crutches were damaging his shoulders and that he should begin using a wheelchair. Vail decided that he could come up with a better solution. With Scott and Jerry's help, Vail worked up a prototype for crutches with built-in shock absorbers, a product that would eventually drive the launch of Vail's company, Keen Healthcare, which has now been on the Inc. 5000 list of the nation's fastest growing companies for nine years in a row.

While they were still developing the crutch, Vail and Jerry went to a trade show in California to learn the sales channels. They started chatting up kids who walked by, asking them what they wanted to be. "Able-bodied kids had great answers," Jerry said. "An astronaut, an ice cream man, a firefighter. But when we asked kids with disabilities, we got this deer-in-the-headlight look—they just shut down. No one had asked them that before, which was really troubling. Vail said on the spot, 'that's handi*crap*,' and we decided then and there that we needed to start a nonprofit for kids with disabilities so that they know what their options are."

When they told Scott about their experience, he volunteered to start up the fledgling nonprofit. His parents had always encouraged and challenged him. "I grew up in a West Linn, [a suburb of Portland filled with] well-off families, nice houses. Kids are on a college path: it's not *are* you going, but where are you going," Scott says. "But for other people with disabilities, that positive messaging wasn't fully developed," he adds.

There's no legal impediment to their success: the Americans with Disabilities Act was enacted by the US Congress in 1990 to prohibit, under certain circumstances, any discrimination based on a person's disability. And yet in the twenty-four years since it passed, the statistics for Oregon's people with disabilities remain virtually unchanged. "Ninety-two percent don't have a significant other. Eighty-four percent don't earn a college degree. Only one in five have a full-time job," Scott says. The problem, he continues, is that "the tradition is largely entitlement and pity. People with disabilities are told, 'It's too bad, it's so sad, but the world's going to take care of you (just not very well).' We talk to students whose teachers don't talk to them about college or vocational training. There's a giant vacuum because people aren't getting positive messaging: it becomes disempowerment." As Jerry explains, "People with disabilities need a purpose in life like we all do. Instead, they are being trained to just exist until their disease takes over (if it's a disease). They learn how to get on benefits and how not to lose them, and there is no excitement or intellectual challenge built into their lives." As a result, people with disabilities often lack the skills and self-confidence to succeed, asserts Scott, and the wider community often reinforces their low self-regard by imposing lower expectations of people with disabilities' capacity and talents.

With Jerry and Vail's support, Scott set out to remove those barriers to success, contributing $5,000 of his own money to get the ball rolling. In

Jerry Carleton (second left), Scott Hatley (center), Vail Horton (right), with two friends. Photo courtesy Jerry Carleton.

2004, Incight was formed. In its early years, it shared office space with Keen, and Scott, its leader, worked long hours for no salary. By 2014, Incight's tenth anniversary year, it had its own office, a staff of ten including Scott and executive director Dan Friess, and an extensive range of programs in four key areas: education, employment, independence, and networking.

Incight's work to combat social stigmas around disability, and to "unlock the potential of people with disabilities," as its mission declares, has been transformational not only for thousands of Oregonians with disabilities, but also for the thousands of Oregonians *without* disabilities who have learned to think differently as a result of their experiences with Incight. Incight's double meaning—to *incite* change in attitudes and experience, and to provide *insight* into others' lives—means that their work takes many forms: job training seminars, internships, scholarships, high school visits and counseling, college tours, networking events, corporate inclusion seminars, assistance with independent living, adaptive sports and recreation programs, and more.

Dan explains that Incight is working to combat an "attitudinal disconnect. There's more economic and social potential that resides in this demographic than is realized, but most of this potential is unfairly locked up due to stigma. We would like to change the entire attitude around disability, and we'd like to make our community the nation's leading disability inclusion community."

Incight works on many fronts to make that a reality. For example, Jerry—now Incight's board chair[15]—says that their scholarship program "is a chance to engage with high schoolers with disabilities to make sure they know college is in their future. I love our approach to it. It's not about academics—we're not looking for just the 'A' students—we want everyone to take that next step into their life path," Jerry says. "I also love our live résumé event. Most people with disabilities have always had others advocate for them: they've never learned how to advocate for themselves. Often for the first time, we ask people to talk about themselves, about their strengths, and to envision how those strengths could be aligned with future employment." One of Incight's cornerstones is fostering independence, including recreation. It co-sponsors a hand-cycling league, and it is also excited about the launch of its hockey cart league, an option for people with greater mobility restrictions. It will be the first hockey cart league in America, reliant on Scandinavian-made pressed plywood carts that are nimble, beautiful, and *fast*. "These things *fly*," Jerry says. "Seeing a kid with joystick mobility sit in the hockey cart and with a flick of his finger *move*—the pure joy on that face rocks me!"

Incight's work with people with disabilities forms a large part of their programming, but equally important is the anti-discrimination education work they do with corporations, government, and other organizations and community members. "We do a lot of corporate culture training," Dan says. "Our program is disability awareness like you've never heard it before." They have led programs for Kaiser Permanente, Portland Metro, NW Natural, and many others, including a series of programs for Daimler, who have asked Dan to travel to South Carolina to lead a workshop on the factory floor of their bus manufacturing plant. This aspect of their programming is, Jerry says, "a little different for Incight in that our outreach isn't *to* people with disability, but it's benefiting them. It's also earned income, which means we can earn money and serve the mission at the same time."

As the folks at Incight regularly prove, they punch well above their weight in programming and impact: with a lean budget and a small staff, they get an impressive amount done. Dan attributes their successes largely to their sizeable and devoted volunteer corps. Volunteer Mair Blatt got involved when her son Mitch, who is legally blind and has cerebral palsy, began an internship with Incight.

"When you have a child with a disability, you become very info-hungry, especially as they approach transitional ages and phases," Mair explains.

"I wanted to know more about Incight, because I thought that was the next phase for Mitch: going to college, working, finding independence." Mair decided that Incight deserved her support, and for the first couple of years, she gave as a donor. As soon as her nest emptied and both of her kids were at college, she started volunteering. "Last year, I helped plan their gala event: it's fun, and you get to grease your creative wheels—Incight likes to be creative," she says. A volunteer for a number of organizations, it is remarkable she could find time for one more. But Incight is special, Mair asserts. "Volunteering can often be thankless, which is just fine, but I'd leave every Incight meeting so inspired and feeling so appreciated. You feel it when you're around them: they truly care, and they're so passionate." Mair's volunteering has helped Incight enact its mission, and Incight's staff laud her devotion and enthusiasm. Mair firmly denies being exceptional. "We live in a great community. I'm not unique [in how much I volunteer]. The Northwest feels very giving. I'm constantly shocked by how much people give here, and how much they'll roll up their sleeves and get the work done."

Vail testing a hand-cycle, with Dan Friess (left) and Scott Hatley (right). Courtesy Incight.

Incight's volunteer corps have enabled them to change thousands of lives, as has the generosity of Vail, Jerry, and Scott, whose personal contributions of time and money got the organization off the ground. But despite its successes, says Dan, Incight still struggles to attract funding. "We've grown our donor base tremendously since we first started. But we know that our mission deserves to invite a much larger donor base than we've currently reached. We've piloted our model here, but it's scalable and transferable, and we'd like to see our work replicated at a larger scale. We've given over 630 scholarships, we've had remarkable employment outcomes, and we're growing. We'd like to have the stature of Friends of the Children and have people recognize us on a named level. We'd really like to *not* be a best-kept secret!"

Mair echoes their plea for more recognition and support. "As Dan reminds us, should we join the disability community tomorrow, he hopes it occurs in a more tolerant society, where you can bring your personality and skills to the party instead of your disability. I look around and see so many people who are not awake, and I wish that the whole world was awake to people with disabilities. Having tolerance, and realizing the potential of this population helps the community, it helps the government, it helps our economies. Every community needs an Incight."

BASIC RIGHTS OREGON: EQUALITY IN LOVE

Oregonians with disabilities have often faced an uphill battle for respect and equality. Many others have too, including Oregon's LGBTQ community. Nicola and Meg Cowie know that all too well. Back in 1987, British-born Meg and Nicola met while in the cast of an amateur play in Britain. Married for almost twenty years and unabashedly in love, they have spent the last two decades moving frequently due to the demands of Nicola's high-powered computer security job. Nicola had worked in Oregon before, so when the news came down that they would be moving to Hillsboro again, they were looking forward to returning. But at the time, American and Oregonian laws disrupted an easy re-entry because during their three-year return to Britain, Nicola had transitioned from male to female. In 2011, American officials declared their marriage invalid because they were now a same-sex couple. Oregon officials, meanwhile, said they could not be registered as domestic partners because they were already married in Britain. Because of this hellish catch-22, Meg struggled to get onto Nicola's health insurance plan; she was not allowed to work because of immigration laws; and both of them had to live with the knowledge that local and national bureaucracies had invalidated their two-decade commitment to each other. "We're just a middle-aged couple doing what middle-aged couples do, living in the suburb with our cat,"[16] explains Nicola. "To be told that we are not entitled to remain married was really painful."

Nicola and Meg Cowie. Courtesy the Cowies.

Frustrated and hurt, they reached out to Basic Rights Oregon, an advocacy organization that fights for justice and equal rights for LGBTQ Oregonians. Basic Rights Oregon, which is headquartered in Portland but is active statewide, grew out of over two decades of anti-gay ballot measures that plagued Oregon, attacking the legal rights and basic dignity of LGBTQ Oregonians. During the 1980s and early 1990s, the Oregon Citizens Alliance waged vitriolic and self-righteous battles against homosexuality that left the state's LGBTQ community reeling and vulnerable.

Jeana Frazzini, executive director of Basic Rights Oregon, says, "we realized we needed to establish an organization that could build power and mobilize in between election years so that we could work for proactive legal changes rather than just stopping the attacks." Since 1988, Oregonians have voted on five statewide and over twenty-five local anti-LGBTQ ballot measures, perhaps most notoriously in 2004, when a clause was added to Oregon's constitution that defined marriage as between "one man and one woman."

Two Spirit Justice Summit. Courtesy Basic Rights Oregon.

At the top of BRO's policy agenda was achieving full marriage equality, with all of the concomitant legal benefits for LGBTQ spouses. When we first spoke with Jeana in December 2013, Basic Rights Oregon was gearing up to put an initiative on the November 2014 ballot to strike down Ballot Measure 36 (which amended the constitution in 2004) and replace it with pro-marriage equality language. They had launched Oregon United for Marriage, a coalition of diverse voices from every community and demographic in Oregon. As 2014 began, however, a new door opened: two couples, a pair of unmarried women and two men already married in Canada, filed lawsuits in the US district court in Eugene challenging the state's constitutional ban on same-sex marriage. On January 22, 2014, Judge Michael McShane merged the two lawsuits, and on February 20, Oregon's attorney general Ellen Rosenblum told the court that she could not and would not defend the state's ban in court. After hearing arguments in April, on May 19, 2014, Judge McShane announced that Oregon's ban on same-sex marriage violated the US Constitution. Marriages started almost immediately across Oregon.

Basic Rights Oregon still needs all of the support it can get. Its policy work isn't finished: near-term plans include a ballot initiative to remove the discriminatory language from the state constitution (the federal court decision invalidates it but it will stay in the constitution until BRO can build up the larger majority it takes to remove it). BRO's lobbying and policy work is strengthened by its community engagement and leadership development programs and by its support of progressive politicians and civic leaders.

Moreover, its advocacy work and service provision remain as essential as ever: legal marriage equality doesn't mean that discrimination will end, as social prejudices and bureaucratic inequities can endure much longer

Two brides on Decision Day. Photo by Beth Olson Creative. Courtesy Basic Rights Oregon.

than legal obstacles. BRO offers a host of services for those affected by housing, healthcare, and employment discrimination; bullying in schools; hate crimes; and other structural and societal prejudices. BRO is particularly attentive to the needs of elderly LGBTQ Oregonians. This generation has experienced some of the most repressive and unfair treatment and still does, Jeana says. "After decades of often passing as brothers or spinster sisters, our elders are now facing segregated care facilities that don't recognize their relationships—they'll respect marriages but not gay marriages." Because racism often travels alongside homophobia, Jeanna adds, at its heart Basic Rights considers itself "an anti-racist organization that focuses on LGBTQ issues." It has built a strong network of supportive allies, ranging from the Urban League of Portland to the Asian Pacific American Network of Oregon (APANO) to CAUSA (also part of the CAPACES alliance).

BRO's work made it a perfect resource for Meg and Nicola: Basic Rights was quick to help them find a lawyer to take on their case. As time passed, the Cowies became deeply appreciative of the community and the support Basic Rights provided. "We started giving back a little, and then we were suddenly sucked in," explains Meg. "We thought, well, the law didn't recognize our marriage so what we need to do is change the law, and so we joined the marriage campaign." Meg and Nicola gave as freely of their money as they were allowed—"as non–US citizens, the amount we can donate to political causes is capped," Nicola explains—but they give their time limitlessly: they are two of Basic Rights' most dedicated and reliable volunteers, working in phone banks, hitting the streets for signatures and conversations, and speaking at countless events about their experiences and love.

John Halseth and Robin Castro are another couple who contribute time and money generously to BRO's anti-discrimination work. Together since 1996, they have been volunteering with BRO for a long time, but, Robin says, "as we got older and more financially stable, we've been able to become financial supporters too." When asked what motivates his volunteering, Robin is blunt. "Gay people are not yet equal. . . . There is a stigma that our relationships aren't valued. It's ironic, because when I was growing up, all of the messaging I got was that homosexuals were promiscuous, yet [until recently, we've been] told we can't settle down and have families."

Robin Castro and John Halseth. Photo by Johnny Shultz. Courtesy Robin and John.

In a relatively short period of time (2004–2014), attitudes toward our state's LGBTQ community have progressed tremendously: at least 58 percent of Oregonians now approve of gay marriage.[17] Because of Basic Rights' staff, dedicated volunteers, and the visionary donors who have supported their work, Oregonians are becoming more tolerant—the message is getting out. Every bit of outreach, every story shared, helps to foster understanding. "The conversations about why marriage matters to gay people really [broke] down the barriers in how people think—it help[ed] people to see that we're more similar than different," Jeana says.

> Everyone knows that marriage means love and commitment and family, and the very reason that gay people want to marry is because they've found that special someone, they want to make that commitment. It's kind of like a "coming-out 2.0": it's not just declaring that you love someone of the same sex, it's opening up your life and sharing what that love means—the joys, the barriers, the sorrows. It's about helping people to understand that you're not taking anything away from anyone else, you're just trying to be happy, to do meaningful work, and to love and have love at every opportunity.

Basic Rights Oregon's model has been hailed nationally as a perfectly structured grassroots campaign—a solid mix of well-researched and strategic policies bulwarked by a cohesive and mobilized network of passionate volunteers and donors. However, because it is a political nonprofit—a 501(c)4 organization—it has had mixed success in obtaining support from philanthropy, with sizeable grants coming in from large national foundations but with underwhelming local support. "It's a particular frustration of mine that we have an organization that's commanding large national grants—$700,000 grants—and yet we can't get a grant from a grantmaker in our own state for $25,000," Jeana says. "There's clearly a need for more education targeted at the philanthropic and foundation community."

That need for education and advocacy persists in the wider community too. "There is a significant gap between legal and lived equality," Jeana says. To bridge that gap, BRO acts as a policy watchdog, making sure that laws are enacted on the ground. It also fights on a number of more nuanced fronts— for example, for the rights of transgendered people to full health benefits, including transition-related care—and it works with the government, corporations, and nonprofits to combat other institutional discrimination. Social discrimination is still a problem, too. Jeana says that when marriages started happening, in May, "people arrived in Portland from all corners of Oregon, many coming because they didn't feel safe going to their own county's office. We had people from Salem saying that they wanted no photos because they didn't want to be publicly outed: it's the capital of our state and they don't feel safe walking downtown. We haven't even begun to scratch the surface."

Most of BRO's clients have experienced prejudice and violence first-hand. "Just a couple of weeks ago, I was verbally abused by a man. He was yelling in my face so close to me that I had to step back. I was attacked for what he perceived me to be," Meg Cowie says in disbelief. Clearly, there is still much work that needs to be done. As Thurgood Marshall said, "[t]he legal system can force open doors and sometimes even knock down walls. But it cannot build bridges. That job belongs to you and me."

Through legislation, advocacy, and the kind of storytelling and outreach that builds those bridges, Basic Rights Oregon has helped make our state a more tolerant and inclusive place for everyone. "On Decision Day [May 19, 2014], we were thrilled," Jeana says. "The fact that marriage equality is now a reality for Oregon families is wonderful. This is historic and tremendous progress, and we'll hope we see a nationwide solution soon." To Nicola, marriage equality makes sense within the state's wider identity as a place of generosity, friendliness, and free-spiritedness. "Oregon is one of the most accepting and pleasant places we've ever lived," Nicola adds. "I think there's a peculiar mindset in the Pacific Northwest because there's so much space and openness . . . there's quite a lot of live-and-let-live because there is space for everyone to be who they want to be, to be who they *are*."

In his ruling striking down Oregon's same-sex marriage ban, Judge McShane agreed. He wrote:

Oregon United for Marriage supporters. Courtesy Basic Rights Oregon.

I believe that if we can look for a moment past gender and sexuality, we can see in these plaintiffs nothing more or less than our own families. . . . With discernment we see not shadows lurking in closets or the stereotypes of what was once believed; rather we see families committed to the common purpose of love, devotion, and service to the greater community.

Where will all this lead? I know that many suggest we are going down a slippery slope that will have no moral boundaries. To those who truly harbor such fears, I can only say this: Let us look less to the sky to see what might fall; rather, let us look to each other . . . and rise.

A MORE UNITED OREGON: PHILANTHROPIC OPPORTUNITIES, PHILANTHROPIC NEEDS

"Some people don't even realize that inequity still exists. How do you fund an organization helping to solve a problem that people don't think exists?"
—Adrienne Livingston, Black United Fund

Many pioneering, creative, and determined Oregon nonprofits are advocating for equality. And although Portland hosts the largest populations of many minority communities, these issues lose none of their urgency in smaller population centers. In fact, a handful of rural counties have a much higher percentage of minority residents than Portland has—for instance, Jefferson County is 38 percent Latino and Native American.[18]

Social justice and service nonprofits are spread across Oregon, and work through diverse methods to diverse ends. Some focus on providing services and advocacy for certain races, languages, or ethnicities: for example, Unete serves Medford's Latinos; the Kommema Cultural Protection Association in Yoncalla advocates for and celebrates Oregon's native Kalapuya culture; APANO advocates for Asians and Pacific Islanders; and Russian Oregon Social Services provides services ranging from immigration help to domestic violence counseling in Oregon's often cloistered Russian orthodox populations. Intercultural organizations—which use solidarity among different racial and ethnic communities not only to provide services more efficiently but also to turn up the volume on shared advocacy efforts—often work at the person-to-person level, bringing individuals of diverse backgrounds together for advancement and aid. Other organizations—the Coalition of Communities of Color, for instance, an alliance of highly respected culturally specific nonprofits—work at an institutional level, making policy recommendations to both government and the philanthropic world to enact legislation and increase funding for racial equity, poverty reduction, and human services.

There are other communities and groups that need tailored advocacy and services. Many social justice organizations work to provide inclusion, services, and advocacy for the elderly; for the equal representation, health, and employment status of women; for victims of abuse, trauma, and neglect; for religious tolerance; and for the provision of health, advocacy, and support services for people living with HIV/AIDS and other medical conditions. Advocacy and service provision tend to go hand-in-hand at most of these nonprofits. A superb example is Project Dove in Ontario, which runs a twenty-four-hour emergency shelter for domestic violence and assault victims. It also helps victims with transportation to court and other court-related costs; pro bono legal assistance; transitional and permanent housing; counseling; and domestic violence avoidance training. Although government funding cuts have reduced its staff from twenty-one to three full-time employees, Project Dove has mobilized grassroots donor support and in-kind partners so that it can continue to protect clients' rights to safety, to freedom from fear, and to legal justice.

United in their advocacy for fairness, inclusivity, and equality, these nonprofits also share the sobering reality of chronic underfunding. Human services as a broad category receives a substantial proportion of overall philanthropic contributions. However, organizations that assist and advocate for minority or marginalized groups often struggle to find a toehold in the funding stream, despite the fact that Oregon is becoming increasingly diverse.

A multipronged strategy is required to combat this trend. Developing a better understanding of philanthropic capacities within marginalized communities may help nonprofits reassure mainstream donors that these organizations have high levels of grassroots support. Kayse Jama of CIO provides an excellent example: in Somalian communities, the most well-off (even if they are diaspora living in America) are asked to contribute a certain amount as a matter of family honor and pride for each new community project—a road, a school, a public works facility. Understanding and mobilizing cultural traditions like this can help empower nonprofits working from within these communities.

Even so, giving from *within* marginalized communities will seldom be sufficient: Oregon's donor community needs to make a more concerted effort to help maginalized groups gain support more broadly. "There's a significant difference in the need of communities of color and the amount of support they're receiving," Matt Morton of NAYA explains, "so I think that what we need to see is a commitment toward philanthropic equity, a commitment of resources toward culturally specific organizations."[19] This translates into more effective philanthropy, adds Matt. "Organizations embedded within communities get better outcomes and provide more targeted services." This applies to individual donors as much as it does to foundations. As Adrienne Livingston, former director of the Black United Fund, puts it, "it's all about relationships: people tend to donate to like people, to their friends. Oregon donors need to get out of their comfort level, to get out of their immediate surroundings, and to look at a wider sense of community."

Better philanthropic reporting and research tools are also required, according to Joyce White, director of Grantmakers of Oregon and South-west Washington. Census numbers routinely undercount or miscategorize minorities, and it and other polls often fail to ask the right questions to assess correct needs and population numbers. Philanthropic institutions fail similarly, Joyce says. "It's hard to know where the gaps in provision are because everyone has their own system of taxonomy and terminology," she explains. "Unless there is a nuanced system, it's hard to know where the cracks are, to understand who's been left out and to understand what constitutes effective targeting."

Having a nimble and open-minded donor pool is also essential. This means accepting philanthropic risks and being willing to look beyond main-stream organizations to smaller, less visible, less evaluated ones. As Harriet Denison declares, "if you don't have any failures, you're not taking enough risks! You can't have all the information!"

A willingness to fund 501(c)4s—political advocacy organizations like Basic Rights Oregon and PCUN—is also necessary to formalize social change. It takes a particularly altruistic donor to support this sort of non-profit organization, as contributors do not receive a tax deduction. But philanthropy and volunteerism are nevertheless essential to progressive change in Oregon: for example, Basic Rights Oregon's work[20] would falter without these willing donors and volunteers, and many of the civil rights victories of the past were also driven by this kind of philanthropic altruism and activism.

In short, private philanthropy is essential to creating an equitable Oregon. Harriet believes that philanthropy "is a way to fill in the gaps, to fund things that are either not considered important by government or, in our case, to fund communities that were struggling to make their voices heard." This should be an urgent and important task for *all* Oregonians to consider, she says. After all, the economic case for greater diversity and equity is strong: "[i]t certainly represents a tremendous opportunity for the state," says Michael Hames-Garcia, chair of the University of Oregon's ethnic studies department. "One of the disadvantages Oregon has faced economically and in competing for businesses in trying to attract top talent is that we don't offer a diverse environment and diverse work force."[21] The moral and social case for a more equal, more diverse Oregon is even more compelling. "It's a team effort," Adrienne Livingstone says. "People need to see the rainbow in all its richness. It's so enriching to build relationships with other peoples, other communities."

Equality and tolerance for all Oregonians is vital to the future success, health, and livability of our state. Writing about her experience volunteering for Basic Rights Oregon, Nicola Cowie is eloquent about why concordance around these issues is key. "It's helped me realize that for human rights to move forward, we must work together, on multiple issues at once, to win freedoms and protections for us all. Some people make it sound as though we are all completely separate groups—as if gay, lesbian, bisexual, transgender people, people of color, people of faith, and immigrants are on opposing teams, working for different causes. . . . In reality, transphobia, homophobia, racism, immigration, and faith are not discrete issues. . . . All these policies impact me and my family."[22] The precedent for this is quite simple, Nicola adds. "At the most basic level, it all comes down to the Golden Rule. I believe in treating others as one would like to be treated."[23]

Ballet Folklórico México en la Piel from Cornelius. Photo by Kristin Anderson.

6
Art for Good: Funding Oregon's Arts, Culture, and Heritage Sectors

"I do not want art for a few, any more than education for a few, or freedom for a few."
—William Morris, "Hopes and Fears for Art"

"The arts are not a frill. The arts are a response to our individuality and our nature, and help to shape our identity. What is there that can transcend deep difference and stubborn divisions? The arts."
—Former Texas Congresswoman Barbara Jordan

"Art is the signature of civilizations."
—Beverly Sills

For millenia, the patronage of art and culture has been regarded as a key indicator of an individual's and a society's prestige and advancement. Philanthropists and civic leaders have placed value on funding arts, culture, and heritage organizations since long before the Renaissance: modern traditions of funding trace their lineage to ancient Rome, Greece, Persia, China, and beyond. Under these systems, buildings were erected, paintings and sculptures commissioned, literature and music composed, and all now form a part of humanity's rich cultural inheritance.

Prints drying at Crow's Shadow Institute of the Arts near Pendleton. Photo by Kristin Anderson.

Today, the enrichment that comes from a robust arts and cultural life is far from being a luxury. A healthy cultural scene fuels our sense of civic pride and duty, thus feeding broader economic and social health as well as sustaining us on deeper levels both individually and communally—after all, experiences that bring us closer to our communities also drive us to give back to them. A strong cultural scene, then, makes for strong communities—it builds a sense of *place*.

When President Johnson signed the law creating the National Endowment for the Arts (NEA) in 1965, he declared, "Art is a nation's most precious heritage. For it is in our works of art that we reveal to ourselves and to others the inner vision which guides us as a nation. And when there is no vision, the people perish." Yet despite the urgency of his assertion and the traditional value placed on arts funding, since at least the early 1980s the NEA has been threatened with abolishment, continually questioned in Congress, and beleaguered by perennial budget cuts. Moreover, the NEA's struggles have trickled down: its difficulties have been mirrored at a statewide level in part because Oregon's arts agencies and institutions receive NEA funding, but also because the NEA's battles are part of a wider trend of both public and private defunding of the arts.

Many Americans regard the arts as nonessential, arguing that either you educate kids and feed the hungry or you fund the arts. As a result, arts, culture, and heritage programs are the first to get cut during government's perpetual belt-tightening. But while times are bad for arts funding nationally, they are particularly bad in Oregon. "It's no secret that state-wise, we're ranking near the bottom in support for the arts," notes Julie Vigeland, chair of the Oregon Arts Commission. Charlie Walker, the founding chair of the Oregon Cultural Trust and vice chair of the James F. and Marion L. Miller Foundation, agrees: "A few years ago, Oregon ranked forty-ninth, next to Guam, on our levels of spending for the arts," he says. "Even now, public arts funding is low, and the need is still great." Oregon's 2014 budget brought the state back to thirty-second in the nation for public arts funding,[1] although our ranking on arts education is probably much lower—in 2012, we give 9 percent of public arts grant dollars to education, against a national average of 28 percent.[2] What this means in dollars and cents is that the Oregon government will be distributing roughly $2.24 million of public funds to the arts in 2014. To the average household, that may seem like a lot, but when there are over three thousand arts organization in Oregon; when the state budgets only $200,000 more for the arts than tiny Rhode Island; and when Minnesota will be granting $34.18 million, our scramble up from rock-bottom seems less impressive.[3]

Private contributions from individuals or foundations make up the bulk of arts and heritage funding in Oregon, and they are not reflected in these rankings. However, as Charlie notes: "There are only a few Oregon foundations today that would list themselves as having arts and culture as one of their key items to address. Having only a few foundations with arts and culture as line items raises a question about where the support for the arts *is*." The answer may be that it is largely absent: philanthropically, although cultural organizations represent 14 percent of Oregon's nonprofits,[4] they received only 5 percent of all individual or foundation charitable contributions in 2011. This figure has been similarly low for over a decade despite herculean efforts within the arts community to elevate it.[5]

The situation is no better with corporate funding for the arts, says Paul Nicholson, emeritus director of the Oregon Shakespeare Festival. "There is a dramatically diminished role for corporate giving now," he says. "In the 1980s, there was still a prevailing belief that corporations could use arts philanthropy as marketing dollars, as a way to polish the image of the company." But, he continues, "as the economy has changed and become more challenging, fewer of those marketing dollars are being directed philanthropically." (Indeed, many corporations are pulling back from philanthropy entirely.) Jerry Hulsman, winner of the Association of Fundraising Professional's Outstanding Volunteer Fundraiser 2013 award for his devoted work with the Oregon Symphony, thinks this plan is shortsighted. "I've said this time and time again: I really feel like the arts tell you what kind of city you've got, whether it's a good place to live. Professionals look for a good arts scene—a good symphony, ballet, opera, theater—when they're changing careers. Oregon's biggest companies, who seek to attract top talent, would do well to remember that."

Because of this decreased funding, Oregon's cultural organizations have been left scrambling. Almost uniformly, they are understaffed, underhoused, and in budgetary survival modes rather than focused on creativity and expansion. There is a disconnect here, it seems, between the value we place on the arts and the level at which we are willing to fund them.

Oregon's art, humanities, and heritage industries—which for concision we will group together under the umbrella term "culture/cultural" organizations—are essential threads in our social fabric: they directly correspond to other needs and bring benefits of all kinds. They are also of significant economic value: many cultural organizations are sizeable employers within their communities and bring in a considerable amount of revenue to local economies. In Eugene in 2010, the total economic impact of cultural nonprofits was $45.5 million, and in greater Portland, their total economic impact was $253.5 million—over one hundred times as much as is granted by the government to cultural organizations across the state.[6]

Beyond the immediate economic benefit, a robust cultural scene has positive effects for an economy over time: quality of life rises, a place

Choristers in rehearsal. Photo by Michael O'Brien.

grows more desirable to the types of professionals who power economies, businesses grow and economies flourish, and philanthropic reinvestment becomes more feasible. Moreover, creativity feeds creativity: innovation in one area (the arts) often leads to innovation in another (business, science, or technology, for instance). Businessperson Mark Golden writes that "it is clear that there is an . . . urgency for creative, innovative thinking that comes from training in the arts. . . . We've lost track of the value of the humanities in creating a well-rounded individual, capable of thinking beyond the old solutions."[7]

A less quantitative benefit is that a healthy cultural industry interacts with and aids the causes of the other nonprofit sectors. For example, cultural organizations and artists help bridge the urban-rural divide (as the Sisters Folk Festival, the Oregon Trail Interpretative Center, Slamboo, and the High Desert Museum have shown). Cultural offerings also often respond to the same unique sense of place that motivates many environmental conservationists, thus uniting our state's conscience around similar issues. Artists and cultural organizations provide exciting educational avenues and help break down barriers between communities of different nationalities, races, backgrounds, and beliefs: robust community cultural programs correlate directly to improved educational achievement and social inclusivity, as we will see. In short, far from being in competition with other areas of need, cultural programs are inextricably linked to them.

Despite Oregon's distressingly low levels of funding, our cultural organizations have managed to remain vibrant and active across the state. This chapter celebrates the vital work of those taking a lead in arts funding and volunteerism, ranging from an advertising mogul to a Skid Row resident to a Japanese American visionary. It also tells the stories of a few of the many extraordinary creators and cultural organizations who, despite difficult circumstances, are bringing creativity, insight, and innovation into our communities.

OREGON'S HERITAGE ORGANIZATIONS: VIBRANT, EXPANDING, ESSENTIAL

For at least the last fifty years, but particularly since 1976, the nation's bicentennial year, historical societies across Oregon have been popping up in even the smallest towns, formed by citizens eager to research and document their regions and communities. Historical preservation societies such as Restore Oregon have appeared too, dedicated to saving the buildings and monuments.

The Oregon Historical Society (OHS), a much-visited, much-loved museum founded in 1898, is the mother of all these organizations. Positioned a block away from the Arlene Schnitzer Concert Hall and opposite the Portland Art Museum, OHS is a cultural pillar of Portland's south park blocks and a monument in its own right. But even OHS struggles for funding. "Most state historical societies are state agencies and are funded by the state government, but we're not," executive director Kerry Tymchuk explains. "We're a nonprofit, so we rely on philanthropy. Like a lot of charities, we've been through some difficult years. A few years ago, there was a perception that OHS was circling the drain. There were a couple of different reactions to that: some people stopped giving altogether, but others stepped up and gave even more . . . People got excited about it again." It is, he says, because of these donors' largesse, and because of a five-year, $12 million levy generously passed by Multnomah County voters, that the Oregon Historical Society is on firmer footing today. And its exhibits and programming—including "Windows on America" (its exhibit on American presidential artifacts and documents), "2 Years, 1 Month: Lincoln's Legacy," and "Clink!" (the story of Oregon winemaking)—have drawn in audiences and garnered acclaim, as has Kerry's leadership: his presence has been transformative to the organization.

But even now, Kerry says, there are a number of improvements and services OHS would like to offer, and finding sufficient funding is always an uphill battle. Remedying that, he suggests, is something that each Oregonian can help with. "The past three years have been ones of great momentum for the Oregon Historical Society, as our attendance has skyrocketed and the number of our exhibits and programs has doubled and re-doubled," Kerry says. "If the momentum is to continue, however, then we also must continue to make the case that a strong and vibrant Oregon Historical Society is a goal that should be shared by *all* Oregonians."

JEFFERSON COUNTY HISTORICAL SOCIETY

If the Oregon Historical Society struggles to find funding in today's philanthropic climate, it is even more challenging for regional historical societies, particularly those located in economically impoverished areas. But their work is important, and often benefits from the legions of volunteers inspired by their local histories.

The Jefferson County Historical Society was one of those founded in the bicentenary decade; Jarold Ramsey, a poet, essayist, and retired professor of literature, is its president. "We have a short settler history here in this county, but it's been an important location both for the state and for the nation, and I worried that our history was getting lost, that our records and artifacts were not being well preserved," Jarold says. "We established a museum in the old county courthouse [in Madras], and our collection is impressive. But the courthouse has now been condemned as unusable, and our entire collection is in archival storage—there is no place to which people can come and learn about their history." The society has created traveling digital displays and presentations as temporary solutions while it searches for a new home. It has also started a history day at the local middle school, is about to resume publication of its journal, and has begun a series of history pubs at the Great Earth deli in downtown Madras.

"We are proud of what we do, but we're constantly frustrated for lack of funds and political support," Jerald says. "We are also entirely dependent upon volunteers, and in a farming community, volunteers are difficult to come by—farmers live hard lives and work very hard." Given what they have accomplished on the backs of their devoted volunteers alone, they certainly deserve additional support: Jefferson County Historical Society's contributions to their

Fourth of July picnic at Elkin's Ranch, 1915. Courtesy Jefferson County Historical Society.

local community, and to Oregon's historical tapestry, are invaluable. Ramsey is eloquent on the cultural impact of local historical societies:

> We are doing essential work. From an academic's perspective, I know how little respect local history gets in the academy, but to me, local history is essential to historical study: local histories are how we flesh out our portrait of America. The way you trace important historical events and figures are through their effect on everyday lives, and the story of small towns' fortunes and demographics are tied intrinsically to broader regional and national trends. If you want to know your history as a society, it's important to document it at this level—it fleshes history out, and connects it to lived experience.

Beyond historical societies' academic and educational value, Jerald adds, they also build community. "Like almost any community in Oregon, our demographics are changing rapidly—we have the most ethnically diverse population in the state," Jerald explains. "A historical society like this lets us document this change while setting up a sense of historical continuity; it lets us recognize and celebrate this change while linking it to what came before. And ultimately, it lets newcomers step into a stream that comes from a long way back and will go a long way forward, giving everyone a sense of place and broader community."

OREGON BLACK PIONEERS

Across the state, organizations with similar missions are working to preserve Oregon's heritage and link it to the future. Some of these societies, however, focus not on a specific town or county but on a marginalized community, ensuring that Oregon's historical narrative is growing both broader and more nuanced. As such, these organizations complement and reinforce the nonprofits profiled in Chapter Five that advocate for the representation and rights of marginalized communities.

Salem residents Willie Richardson and Gwen Carr are the driving forces behind Oregon Black Pioneers, Oregon's preeminent African American public historical society. In a small office above Pioneer Trust Bank on Commercial Street in downtown Salem, they tell us about their work. "We want greater Oregon to be aware of the impact African Americans have had on the development of our state," Willie begins. "Ours is a rich, rich culture and history, and it's important that people know that, far from being exclusive to Portland, African Americans have lived across the state, in small and large communities alike, and have had a major impact on our statewide history."

(Left) Part of the "All Aboard" exhibit at the Oregon Historical Society. Courtesy Oregon Black Pioneers. (Right) Willie Richardson and Gwen Carr of Oregon Black Pioneers. Photo by Kristin Anderson.

As Gwen explains:

> What is unique about Oregon's history is that Oregon was a free territory and a free state and yet had black exclusion laws on the books to prevent black settlement. Our racial history is pretty bleak, and Oregon's small black population today is a legacy of those laws. But people don't realize that black people were among the first settlers of Oregon: they were on the ships exploring its coastline; they came over on wagon trains. We didn't just arrive in the 1920s and 1940s—we have a long history here.

Documenting that history is important for several reasons, Gwen says. "When you leave out information from historical record whether you do it intentionally or not, you give an inaccurate picture of how we came to be as a state. And for the individual, when history leaves out a particular segment, whether it's black or Latino or Asian or gay . . . if it looks like you weren't here, then you have no sense that you're important, that you have ownership of the state and a connection to it."

Oregon Black Pioneers does not just celebrate and publicize the history, Willie adds. "We also uncover it. . . . We are piecing together a fuller history so we can know *what* to celebrate—that's the charge and the mission, really getting to know African American history here." The records they have discovered have been substantial and surprising: they have found African American influence in every corner of the state. "Ultimately, we want to make sure that in the future telling of the Oregon story, it is inclusive and reflects African American impact. Things get glossed over." There was a historical marker on the coast documenting the site where, in 1788, an unnamed crewmember of Robert Gray's ship the *Lady Washington* was killed, Gwen recounts. Oregon

Black Pioneers lobbied for the marker to be updated: the crewmember killed was Marcus Lopeus, the first documented person of African descent to set foot in Oregon.[8]

Like most historical societies, the organization's budget is tiny. While Gwen and Willie dream of having a paid staff person and a permanent museum rather than temporary exhibits in other facilities, Oregon Black Pioneers would need considerably more support to reach that goal. But in a sterling example of local corporate philanthropy, Pioneer Trust Bank (a Salem heritage institution in its own right, started by Asahel Bush and William S. Ladd in 1869) has been incredibly generous with its support of Oregon Black Pioneers, underwriting exhibits and even donating rent-free office space in its own headquarters.

Like the Jefferson County Historical Society, Oregon Black Pioneers embodies the essential and enormous role volunteers play within Oregon's cultural sectors. Its exhibits, including "All Aboard!: Railroading and Portland's Black Community," presented at the Oregon Historical Society in spring 2013, have helped expand Oregonians' awareness of the diversity of our history. Without Willie Richardson, Gwen Carr, and the diligence, passion, and scholarship of Oregon Black Pioneers' other volunteers, Oregon's history would be less complete, less *true*. "As a culture, we forget that we're intertwined, that we're dependent upon each other," Willie says. "Your history isn't yours alone: others impact you. The good, the bad, the awful—it's all relevant to who you are, to who we are. It's *our* story—it's *Oregon's* story—and it needs to be told."

OREGON NIKKEI LEGACY CENTER, BILL NAITO, AND THE NIKKEI ENDOWMENT

Oregon's Japanese American community has been working with similar vigor to uncover, preserve, and share its history. For twenty-five years, landscape architect Robert Murase had been working on his dream to build a memorial to the incarceration of Japanese Americans during World War II, but it was not until he teamed up with the formidable visionary Bill Naito in the late 1980s that the project became a reality.

Slight of build, with a neatly trimmed beard, Bill was a Nisei (second generation Japanese American). He fought in World War II as an infantryman and translator, and later became a pillar of the Portland business community, with boundless energy for work and volunteer activities. His love of urban Portland was legendary: he is generally credited with providing the leadership that halted the further decline of downtown Portland by cleverly rebranding the derelict Skid Row district of Portland as "Old Town" and by providing substantial investments to renovate and preserve old historic buildings.

(Left) Bill Naito. Courtesy Erica Naito Campbell and the Naito family. (Right) Oregon Nikkei Legacy Center installation about G2 Assembly Center. Photo by Rich Iwasaki. Courtesy Oregon Nikkei Legacy Center.

As a demonstration of both his commitment to the city and to his cultural heritage, Naito worked with other Japanese American leaders to form the Oregon Nikkei Endowment in 1989. Naito, Murase, the Endowment's new board of directors, and its president, Henry Sakamoto, together rallied the community to build up the Endowment in order to erect the first monument in the country to memorialize the Japanese American experience during World War II.

In 1990, Portland hosted the first reunion of Oregonians of Japanese descent who had lived in the state before the start of World War II. Over nine hundred people attended from all over the world. And as part of the ceremonies, the Japanese American Historical Plaza, the new permanent monument to the lives of Oregon Nikkei, was dedicated in Tom McCall Waterfront Park. A couple of years later, in the spring of 1992, the Nikkei community marked the fiftieth anniversary of the signing of executive order 9066, which directed the military to incarcerate all persons of Japanese ancestry living along the West Coast. The anniversary events included a dramatic program that recounted the fear and indignation that swept through the Nikkei community in 1942 as entire families were herded into makeshift quarters in Portland before being transported to distant internment camps for the duration of the war.

Following the success of these two events, Portland's Nikkei community decided to create a museum where their oral and written histories could be preserved in an era when the numbers of Issei (first generation) and Nisei (second generation) Japanese Americans were declining. A broad cross section of Oregon's Nikkei contributed to the project and were joined by a huge array of national and international Nikkei donors, an example of community philanthropy at its finest. In 1995, the Oregon Nikkei Legacy Center opened its doors.

Lynn Longfellow, the executive director of the Oregon Nikkei Legacy Center, is Sansei, or third generation Japanese American. She explains that what inspires their work are the sacrifices of the Nisei generation, who fought so hard and humbly during World War II for the United States while their families were imprisoned and undergoing enormous hardships. As Lynn describes, "Our mission is to share, preserve, and honor the history and culture of Japanese Americans in the Pacific Northwest, and to educate the public about discrimination and civil rights." On a minimal budget but with widespread community support, the Oregon Nikkei Legacy Center is doing precisely that.

TAMÁSTSLIKT CULTURAL INSTITUTE

Rising up from the Columbia River plateau near the Blue Mountains is the Tamástslikt Cultural Institute, on the Umatilla Reservation near Pendleton. A striking, low-slung structure made of stone and wood, it reflects its big-sky setting and emerges gracefully from the grasslands and hills around it. Like the Museum at Warm Springs and the Siletz Tribal Arts and Heritage Society, Tamástslikt is a tribal research institute and museum, in this case celebrating the history of the Cayuse, Umatilla, and Walla Walla tribes.

Its director, Roberta ("Bobbie") Conner, was born on the reservation and educated at a number of prestigious universities. She worked in various government and policy roles before returning home to become Tamástslikt's first director. It was a job she accepted willingly: "I think I've been aware of cultural preservation for my whole life," she explains. "People used to come and interview my grandfather for history books, and a scholar lived with my great-aunt to study our language when I was a girl. There were always people talking about history. Old Nez Perce men would come and visit with my grandfather, and I was scolded in Indian, our pets had Indian names. . . . The

(Left) A child's moccasins preserved at Tamástslikt. (Right) Bobbie Conner in Tamástslikt's foyer. Photos by Kristin Anderson.

reason I am in this work is because my grandfather, my grandmother, and my mother were already devoted to sets of behaviors that were about preserving who we were."

Bobbie threw herself headlong into establishing Tamástslikt. The fundraising process was arduous and fraught with difficulties, she explained, although when OCF came on board, the Meyer Memorial Trust and a few other foundations followed suit, and Wild Horse Casino also helped bankroll it. They still struggle to make ends meet, Bobbie says, but that shouldn't come as a surprise. "These are eighteen wheelers on our freeways, not tourists. Why anyone would ever think we'd be profitable is beyond me. That's not why we did this. I don't want to pare this back to affordable: the goal is to fulfill the mission!" In some other organizations, this determination might seem a little impractical, but in this case, Bobbie's right: their mission is to protect, research, and share an entire heritage, so there is no room for cutting corners.

Tamástslikt—which means "to translate," "turn over" or "turn around" in the Wallulapum language—lives up to its mandate, providing programming and services on multiple levels. It celebrates and documents local culture through its vast permanent collection; provides educational outreach to children, schools, and the elderly; raises awareness among casino-goers and other tourists; and archives, preserves, and guards important historical relics. The institute also conducts scholarly historical and linguistic research: for instance, Bobbie is working on an atlas of native place names, and the education department is gearing up to publish two dictionaries of native languages. Tamástslikt also has rotating shows brought in from other museums. In autumn 2013, for example, an exhibit of Andy Warhol's representations of cowboys and Indians was featured alongside the native arts and artifacts that may or should have influenced him. The show was a huge success, Bobbie says: "it's been the best shoulder season attendance we've had—people have been drawn to it like a moth to a flame."

The permanent collection has also garnered praise because of its thoughtful curation. It is divided into three sections: "We Were," "We Are," and "We Will Be." The past section contains key artifacts and historical data; the present section focuses on native leaders, heroes, innovations, and accomplishments; and the future section presents their dreams for the future and various pathways to get there. The emphasis on leadership, hope, and progress is intentional, says Bobbie. "One of the things that's challenging for us is that whatever ills the nation has, we have it in spades: hypertension, diabetes, meth addiction, teenage suicide, apathy, whatever it is, we have more of it per capita. Proportionately we have more men and women in prison than we should, more men and women in the armed forces, fewer

The Umatilla Reservation near Tamástslikt. Photo by Kristin Anderson.

jobs, poorer health care." Systemic inequities, and mainstream apathy or ignorance about the persistence of those inequities, have allowed them to become entrenched. "My mother was a counselor at Warm Springs High School and one of the things she found was that Indian kids are overlooked in their needs: problems went undiagnosed. If they can't see the board, or if they can't hear the teacher, or if they haven't had breakfast, how do you expect them to be a STEM[9] student? How can a kid be ambitious about college or employment when no one in his family has had much of either? Thinking ahead won't be part of his horizon."

Tamástslikt presents a counter-narrative: while it is blunt about real-world challenges, it also delineates a long and progressive cultural lineage and proud accomplishments from modern times. "We're the beneficiaries of a culture that says no one should be left alone or living in isolation," Bobbie explains. "We have rips and tears in our social fabric that we wish we could mend sooner, faster, or stronger; but we also have inherited certain behaviors that say we're still connected to everyone. That's the gift of our culture, and one of the blessings of having a reservation in our homeland[10] is that we have a stronghold for our culture." Tamástslikt Cultural Institute, then, is a stronghold for a stronghold: it is a remarkable testament to the vitality and heritage of the Cayuse, Umatilla, and Walla Walla tribes, and it is a glowing addition to Oregon's heritage landscape and narrative.

Ultimately, all of Oregon's heritage organizations are working toward similar ends: they seek to flesh out our state's complicated and fascinating history by telling the stories of those Oregonians who shaped it—many of whom previously lacked a platform to spread their stories to a wider audience. Heritage organizations strengthen Oregon's civic structure through advocacy, diligence, and scholarship, and they do so often through the passion of many dedicated volunteers. Yet their work is habitually undervalued by those unfamiliar with it. "The heritage community is low-visibility: their work is quieter than some arts organizations, and thus they don't have the same established structure of donors," says Kimberly Howard, former manager of the Oregon Cultural Trust. "They need our help desperately and are doing such crucial work. After all," Kimberly adds, "unless we have a strong sense of who we are and where we've been, we won't know how to move forward."

THE ARTS IN OREGON

Oregon's heritage organizations are complemented by a number of creative arts organizations, many of which share common goals with the heritage sector—the expression and preservation of cultures, the creation of social cohesion through shared experience, and the celebration of beauty, innovation, history, and solidarity.

HALLIE FORD, MARIBETH COLLINS, AND THE HALLIE FORD MUSEUM OF ART IN SALEM

Numerous institutions straddle the boundaries between arts and heritage. Tamástslikt does: many items in its collection are stunning pieces of art that are also artifacts of cultural significance. Similarly, the Hallie Ford Museum of Art defines art as its primary focus, but cultural heritage readily accompanies it.

Although widely respected, the museum is not nearly as well known as it deserves to be. Located in downtown Salem just steps away from the capitol, the Hallie Ford Museum of Art occupies a novel position for a number of reasons. It houses an art collection from around the world that would make

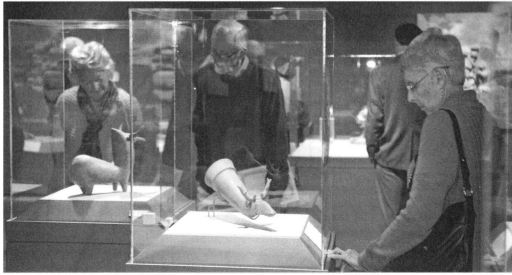

The wonderful "Breath of Heaven, Breath of Earth" exhibit, Fall 2013. Courtesy the Hallie Ford Museum of Art.

The Hallie Ford Museum of Art in downtown Salem. Courtesy the Hallie Ford Museum of Art.

many larger museums envious and has attracted touring exhibits from some of the world's top museums. Part of Willamette University, it presents exhibits that are curated to a high scholarly standard, and it boasts a collection that ranges from contemporary Pacific Northwest painting to classical sculpture, Asian art, and other global collections. Perhaps most novel of all, the museum has acquired endowments that have, through the generosity of a handful of key funders, settled it on a comparatively firm financial foundation.

John Olbrantz is the Maribeth Collins Director of the Hallie Ford Museum of Art; his title offers a clue to the identities of two of the museum's chief benefactors. Hallie Brown Ford and Kenneth Ford ran Roseburg Lumber Company and, in 1957, started what would become the Ford Family Foundation. Over the years, Hallie built a reputation as an artist and as someone dearly interested in funding the arts, and in the 1990s, while she was living in Salem and a trustee of Willamette University, Hallie leapt at the opportunity to start a museum to house the school's already exquisite collection of art and artifacts, many of which had been given generously to the university by Professor Mark Sponenburgh. Through the Ford Family Foundation, Hallie initially gave $2 million to purchase and renovate the vacant US West Communications building in downtown Salem. After the museum opened, her largesse continued: Hallie provided half a million dollars in seed money for an endowment fund to support the museum's operating expenses—a rare and visionary contribution, as few funders prioritize behind-the-scenes needs like keeping the lights on, the staff paid, and the facilities in good repair.

Longtime benefactor Maribeth Collins, former president of the Collins Foundation and chair of the board of the Collins Companies, also made an impressive long-term commitment. She endowed the museum's directorship and provided an endowment for a biennial regional art exhibition. At the same time, the Confederated Tribes of Grand Ronde endowed the museum's Native American art gallery through their Spirit Mountain Community Fund. "So," says John Olbrantz, "within a year and a half of opening, we had an endowment for my position, an endowment for a biennial regional art exhibition, and an endowment that supported a biennial contemporary Native American exhibition."

The museum then hunkered down, cautiously building the endowment funds for several years. Through Willamette University, funds became available to hire a collection curator, and during the same period, Maribeth approached John again and said (as he tells it), "'John, what's your biggest need?' I said we really want to be able to reach out to the community through K-12 educational work, and so we really need to hire an education curator." Maribeth provided the funds to endow a permanent education curator position soon thereafter. Moreover, a couple of years before she died, Hallie Ford provided a sizeable endowment for a major biennial art historical exhibition.

Today, the museum's collection and exhibitions are the envy of many. "We've carved out a unique niche," explains John. "We do major art historical exhibitions—the Chinese bronzes from the Arthur M. Sackler [Foundation, New York], Italian drawings, this year's 'Breath of Heaven, Breath of Earth.' . . . We do these major exhibitions, and then we are also experts in historical and contemporary regional and Native American art and have organized major retrospectives of prominent regional artists." The museum has also published several books about regional art, cementing its position as an authority on artistic trends in the Pacific Northwest.

Maribeth Collins. Courtesy the Hallie Ford Museum of Art.

These curatorial and scholarly successes are entirely the result of sound planning on John's part and of the pragmatism, generosity, and trust of the museum's noteworthy funders. "We're in good financial shape," John says, "because we've slowly and strategically built our endowment to match our expenses . . . That's not to say we don't have holes in our funding and areas of challenge," he adds. "Our memberships are low, we don't get much revenue from admissions, and I would really like to be able to endow our collections curator position. We are also running out of space in this facility—we have this wonderful and growing collection of African and Oceanic art and we have no place to display it. So we are definitely not in an ideal position." Nevertheless, he says, they could never be where they are now without Hallie Ford's sustained generosity. "And god bless Maribeth Collins. She's really emerged as a major patron of this institution."

Maribeth receives this comment modestly and speaks of her love for the museum. "It's just been such a wonderful experience for me, and anything I've done there has been sheer joy. I think John Olbrantz is just the best—I've so enjoyed getting down there and seeing his various exhibitions, and I think he really has a dream for what he wants it to be and is gradually realizing that dream. Salem needed something like that," she notes simply. "It's a first-rate museum." When asked why she donates to the arts more broadly, Maribeth's answer is equally straightforward. "I just believe wholeheartedly that arts, culture, and the humanities are really important. I learned it from my husband's family: they all really gave to the arts, and we passed that along to our children." Ultimately, she says, "the humanities and the arts are just a part of our lives. We need to contribute to them where possible—it's really important to quality of life."

DISJECTA CONTEMPORARY ART CENTER

The Disjecta Contemporary Art Center could not be more distinct from the Hallie Ford Museum of Art in either ambiance or curatorial goals. Housed in a former bowling alley in industrial North Portland, Disjecta's space is cavernous, spare, and minimalist—a blank slate on which to present some of the most challenging, provocative, and up-and-coming names of contemporary visual and performance art from across the country.

Relatively new to the scene—it began in 2000—Disjecta was first housed in a run-down Masonic lodge before it moved to its new twelve-thousand-square-foot facility. The barrel-vault structure's soaring ceilings and open expanses provide the perfect venue for large-scale installations,

Score, an installation by Avantika Bawa, April 2, 2011 – April 30, 2011. Photo by Mark Stein. Courtesy Disjecta.

site-specific work, and performance art. Disjecta's programming lives up to the space: a curator-in-residence program keeps their offerings fresh, and the Oregon-focused Portland Biennial has proven a landmark addition to Oregon's arts community. Despite the organization's youth, its success has been impressive. It has won international praise and has been celebrated in an article in the *Guardian* (UK) newspaper as one of the top sights to visit when in Portland. More locally, *Willamette Week* called Disjecta's 2014 biennial "one of the highlights of this year's cultural calendar," asserting that "if there's any entity on the scene today with the resources and curatorial finesse to cut through . . . hype and showcase emerging talents outside the mainstream, it's Disjecta."[11]

This high-profile presence can be both good and bad, explains executive director Bryan Suereth. "People's understanding of Disjecta in the community can be skewed. Because we have a robust programming calendar, we act like a $1 million organization—it's not necessarily evident that we only have two staff and a $300,000 budget," he says. "I think people view Disjecta as a successful organization, which is fantastic, but if it prevents them from contributing because they imagine we're financially complete, then it's problematic." Disjecta had none of the institutional or academic connections that the Hallie Ford Museum started with, and while they acquire some foundation funding, they have struggled to find individuals to contribute to their innovative and frequently rotating exhibits. Theo Downes-Le Guin, Disjecta's board chair and the owner and director of Upfor, a prominent Portland gallery, explains that Disjecta's funding breaks down to 35 percent earned revenue, 50 percent grant support, and 15 percent individual giving. "It's very difficult for any visual arts organization to reach high rates of individual support," Theo says, but it is particularly difficult for Disjecta because both the organization and its audience are relatively young.

Theo is eloquent on the challenge of funding a new, contemporary-minded arts organization in today's philanthropic climate. "The generation of wealth that was formed in the late nineteenth/early twentieth century and that started up most of the prominent East Coast galleries and museums wasn't really here on the West Coast. Not as many businessmen here used art as a way to increase their social status, so we have always been at some disadvantage in arts funding," he states. "Now, three generations later, we don't have many grandchildren who were raised with the assumption that it is part of their duty, part of their stewardship of their city, to support art. And if they were raised with that assumption, that support is typically not channeled into contemporary art."

Disjecta faces additional challenges, says Bryan, because of its focus on new work and taking risks—sometimes the results are unpredictable, even unsuccessful. Another challenge is that Disjecta is not a collecting institution. "People know what museums are, there's a presumed social good," he says. "But when it comes to funding institutions that provide artists with formative experience and help them build up their reputation so that they one day *might* be acquired—we often don't trace the value back down the chain." Not that being in a museum is or should be the end goal, he adds: Disjecta makes a point of including artists whose works will never, in either medium, intention, or content, suit or court museum acquisition.

To compensate for these in-built funding obstacles, Disjecta has assembled a proactive nonprofit board, ably captained by Theo. "My role on the board is to counterbalance the entrepreneurial spirit Bryan's brought to Disjecta," Theo explains. "As an organization grows in success and reputation, it needs increased governance: funding sources have certain expectations about transparency and management, and a board provides responsibility and oversight. So our role is to make things happen, to provide opportunities," he says. "What I think the board has done—and what any board needs to do—is to provide a network, to broaden the influence of the organization, to raise awareness of it, and to bring support in. I can also give Bryan a—" he pauses, searching for the right phrase—"diversity of opinion on how best to do what we're doing," he finishes with a smile. "Yes, it's a very hands-on board," Bryan agrees, grinning.

With strong support from its board, Disjecta has become an important resource in Portland's contemporary arts scene. In a short space of time, and despite an uphill battle for private funding, Disjecta has demonstrated that it is possible to run a modestly scaled organization that has national influence. Bryan notes that Disjecta also "has managed to navigate a path between Portland's scrappy DIY arts culture and pure establishmentarianism, and to help artists do that as well." However, although it has been successful on a small budget, Disjecta would very much like to escape survival mode, and to do so, it needs more supporters. Bryan elaborates.

> If you're someone who accepts the value arts bring to a city, *buy art*. But also find an organization that supports artists with minimal overhead. Putting money into the hands of artists so that they can do what they do with very few strings attached is a powerful tool. How do you affect society when you support that kind of experimentation? You have to place value in the process. It's akin to a science lab: there are so many failed experiments, but successful results in the art world are transferred to design, to habitat, to so many areas of our daily lives.

"But you can acknowledge that artistic innovation affects other disciplines and industries, most foundations that support the arts, and most individuals who do, do it for very different reasons," Theo adds. "They accept the notion that art is a common good and that young artists are part of a healthy community. You invest in science because .01 percent of it will be transformative for society. We also need to invest in art with the same ideology, that the transformative quality of art is of value in itself."

Whatever one's rationale for funding the arts, it is easy to believe that Disjecta is a crucible for the great works of the future. A healthy arts scene needs institutions like Disjecta that devote themselves to commissioning and publicizing new works of art, and that incubate, mentor, and support promising young artists. With its rotating curators and global gaze, Disjecta also connects Portland's arts scene to a national and international conversation, bringing innovative artists with national reputations to intersect with Oregon's own creative community.

Disjecta's structure also demonstrates the utility and stimulation that comes from having a warm, frank, and engaged relationship between a nonprofit director and the board. For Disjecta, the benefits of this relationship are clear enough, but Disjecta's board members also benefit. When asked why he was motivated to volunteer with Disjecta, Theo responds quickly and passionately. "There are ideological reasons that I joined—I think Portland *needs* what Disjecta provides—but I also just found them exciting. I went to the first biennial that Disjecta ran and I loved the eccentricity, the randomness, the excitement of their works. It's what I've needed in this life."

NESKOWIN CHAMBER MUSIC AND THE GRANDE RONDE SYMPHONY ORCHESTRA

We hear, and consume, music everywhere: while waiting for a coffee, while driving or walking, while working, and often in our leisure time. Music is part of what creates our quality of life, and yet few of us realize the time and money required for the composition and performance of our favorite works.

When the former president of Linfield College, Charlie Walker, and his wife Cherie retired to the small coastal town of Neskowin, they quickly realized how much they missed having access to live music. "We built a house at Neskowin, but were driving to Portland or Astoria to go to concerts," Charlie recalls. "One day, I asked our builder Nick Dusic whether he liked classical music, and he said 'I love it.' I said to him, 'well, if you'll sell the tickets, I'll bring the music.'" Out of two enthusiasts' love, Neskowin Chamber Music (NCM) was born. "We were risking our own money," Charlie says, "but we managed to bring in ensembles from all over, and we got the very best! We had the Juilliard String Quartet; we even had the Kremlin Orchestra—thirty-five people!"

Accessibility has always been the most important attribute of their series, Charlie notes. "When we started in the fall of 1994, we provided five concerts for $29 per person total. I heard people say that this was the largest amount of money per year they spend on entertainment. If the fee was $129, they'd have never come." The question, he says, is how many people do you want in your audience, and how diverse an audience do you want? You can have ticket prices that raise the amount that you need to operate, or you can seek subsidy for ticket prices so that you can keep them low and the doors open to everyone.

Neskowin Chamber Music has always pursued the latter option. To ensure that access starts at an early age, and to compensate for local schools' diminishing music programs, NCM also runs a program for third to fifth graders in the schools from Tillamook to Newport. The goal is to develop in these children an understanding of, and interest in, classical music, and to sustain that interest not just through their outreach program but also through regular exposure to classical performances and access to music lessons. "If you want to learn the violin or the viola, we'll provide you with an instrument and instruction free of charge, and we'll give you complimentary seats at our seven-concert series," Charlie explains.

Anthea Kreston, violin, and Jason Duckles, cello, of the Amelia Piano Trio, played for students at Neskowin Valley School, April 14, 2014. Courtesy Neskowin Chamber Music.

The organization has kept costs down by relying exclusively on volunteer labor, a luxury most larger organizations (or small organizations in larger communities) could never manage. It also relies on community donations to cover musician fees and outreach costs, and in-kind donations for many services, including accommodation, food and drink for visiting musicians, and tutors for NCM's school outreach programs.

Like NCM, the Grande Ronde Symphony Orchestra (GRSO), based in La Grande, works to serve rural populations by ensuring community members have regular access to classical music. Despite the loss of historic corporate support to area nonprofits, the GRSO has maintained a strong presence in the region, performing regularly in La Grande, touring to other towns, and drawing musicians and audiences from hundreds of miles.

Accessibility and availability are essential cornerstones of the GRSO's mission. Ticket prices are deliberately kept low, and community building and education are also mainstays: before each performance, GRSO presents a social with complimentary drinks and hors d'oeuvres accompanied by information about the music and composers featured that evening. GRSO also runs the Grande Ronde Student Symphony (GRSS), a branch of the orchestra for beginning and intermediate music students of all ages (more accomplished students play in the main orchestra). Because many regional towns do not have any orchestra, the GRSS fills a significant need, and each year it draws from a wider geographic area, with many students driving in from Baker and Wallowa counties. Eastern Oregon University students also serve as mentors to younger students, which helps establish a broader sense of musical community and delineate a clear musical progression from elementary and secondary school to university. Moreover, to keep the student orchestra accessible to students of all income levels, participation in GRSS is for free to many, and GRSS provides compensation for mileage costs to offset the long distance some students must travel.

GRSO's vital work is made possible through the determination of its stalwart volunteer board, which handles everything from fundraising to performance planning. "We're not just a decision-making board," says longtime board chair and honorary lifetime president Lorna Spain. "We're an all-volunteer working board: we put on all of the concerts, design and place the advertisements and posters, and do all of the fundraising. We work all year for the symphony." The board works miracles to keep the orchestra afloat and as professionalized as possible: it built an endowment, runs annual fundraisers and a ticket subscription society, and pursues numerous monetary and in-kind donations from community members. It has also leveraged a network of partners within the community, most extensively with Eastern Oregon University, which provides performance space, credit hours and associated coursework for college student members of the orchestra, and a professorship for Leandro Espinoza, the orchestra's longtime conductor.

Lorna Spain. Photo by Kristin Anderson.

While a number of board members, like Lorna, are musicians who play in the orchestra, others are enthusiasts who offer non-musical skills. As for her own talents, Lorna admits with a laugh, "I'm a better board chair than I am a musician." Known as "the Mother of the Orchestra" by some fellow volunteers, Lorna has been tenacious and tireless as a leader. "I've put in full-time and more for quite a few years," she acknowledges, "and you don't find many volunteers that have that kind of time. But I turned eighty awhile ago, and I've got my bucket list, so I'd like to step down one of these days if I can find someone who can take it on." Succession is a big problem, she says, because the burden is so onerous.

> We do a lot of fundraising, and you get burned out. I have a lot of energy and passion, but between the grant writing and auction planning and the appeals and ticket sales, it's tiring. We're always

trying to find that continual supply of dollars and to keep a committed corps of volunteers. Our largest donors are no longer the railroads or timber or paper companies: they're individuals. Our annual budget is only $36,000 [which is incredibly lean], but we work very hard to raise that money.

Fundraising burnout is a real and familiar problem for all nonprofits, but because they often rely more heavily on volunteer labor, arts nonprofits may face this burnout more than those in other sectors. With additional monetary support, the Grande Ronde Symphony Orchestra could professionalize further and pay its musicians a living wage, Lorna says. Just as importantly, it could expand its outreach and performance opportunities across eastern Oregon's far-flung communities, thus giving additional audiences the joy of watching them perform.

BODYVOX: CONTEMPORARY DANCE WITH A TWIST

Anyone who has been to a dance performance—whether ballet, contemporary, hip-hop, jazz, folk, or any other genre—knows how transformational watching dance can be. Its aerial grace can take your breath away and the percussive staccato of dancers' rhythms can make your heart pound. But dance organizations often face attitudinal challenges when courting audiences and

Bodyvox headstand (Ashley Rowland, center). Photo by Lois Greenfield. Courtesy Bodyvox.

funding: some assume dance to be inaccessible—too cerebral, old-fashioned, abstract, or elitist. This assumption couldn't be further from the truth.

"Dance is an exciting part of what makes this place and time somewhere you want to be: it's important to and reflects Oregon in 2014, in 2015, in 2016—it's not a thing of the past," says Kevin Irving, artistic director of Oregon Ballet Theatre. Dance also brings communities together around something to which we can all relate, Kevin says. "As children, we dance . . . Dance connects us back to our very earliest senses. It enlivens us, reinvigorates us, it gives us that sense of freedom and abandon. . . . And part of that wonderful experience is that you are having it at the same time as all the other people in the audience around you." Oregon Ballet Theatre and other dance companies across the state—ranging from Dance Kaleidoscope in Ashland to the CABA Chinese Lion Dance Troupe of Eugene to Ballet Folklórico México en la Piel of Cornelius—are doing just that: building community cohesion through shared experience, entertaining and delighting us, and gripping us in the thrall of the present moment.

Portland's Bodyvox is a perfect example. Led by artistic directors and husband and wife Jamey Hampton and Ashley Rowland, Bodyvox's specialties include innovative choreography, creative and often humorous staging, and community visibility. "We knew at the beginning that for people to support us, we needed to be present in the community," Jamey explains. "So we started early on to create opportunities for community engagement: classes, workshops, outreach to places around the state, collaborations with other organizations, rental of our performance space. Bodyvox has performed at [Portland's] Jamison Square and in the [Portland Rose Festival's] Starlight Parade. We are constantly working really hard at being a part of the community. Fortunately, it's really a blast to be a part of it!"

Because of this hard work, they are staying afloat, Jamey says, and their ratio of earned to contributed (donated) income is high for a nonprofit. "We earn 60 percent of our annual budget. There are two reasons that number is high: we put a lot of effort into making money and getting out there. But also the contributed income isn't what it needs to be." This affects staffing—they have no full-time development staff—and it also affects benefits: it has been a goal of the company to provide health insurance for their dancers and employees, and it was only in 2014 that they were finally able to, thanks to a major philanthropic push from a longtime supporter. "Dr. Joe Campbell, a really wonderful, thoughtful gentleman and a visionary philanthropist, spearheaded the campaign," explains Una Loughran, Bodyvox's general manager. "He owns Elk Cove Vineyards and hosted a fundraising dinner for thirty people at $500 a ticket. And when that didn't raise quite enough, he issued a challenge grant to the organization, promising us $10,000 if we could

Bodyvox DanceCamp 7. Photo by David Krebs. Courtesy Bodyvox.

raise another $10,000. We did, and now we have health care! It really was a case of a community member stepping up to make things happen, and it took fewer than forty generous individual donors to make it a reality."

Bodyvox's programming and ability to create new work also relies heavily on the largesse of individuals and foundations. "A new show can cost as much as $200,000 to build, which seems like a lot of money until you know that that's for twelve months of concept and design and rehearsal and work-shopping, and that there are anywhere between six and fourteen people that are hard at work in the studio to make it," explains Una. "Our goal is to show individual supporters more about the process of making new work—the way these dances get built—to learn what it takes to have something beautiful appear on stage for five minutes," Una says. "Not only does it help from a fundraising perspective, but it gets people excited and engaged about the work. Dance is an intriguing process, and our patrons love to see how they do it—it's just fascinating."

To facilitate and encourage greater levels of giving, Bodyvox started the Carol Hampton Creative Fund, named after Jamey's mother and the wife of John Hampton (both profiled in the Introduction).[12] "Its goal is to build dedicated and stable support for the idea of creation, to bring about new works on stage and to underwrite the development and rehearsal time needed," Jamey says. They hope people will contribute to the fund generously. There is good reason to, Jamey says: "We do a lot of teaching. For example, for summer dance camp, we have two hundred kids ages three to ten for two weeks." Bodyvox's choreographic style is unique, too. "There's a lot of great dance happening almost everywhere right now," Una says. "But I can say quite honestly that there's not anything out there like Bodyvox, with its mix of theater and acrobatics and beautiful dancing, and with its international and outreach reputation. It's great working at front-of-house during the shows," Una adds. "When our audience leaves, people come out grinning from ear to ear and they're so excited and energized. I don't think that you get that elsewhere."

THE HEART OF THE COMMUNITY: MEDFORD'S CRATERIAN THEATER AND PORTLAND'S MIRACLE THEATRE GROUP

Theater groups face similar challenges in finding funders who understand and value the creative process, rehearsal time, and production costs associated with performance and new works, and even prominent theater companies like the Oregon Shakespeare Festival and Portland Center Stage struggle to find sufficient long-term support.

Theater facilities management and renovation are costly budget items, especially when a company is housed in a historic theater. The past few decades have seen a number of prominent fundraising campaigns, part heritage enterprise, part theater company operating expenses, to save crumbling but historically precious old theaters. The Liberty Theater in Astoria, the Egyptian Theater in Coos Bay, the Elsinore in Salem, and the Craterian in Medford have all benefited from dedicated and determined volunteers who have fought through drawn-out campaigns to secure the future of these valuable and useful performance palaces.

Salem's historic Elsinore Theater.
Photo by Kristin Anderson.

Lindsay Berryman, the former mayor of Medford and the leader of the charge to save the Craterian, says that the restoration of the theater was essential to the town's urban renewal and has brought new cultural life to downtown Medford. But it took a herculean effort by Lindsay and the other all-volunteer fundraisers to raise the necessary public and private funds and grants. Along the way, they were helped by Ginger Rogers, former Hollywood star, adopted Oregonian, and one of the Craterian's most enthusiastic champions. The community benefit of the restoration has been remarkable, says Lindsay. "The Craterian project has infused a lot of people into the downtown. It's also boosted the arts community and its wider well-being.... We now have public art on the streets, and galleries. Our town used to be called 'Deadford' or 'Dreadford.' You don't hear that much anymore. The Craterian's restoration was a raising of the town's self-esteem."

That the Craterian's restoration could have such a wide impact on Medford as a whole makes sense. Theater has played a prominent role in societies for almost as long as storytelling has, and in America, theaters historically have been central to the social and civic life of towns of all sizes. The rejuvenation of these old theaters as places both of historic and contemporary value makes sense—they help ground a community.

New theaters and theater companies do as well. Portland's Miracle Theatre Group plays a similar role within its inner southeast Portland community. Founded in 1985 by wife and husband team Dañel Malán and José Eduardo González, Miracle's mission is straightforward and broad: "to provide extraordinary Latino theater, culture and arts education experiences for the enrichment of all communities."

Dañel Malán and José González.
Photo by Kristin Anderson.

Brightly colored and attractive, the façade of its building—El Centro Milagro—stands out from the warehouses and auto-body repair shops surrounding it. Inside, the building stands out too: a converted ballroom, it functions as a stage, studio, classroom, and community gathering place. The building's and the company's prominence result largely from the determination and charisma of Miracle's founders. Their backstory is charming: José met Dañel while in graduate school at UCLA studying theater set design. "I saw this cute girl walking around, and I was really shy and didn't do anything about it." Eventually, he recalls, "she walked up to me and said, 'we gotta talk,' so it's all her fault!"

When he graduated, they both moved to Portland, where José had been working on a show. After producing a number of shows for other theater companies in town, they finally started to think about starting their own company. "We definitely weren't going to succeed as a for-profit, so we applied for nonprofit status," José notes. "There was a line in the form, something like 'we shall create this company in perpetuity,' and I thought, 'this is serious stuff!' We thought hard about what was involved to establish a theater company in perpetuity, and we also thought hard about our name. We settled on Miracle because it meant two things. One, that we believe in miracles—otherwise we wouldn't be doing it—and two, it was a miracle that we could get a show running at all! We also liked the resonances with the miracle plays of medieval theater."

Miracle Theatre Group was not, however, immediately a *Latino* theater company. It started out doing Greek plays, but when, in 1989, they started the first Hispanic Cultural Festival, they fell in love with the work. After a couple of tough years of borrowing money from families and draining their own bank account dry, José sat down and wrote three grant applications.

One, to the Collins Foundation, came back positive and "out fell a $4,000 check," he says. "That saved our bacon: we could pay all of our bills and actually start earning back some revenue." They haven't looked back.

Miracle has had other transformative moments as recipients of philanthropy: in the mid-1990s, for instance, after applying for a small program grant to the Northwest Area Foundation, they got a call saying that the foundation wasn't interested in supporting the program, but they were interested in offering ongoing operating support, a rare and indeed miraculous intervention. The theatre's budget at the time was $60,000; Northwest Area Foundation offered them $250,000 over three years to build their capacity. Shortly thereafter, they moved into their present location, doing most of the renovations themselves. "We built the risers: Jamey Hampton got Hampton Lumber to donate the wood, and Northwest Natural donated pipes that provided the risers' structural support," José says. Dañel was on tour in Salem and noticed that the Elsinore Theater was replacing some seats: El Centro Milagro ended up with their old ones. Everything about their space has been built with hard work and lots of community support, they explain gratefully.

In its thirty years, Milagro has acquired a glowing reputation not only for its creativity and artistic direction, but also for its educational content and tireless outreach. Dañel is the more activist of the two, José says. Dañel agrees: "I don't really delineate between art and activism and education: activism is education and we use theater as a vehicle." She elaborates:

> Theater is an effective educational tool because it creates teamwork, leadership, and responsibility. It allows people to step outside of norms and to reverse roles. We've worked with the health department, the Cascade Aids Project, the Pride Foundation, and Planned Parenthood to engage people in conversations about sexual health; we've worked with Nike and the Timbers and Frank Jansen of the Crow's Shadow Institute. We've done work on prenatal health, breast cancer, youth homelessness, health and fitness, positive self-images, and of course all sorts of arts and cultural topics—El Salvador, the Zapatistas, Frieda Kahlo, *Don Quixote*, border crossing, you name it. And we work with a lot of communities on immigration issues and literacy: literacy is a big deal.

Miracle also works to combat racism between communities. It's important work, Dañel says, recounting an example from a diversity training event she led during which a person stood up and admitted, "I think Mexicans smell of grease because they go home and fry tortillas." People who are racist, Dañel explains, "often don't know it: it's built-in. I ran a training at a hospital where the nurses were complaining that their Latino patients were always late, but what they didn't understand was that they were late because they would walk from the fields for three miles to get to the appointment." She continues, "I really believe in the one-person-at-a-time theory. You can't change the whole world, but there's a chain reaction: you touch someone, they touch someone else. Our goal is to make people more tolerant and to open their eyes."

It's not just about education and activism, however, José notes. Both their touring productions and educational events and the bigger dramatic productions at their headquarters in southeast Portland have received critical praise for their artistry, depth, and theatrical ingenuity, and Miracle has a loyal and ever-swelling audience. José attributes their success in part to the generosity of their volunteers. "Our fundraisers are run by volunteers; our shows and other events are too. They're ambassadors for us, and we're so grateful to them," José says.

The organization is also grateful to their grantmakers (especially catalyst funders like the Collins Foundation and the Northwest Area Foundation) and its many individual contributors. There are several ways people give, José explains: through a gala and a Day-of-the-Dead celebration, through *Willamette Week*'s Give!Guide, an annual Christmas appeal, their subscriber base, and also one-off opportunities, such as a theater-seat naming campaign. But much of their support comes in the form of small donations by devoted contributors. One of them is Thom Jenkins, a board member who worked with Miracle in its early days, helping to create their first children's productions and contributing endless creative input as well as financial help. "He lived in Skid Row," José recalls, "and was a recovering alcoholic. One day, he brought us a paper bag filled with coins and crumbled bills—he'd gone around Skid Row's streets and asked all of his homeless friends to contribute."

When asked about his vision for Miracle Theatre Group in the future, José pauses, and then replies, "if I walked into this place in twenty years, I'd love to see packed houses, vibrant lively accelerating theater on stage, communities intersecting from all parts, a stable operation, and a real sense of aesthetics as well as a sense of responsibility to the greater community. If the spirit is not there, there's no point." Meanwhile, they keep working, he says, because as artists, their work is important. "The arts are integral to an individual's and a society's well-being," José notes. "You can't have a civilized society without arts and culture. . . . The arts provide an incredible way to express something that's deep and human and important, and theater is part of that. Theater is storytelling, and engaging people with ideas and emotions

Milagro production "Corrido Calavera." Photo by Russell J. Young Photography. Courtesy Milagro.

to change and impact them, to uplift and entertain them. I truly believe that the arts are transformative."

FISHTRAP, LITERARY ARTS, AND LITERARY PHILANTHROPY

If storytelling is at the heart of good theater, it is also at the heart of our daily lives. "We tell ourselves stories in order to live," wrote Joan Didion. We seek narrative, whether in our internal monologue or in our interactions and entertainments—it's part, some might say, of what makes us human. Literature satiates that need: for many of us, a book can provoke thought, deliver entertainment, and open doors onto other traditions and lives. Oregon has been feted as a state with a uniquely strong literary community. We cherish independent bookstores like Paulina Springs Books in Sisters and Powell's Books in Portland; we laud homegrown authors like Ursula Le Guin and Mary Szybist and Barry Lopez; and our literary strengths certainly feed into our wider identities as Oregonians—our sense of place, our appreciation of difference, and our desire to protect valuable ecologies have in part been sculpted by the work of Oregon's great writers.

Oregon's writers have succeeded because of their own talent and tenacity, and also because citizens across the state have coalesced around literature as something to value and support. From Write Around Portland to Playa, an artists' retreat in Lake County, nonprofits and arts funders across the state are dedicated to preserving Oregon's reputation as a great place to be a writer and a reader.

One organization, Fishtrap, focuses specifically on what it means to be a writer working within a wider region and ecology. "Our mission is to promote clear thinking and good writing about the West," says Ann

Wallowa Lake. Photo by Kristin Anderson.

Whitfield Powers, Fishtrap's executive director. It's in a good position to do both of those things: located near Joseph, high up in the Wallowa Mountains, Fishtrap is surrounded by the kind of natural beauty that clears heads and inspires. Its main retreat facility is at the end of Wallowa Lake. To reach it, you drive through the tiny, artsy town of Joseph, past some beautiful farm country, along Wallowa Lake's famous glacial moraine, and into the forested foothills at the head of the lake. "Fishtrap is very place-based," Ann says. "It started in reaction to a gathering of writers in Portland that was supposed to be a statewide representation but was really only those from the I-5 corridor. Folks here felt like there's a lot of great writers in the rest of the West, too. We're remote in a quintessentially western way, and when people come here, they are making a conscious effort to step away from their regular life."

The organization's flagship program is Summer Fishtrap, held at its Wallowa Lake facility. "We bring together creative writers, readers, and thinkers for a week of conferences and conversations, and we've done that for twenty-seven years," Ann says. In addition, Fishtrap runs a writers' retreat in Imnaha Canyon (at a cabin generously lent to them by longtime supporters) and offers writers a chance to interact with the nearby Zumwalt Prairie at its Zumwalt outpost. Whatever the location, Ann says, "community is a big part of the Fishtrap experience. Writers always need community and connection, but we need it even more out here. Here you can be surrounded by two hundred writers from different walks of life. It's refreshing to meet someone who shares your passions and is completely different from you."

While writers come from both near and far for Fishtrap's retreats and conferences, Fishtrap also runs year-round programs for the local community from its center in Enterprise. "We do the Big Read, and the whole county (population 7,000) celebrates a great work of literature every year," Ann says. "And we do book discussions and arts classes; we've just started

Fishtrap Fireside, a monthly reading series and open mic night; and we've also just started a new program with OSU where they send two of their graduate students to work with us for a year. One of them is currently teaching a college-credit Fishtrap class for high-school seniors."

Accessibility is a key part of all of these programs: fostering both local and regional aspiring and emerging writers is one of Fishtrap's principal aims, which often means offering direct financial support to writers interested in participating. "We give fellowships to those who have the potential to be strong voices out there in the world," Ann explains. "They can attend Summer Fishtrap for free—it's a real mark of encouragement for writers." It can also be a launchpad: for example, Amanda Coplin, author of *The Orchardist* (2013), was a Fishtrap Fellow, and Fishtrap's teachers have included Sherman Alexie, Terry Tempest Williams, and David James Duncan. "We can really play a part in launching people into their writing life and helping them to have the courage and skills and support to maximize their potential," Ann says.

Amy Zahm and Jim Hepworth. Courtesy Fishtrap.

None of this would have happened were it not for Fishtrap's founder and longtime executive director, Rich Wandschneider. Rich's vision for Fishtrap as a nexus of Western writing, and his commitment to developing both local and regional cultural capacity, established Fishtrap as a central presence in Wallowa County. For Rich, part of what makes Fishtrap exceptional is its inclusivity: in its programs, "all kinds of writing are considered. Poets meet historians meet journalists meet song-writers."[13] That diversity of voices is also represented in its geographical draw and the artistic empathy it fosters, says Rich. "I always thought that Fishtrap was a window on the world for the people who live in rural Eastern Oregon, and a window to us for the people from other places—urban and suburban Oregon, the larger Pacific Northwest, and the world, really."[14] "Rich was the heart of Fishtrap," says Ann. "It wouldn't be what it is if not for the generosity of spirit that Rich had and has to this day. He's a big-hearted, inspiring guy and he really took an idea, brought it to life, and cultivated it."

Nor could Fishtrap survive without a loyal army of volunteers to help run their programs and raise their funds. A Fishtrap supporter for twenty-six years, Sara Miller is a volunteer and now a board member as well as a participant in workshops and conferences. She says that she volunteers because "the organization is really important for the literary community across Oregon and across the west. Its benefits are being generated both locally and society-wide, and the bottom line is that I really believe in the mission." It is an exceptional writer's resource, she says, partly because of "its physical

Cheryl Strayed's keynote address at Summer Fishtrap 2013. Courtesy Fishtrap.

location. The valley, with its heart of Wallowa Lake, the moraine, the mountains . . . it's been a spiritual aperture for cultures as long as people have been here." Ann agrees. "This is really a sacred place, a place of peace and quiet, but also a community of passionate people. I hate to use the word 'magical,' but there are many magical moments here."

In addition to her time, Sara also donates what she can. "We gave an auction item—a day at our ranch, which sold for $350. During the verbal appeal, I agreed to do a challenge of $300, but that was a lot of money for us. I've personally benefited from Fishtrap's scholarships, so I'm not always in the position to contribute money. An old guy once told me that Wallowa County is like a bushel of apples: sometimes you take a few apples out, sometimes you put a few apples in."

That's a good model for community in general—a willingness to be helped and to return the favor. Sara's generosity of time, and, when possible, money helps underwrite an organization that contributes a lot of apples to the communal bushel. To locals, Fishtrap is a precious thing. "Whether or not you can come out to Fishtrap, it's important to support us and other organizations like us. A lot of arts organizations have come and gone in the time we've been here, but we have deep roots. Fishtrap is beloved in this county," Ann says. "It's really wonderful to see. That's one of the things that happens in small communities: no one takes anything for granted, and they work hard to keep good things alive. It's really impressive to see how many great creative voices there are in this county, and how many good stories people have to tell."

Around thirty years ago, a few Portland-based literary enthusiasts independently realized something similar: there were a lot of good stories out

there, and not enough celebrations of them. In 1984, Karen Frank founded a
speaker series called Portland Arts & Lectures, which brings famous authors
to speak to Portland's lovers of literature, and shortly thereafter turned it over
to Sherry Prowda and Julie Mancini. In 1986, Brian Booth, a founding partner
at Tonkon Torp law firm and a famous devotee of Portland's
poetry scene, wrote a letter to Ursula Le Guin proposing "to
assist Pacific Northwest writers and promote the literary
arts in the Northwest."[15] What emerged was the Oregon Institute of Literary Arts and its central programs, the Oregon
Book Awards and the Oregon Literary Fellowships.

In 1993, Oregon Institute of Literary Arts merged
with Portland Arts & Lectures to form Literary Arts, a
move that ensured the longevity of the Oregon Book
Awards & Fellowships (OBA&F) by linking them with the
more financially profitable lecture series, but Brian Booth
remained a strong advocate for Oregon literature and for
the OBAs. Andrew Proctor, Literary Arts' executive director, says that "Brian cared about Oregon writers before

Brian Booth. Courtesy the Booth
family and Literary Arts.

a lot of people did. He collected even the rarest of their
books, and arguably he helped shape the Oregon canon. As a state matures,
it's a big deal to have someone so supportive of its literature. For Brian, it
wasn't about public recognition: his interest in Oregon's literary culture was
deeply sincere." New work excited Brian, and many evenings he could often
be found at the back of dive bars mingling with young writers while waiting
for a poetry reading to begin. His own work excited him too: he edited a
number of collections and texts, and enjoyed digging into scholarly projects.

Through Brian's dedication; through the support of his wife, Gwyneth
Gamble Booth, after his death in 2012; through Literary Arts' perseverance;
and through the contributions of thousands of book-loving Oregonians, the
Oregon Book Awards & Fellowships today have honored over five hundred
Oregon writers and publishers, and have distributed over $700,000 in fel-
lowships and awards. For almost thirty years, the Oregon Book Awards &
Fellowships have been transformative to writers struggling to earn a living
and to feel validated in their work. Cheryl Strayed, author of Oregon Book
Award–winning *Wild* and recipient of a Literary Arts Fellowship, writes
that the fellowships "affirm the importance of literature made right here in
Oregon, and they provide vital financial and emotional support to writers at
all stages of their careers. The simple message that each and every fellowship
communicates—*your work is important, we believe in you*—can make a key
difference in a writer's ability to keep writing." Author Molly Best Tinsley
agrees: "the Oregon Book Awards perform a really vital function in times

like these when literary publishing has become such a hard-to-crack industry, and so many of us feel ready to give up trying."

As with Fishtrap, *place* has been essential to Literary Arts since its founding. Brian's sense of place motivated all of his service work, and he often quoted authors who had a sense of the Northwest, its history and its substance, its *zeitgeist*. "It was very important to [Brian] that he was an Oregonian," said Ursula Le Guin, "and that this was an *Oregon* book award."[16] Although Literary Arts offers a range of programs that are, for funding and resource reasons, mostly Portland-focused—high school outreach workshops, literary seminars, slam poetry competitions, and its popular and much-lauded lecture series—the Oregon Book Awards & Fellowships (OBA&F) has a truly statewide impact, deliberately courting and supporting writers across Oregon's four corners.

Ismet Prcic, author, on an Oregon Book Awards & Fellowships tour to Astoria High School. Courtesy Literary Arts.

These days, the OBA&F program includes a very successful author tour, designed so that communities across the state can meet and experience Oregon's most celebrated writers and works. The tour authors give readings, hold workshops, and do outreach in schools. Responses have been overwhelmingly positive. Laurie Nordahl, a librarian at North Bend Middle School near Coos Bay, writes that the tour was wonderful because, "with our low socioeconomic population, many of our students are not able to travel to Eugene or Portland to see authors, so the chance for them to hear an author promote reading, to make the connection of print to a real person, and to encourage young writers is rare."

To celebrate its thirtieth anniversary year in 2014, Literary Arts launched a campaign to raise $2 million with which to endow the Oregon Book Awards & Fellowships—an endowment called the Brian Booth Writers' Fund. This kind of support for writers couldn't be more timely, Andrew Proctor explains.

> Very few people make any money from their publisher as a writer. The fact that there is a portion of writers who do make money from their books can lead people to believe that this isn't an area that requires philanthropic investment. But below the surface, if you look at the acknowledgements page of your favorite books, you'll likely see a long list of foundations and nonprofits who have granted money or resources to the project. This kind of financial and creative support is particularly important for younger and midlist writers. You *need* this kind of infrastructure

to support new work. If some of it becomes commercially viable, that's the best outcome possible, but in this publishing climate, that is highly unlikely.

Even getting to the publication stage requires a long investment in one's art, Andrew continues. "It can take years and years to build a writer's career, and not everyone can be supported by a spouse or come from wealth. If we really want disparate voices from our community, if we want a diverse and multicultural selection of books to choose from, then we need to acknowledge that the old adage that time is money is true: people need help to find the time and space to make art." Literary Arts' Fellowships "buy time for people so they can live up to their literary potential," Andrew says. "One of our most generous donors, Diane Ponti—she contributed $228,000 to the Brian Booth Writers' Fund endowment—says that books are like breathing: we don't pay much attention to oxygen, but if it wasn't there, we wouldn't be either. Writing happens behind the scenes: there's no big spectacle, no leotards or flashing lights or music. Books arrive quietly into a noisy world. We need to pay attention to, and protect, that process."

ARTS EDUCATION: PORT ORFORD ARTS IN THE SCHOOLS AND DAN AND PRISCILLA BERNARD WIEDEN'S CALDERA

Teaching young people the value of arts from a tender age is important, but the number of arts programs and courses offered to public school students is decreasing every year, especially in low-income communities. Moreover, far from filling the gaps in state and local funding, the federal government has significantly reduced its own levels of arts funding, including its support for arts education. This means that in Portland public schools, for instance, only 18 percent of students have certified visual art instruction (compared to 83 percent nationally) and only 58 percent of schools have certified music instruction (compared to 94 percent nationally).[17] As one Oregon arts advocate recently commented, "we're really fortunate that all of our grandchildren are in California, where they have much more arts in the schools than we do here."

Hundreds of arts nonprofits throughout Oregon have outreach programs for young people precisely for these reasons, and for many students, nonprofit outreach programs may be their only exposure to arts. Why does this matter? Study after study has shown that arts education can help narrow the achievement gap and increase students' test scores across the board.[18] Low-income students with intensive arts experiences in high school were three times more likely than students who lacked these experiences to earn a bachelor's degree, and were more likely to earn "mostly A's" in college.[19] A longitudinal analysis of over twenty-five thousand students demonstrated that participation in the arts correlates with higher academic performance, increased standardized test scores, more community service, and lower dropout rates.[20]

Mom, teacher, and artist Allandra Emerson, of Port Orford, knows how essential arts education is. "We have a healthy arts community here, but there's not much overlap between the artists and parents of school-age children," she says. Seeing how little arts education her children received in the local elementary, Allandra helped bridge the two communities, leading the local Port Orford Arts Council to create first a Saturday arts program for children. Soon, Allandra says, they realized it was more useful to integrate their program with the school district directly. "That way you can reach the maximum of kids, not just kids whose parents are interested in the arts." Now, the arts council provides every kindergarten to fifth-grade student with sixteen contact hours of art per year, and the school district has written the programming into the curriculum.

"We're also doing a summer program at the library that links the arts and literacy, using illustrations to help kids get interested in books," Allandra explains. But the arts tuition that they are providing, she says, is far from sufficient. "It'd be great to offer these opportunities to sixth to eighth graders," says Allandra, "and my personal dream would be to see this program become much larger and expand to Gold Beach and to Bandon. It's important to try to get these things going elsewhere: the sense of creativity you can cultivate in a child works to create a well-rounded individual in the future. And it's wonderful to get these small, rural, impoverished communities going on art!"

The reduction in public arts education funding has, as Allandra suggests, hit small, rural, impoverished communities hard. Urban low-income communities have suffered disproportionately too, a fact that hasn't escaped the notice of Dan Wieden, whose Portland-based advertising firm Wieden+Kennedy has been responsible for some of the most iconic and lauded ads of recent decades, with clients ranging from Nike to Coca-Cola to Old Spice ("The Man Your Man Could Smell Like"). Dan is frank about the impact decreased arts funding has had on his business: he wasn't seeing applicants coming from low-income and minority backgrounds with the right creative skills. "In our profession, advertising, there are almost no people of color that are in this industry," Dan says. "What I end up hiring is a bunch of white middle-class young people to create communications aimed at inner city audiences and who try to expropriate that culture and sell it back to them in order to move goods and services. That's not right."

When the agency was young, former governor Neil Goldschmidt convinced Dan that a leading local business's responsibility is "to learn from and support the community," Dan recalls. The message stuck, and after decades of civic engagement and philanthropy, Dan found himself contemplating his eventual retirement. "My late wife and I thought that we'd head to the coast, but after two weeks," Dan says, "we ran back screaming to Portland. It made me really think about what mattered to me and what bothered me that I'd love to change." That's when the idea for Caldera was born, with the simple mission to "bring kids with limited opportunities, both from the city and from the country, together to make art."

It was both a professional and an altruistic decision, Dan says. "The idea was to help build up and diversify the next generation of professionals in my industry, and to help change young people's lives through art education and the freedom to experiment creatively. So my retirement program became to start a camp that taught the creative arts!" Dan's second wife, Priscilla Bernard Wieden, has been every bit as enthusiastic about and generous to the camp as Dan is. When she met him, she says, "I knew nothing about Wieden+Kennedy except for the name of the building. I had a background in alternative medicine, and I decided I didn't want to learn anything about Dan's public face: I wanted to meet the real man," she says, smiling, "and he's a kid at heart, just like all of these kids."

At their suggestion, we meet with Dan and Priscilla during one of the camp's summer sessions. The turnoff to Caldera falls just as the Santiam pass begins to curve down toward Black Butte, Sisters, and the red-gravelled expanses of Central Oregon. Caldera rests on the shores of Blue Lake, which lies behind and above Suttle Lake. The drive around Suttle Lake is scenic: ponderosa and sugar pines creep down toward the waterline, and on the

Inside a studio at Caldera. Photo by Kristin Anderson.

A Caldera staff person, Dan Wieden, and Priscilla Bernard Wieden. Courtesy Caldera.

horizon, Mt. Washington's sharp silhouette punches up into the sky. The blackened snags of a forest fire that threatened the area a few years ago are still visible, but Caldera's campus is comparatively verdant. Its main hall, a striking, vaulted, wooden-beamed contemporary lodge, blends organically with the cabins and teepees and tall trees that surround it. Up the hill lies Blue Lake itself, a deep, crystalline body of water that, like Crater Lake, formed in a volcanic caldera, after which the camp is named.

Dan—or "Papa Bear," his camp name—and Priscilla—or "Moon-flower"—meet us in front of the main hall with another visitor in tow: Reena Evers, the daughter of civil rights leader Medgar Evers. Together, Dan and Priscilla give us all a sense of the bigger picture. "Some of the effect of Caldera is that you're taking [low-income, disadvantaged, often urban] kids out of one situation, putting them into a totally different geography, and giving them chance to choose a new name and to have a different experience than they've ever had before. Kids can create new identities here," Dan begins. Time is very structured at camp, which means that kids who "have had enough responsibility to last centuries" are given freedom from responsibility and thus the space to experiment, create, and play around. Taking urban kids and putting them into a place where, as Dan puts it, "there's dirt and bugs and real darkness" can be both tense and transformative. "The first time we brought kids here, the bus from Portland pulls up and little vans from Central Oregon start arriving and suddenly there are Native American and black and Hispanic and white kids all staring at each other." But pretty soon, Dan recalls, "it turned into a trading post of games and stories."

At this point the campers begin to file in for lunch, and we distribute ourselves among them. At our table, six girls—a Latina, a Native American, a couple of African Americans, and a couple of white kids—pile their trays onto the table and sit down. They hail from Portland, Madras, and La Pine, and they are getting along together like a house on fire. Like kids everywhere, they moan over and celebrate the food in equal measure, but they also talk about what their favorite activities have been that day—drawing, a nature walk, photography. Popsicles are passed around for dessert, and as their tongues turn bright orange and purple, the campers' excited conversations continue. They look forward to more photography, to pottery, to a ropes course, and to swimming in the lake; they think the teepees in which they sleep are awesome but sometimes noisy; and they speculate widely about the depth of lake—when told it may be as deep as the US Bank tower ("the Big Pink") is tall, the Portlanders gasp and fall silent. Announcements echo through the hall and are met with affirmation and enthusiasm, and after a polite and organized tray clearing, the campers are gone, dispersed to their next activities.

It's a pointedly affirmative and respectful atmosphere here, explains Priscilla. "There are no putdowns here, only put-ups." At the final day of each session, everyone sings a song called "we are the ones we've been waiting for," she says, and each kid writes a word down that positively describes each other camper. All campers go home with these words of affirmation.

Camp attendees have such positive experiences that many of them return to work at the camp themselves. Addy (that's her camp name) has worked her way up through the camp hierarchy to become an Advocate Female Supervisor. Coming from Portland, she recalls her first night at Caldera. "It was strange: I was nine and it was my first time away from home. I cried every night, but being able to act and do art and yell and be crazy really brought me out of my shell. It was wonderful." Just seeing the stars properly was transformative, Addy says. "The other night, I wrapped up in blankets and watched a meteor shower. You could never see that at home. This place is inspirational: it changes lives and it affects so many kids. Everyone loves Caldera when they come here." Beyond her sterling work as a camp employee, Addy is one of Caldera's many successful graduates. She recently graduated from Howard University in pre-med and will be continuing her studies in the autumn.

"Big Bird," another camper-turned-staffer, has been coming to Caldera since 2001. Big Bird has done similarly well for himself: he gigs regularly with his band, Bel Mizik, and works as a SUN School program coordinator in Portland. But in the summer, he gives himself over to Caldera. Big Bird is huge, dwarfing the campers and most staff by some measure. "When I first came, I was really short—five foot two. The summer between eighth and ninth grade I grew a foot. I came consistently each year. . . . Campfire was the best, because I've always been a performer. You get to sign up to do poetry or songs or tell a joke: it's an outlet, and you get good at it. There was a gentleman named Robert who couldn't write when he came for his first year. This year, his last year as a camper, he won the poetry slam for all of Portland."

Big Bird, incidentally, refers to all male campers as gentlemen. One session, the story goes, he heard a young man call a girl a "bitch" and started plotting how to improve young campers' levels of respect for one another. "I started running my teepee group like a company. I was CEO, the company was called D4G ('Destined for Greatness'), and the boys could never talk to me about problems without going through a manager first. The goal was to teach them to advocate for themselves and to peer-to-peer problem-solve, and it worked. We also had etiquette sessions," he says, grinning. "Every meal, a formal invitation was given to a lady to join us. 'On behalf of D4G, we would like to invite you to breakfast.' One guest was Chow, Caldera's caretaker. A lot of kids looked at her as a janitor, but we spoiled her, pulled out her chair, poured her water, gave her gifts."

Camp staff Addy and Big Bird pose in front of Caldera's grand fireplace. Photo by Kristin Anderson.

Both Addy and Big Bird agree that Caldera yields young people who are more empowered, independent, and respectful of others, in part because of the camp's discipline, but mostly because of the camp's emphasis on personal exploration and on finding one's voice and talents. "My little brother, Little Bird, comes to Caldera," Big Bird says. "He can play, like, seven different instruments." Other campers show similar genius. "We had a Columbia University professor of writing come to camp to teach writing," Dan says. "She was teaching kids metaphor and analogy, and she gave them the first line of a poem she asked them to write. 'Blue Lake is like—GO!' One Hispanic young lady wrote, 'Blue Lake is like love: in the beginning, it's very shallow, but if you keep going, it gets deeper and deeper.'" Dan pauses, still wowed by the moment. "I mean, how did she even *learn* that?"

The campers also participate in a wide range of visual and musical arts, and have the chance to continue their artistic study throughout the year: Caldera runs programming in twelve middle schools throughout Portland and Central Oregon that have a high percentage of low-income students. Like the "I Have A Dream" Foundation, mentorship is a key, and they stick with kids

Campers in Blue Lake. Photo by Kurt Hettle. Courtesy Caldera.

all the way through their high school graduation and beyond. "The thing that I love about Caldera is that some people think we're trying to train up artists, but really we're just trying to train people to think creatively. It's a critical foundation piece for a productive life," Dan says.

Reena Evers chimes in. She is impressed, she says, because "the arts they're learning here are a survival tool. What is given here are tools of life: it might be learning woodcutting, but it's also being out in nature, and learning about traditions, and bringing together what's available in this life. I feel safe here, coming from a place before that's not been safe, and I connect with a lot of the kids here. These kids embody the spirit of my dad [slain civil rights leader Medgar Evers]. They inspire us to go forward." Both Dan and Priscilla look surprised and gratified. ("Reena was eight and a half when her father was shot in the driveway of their family home," Priscilla says later, "so she knows fear, and for her to say that about Caldera, and about her father, is incredible.") Reena's comments cut to the quick of Caldera's mission. Their bridge-building summer camp, as well as the arts mentorship programs they run all year for some of Oregon's most low-income and at-risk students, have meant that young people are finding a safe space in which to develop their voice, their talents, and their power.

When asked why they give to Caldera, Priscilla urges Dan to tell a particular story. He acquiesces. "My parents were middle-class folks when I was growing up: my mom was the head of the PTA, and my dad worked in advertising. They were generous with their time and with their money, although we didn't have a lot of it," he recounts. "After we were married, my late wife and I lived for a while in a little house on Eighty-Fifth off of Sandy [in Portland], and we were really watching our finances closely. One day, my aunt Dot came in with two big bags of groceries." ("She's the sweetest person ever," Priscilla interjects.) "I said, 'no, we're fine,'" Dan continues, "and I kept arguing with her. She said, 'let's speak outside for a minute.' When we went out, she said, 'if people don't accept gifts, then it doesn't allow people to give gifts.' I thought about that, and I said 'OK.' She had a good point."

After lunch, and after a visit to the stunning wood-and-glass Caldera library and an airy, naturally lit, purpose-built studio that houses drawing and photography workshops, we head up the hill, past a trust-building zip-line and slack-line course, and to the lakefront, which is quiet—at least temporarily. A monolithic, monster-truck-sized inner tube bobs against the dock, the sun scatters across the clear, cold water, and a few faint clouds hang high above the hills. "There's something about this place," Dan says, "something that just happens here." Priscilla adds, "we know this spot had been inhabited for hundreds of years by Native Americans, and we imagine it was considered a fairly special place."

It certainly is to the campers they host each summer. "It's an amazing organization," Addy says. "I would never think of acting or drawing or painting or knitting, and now I do all of those things." Big Bird agrees with Addy, saying that his experience at Caldera "puts me in a place where I want to make a difference. That's what I was taught, and it stuck, and I want to do the same. At Caldera, I had an opportunity that not everyone had, and it's a privilege and an honor to be a part of it." A bell rings, and young artists from every walk of life come tearing onto the docks, hurling themselves over the inflatables and into the frigid lake.

OTHER PLATFORMS, OTHER OPPORTUNITIES, OTHER NEEDS

Caldera's educational mandate is just one tiny piece of the wider arts and heritage patchwork that makes up Oregon's cultural sector. There are many pieces missing from this chapter's discussion. For example, direct grantmaking to or private patronage of individuals or artists' collectives forms an essential aspect of cultural philanthropy. Certain artistic media—film, for example—also deserve more coverage, as do events like the Britt Festival, the Wheeler County Bluegrass Festival, the Mt. Hood Jazz Festival, and PICA's Time-Based Art (TBA) Festival, which play an important role by giving an economic boost to their host communities, opening doors to new audiences, and providing platforms for the debuts of new works. Lecture and reading series, public discussion forums, and the many new history/science/ humanities pubs, where experts present topics in informal settings, also represent economic as well as intellectual stimuli. From the Baker City Arts Center, The John G. Shedd Institute for the Arts in Eugene, the Four Rivers

Portland's Lan Su Chinese Garden. Photo by Kristin Anderson.

Cultural Institute in Ontario, and the wonderful Sitka Center for Art and Ecology in Otis, multipurpose art centers often play a vital role not only in community life but in inspiring creative partnerships between arts, culture, and heritage disciplines. Nonprofit recreational and meditational spaces like Portland's Lan Su Chinese Garden, Japanese Garden, and Rose Garden also need to be celebrated, as do the public spaces—the gardens, parks, squares, gazebos, and piazzas—that unite communities around shared experiences. Moreover, there are whole towns, like Joseph, Ashland, and Sisters, whose strong artistic centers have provided regional entry points to the arts for their surrounding communities, and who are tangible examples of the good a robust arts scene can do for local communities' social and economic well-being. All of these would reward higher levels of civic investment.

LEADERS IN ARTS FUNDING

In our introduction, we highlighted the Schnitzers' historic lead gift to the Portland Center for the Performing Arts and the Hults' support for Eugene's Hult Center for the Performing Arts. Pete and Mary Mark have had a similar impact on the arts scene. Teaming up with other architects of Portland's urban renaissance like Bill Naito, Bing Sheldon, and Ira Keller, the Marks gave significant amounts of money to renovate the Multnomah County Central Library, to construct Pioneer Courthouse Square, to modernize the Oregon Historical Society's building, and most famously to overhaul the Portland Art Museum. Their gifts have helped create and cement Portland's reputation as a city with rich cultural offerings.

Other monumental events in arts philanthropy include the bequest of Portland manufacturer Fred Fields. When Fields passed away in 2011, he left the bulk of his estate to thirteen nonprofit organizations in Oregon for a total bequest of $191.5 million. "Fred was incredibly secretive about this," said

A reception with authors Barry Lopez and Cheryl Strayed at Literary Arts. Photo by Kristin Anderson.

Richard Canaday, the lawyer for Mr. Fields estate. "People didn't realize how wealthy he was."[21] In making his gifts, Fields gave the beneficiaries maximum flexibility on how to use the funds, placing no restrictions on twelve of the bequests, and designating only that his $150 million bequest to the Fred and Sue Fields Fund at OCF be used to support arts and education. This kind of institutional trust is highly valuable to grantmaking institutions, as well as to the public, who will benefit from his legacy to Oregon's artists.

Although too few foundations cite cultural funding as a priority, a handful of private foundations are also taking a leadership role in the sector. The Collins Foundation has been responsible for funding and sustaining a great deal of our most treasured and famous arts and cultural organizations, in addition to funding many smaller projects. The Meyer Memorial Trust has also been instrumental to a number of arts organizations. Under Director Martha Richards' leadership, the James F. and Marion L. Miller Foundation has taken an active role in helping to restructure their grantees' financing so that they operate on firmer financial footing and meet certain stability benchmarks. Their work with the so-called big five major arts organizations in Portland (Portland Opera, Oregon Symphony, Oregon Ballet Theatre, Portland Art Museum, and Portland Center Stage) on deficit reduction is a well-thought-out management plan and an interactive, engaged mode of philanthropy. Beyond the big-five initiative, The Ford Family Foundation has just created a special fellowship for practicing artists. And under President and CEO Max Williams' leadership, the Oregon Community Foundation is moving toward a greater involvement with arts, fulfilling its responsibilities to the new Fields' gift, which will make OCF the largest arts funder in the state.[22]

There is a burgeoning recognition among some leading arts funders of the importance of general operating support. Many cultural organizations agree that the type of funding being offered is just as important as the amount. Currently, many cultural nonprofits are forced to rely overly on earned income (for example, ticket sales) and program grants because so few funders offer grants for day-to-day expenses. This trend often prompts the creation of new programs to attract grants, when in reality unrestricted multiyear grants to shore up operational expenses would create more resilient, robust arts organizations and would strengthen existing programs. Oregon's most progressive arts funders are realizing this and offering more unrestricted operating support.

PUBLIC-PRIVATE PARTNERSHIPS AND THE OREGON CULTURAL TRUST

Here in Oregon (and across the nation), various schemes are being discussed or enacted to help raise the levels of public funding for arts, cultural, and heritage sectors: license plates, room taxes, income taxes, sales taxes, cultural districts, Multnomah County's art tax (which may or may not be renewed). Those schemes that have been implemented have had some positive effects, but they cannot easily counter decades of funding cuts and the overwhelming needs that have resulted.

One promising public-private partnership—still underutilized and underfunded—is the Oregon Cultural Trust (OCT). Created during Governor Kitzhaber's second term with nearly unanimous support from the Oregon legislature, the Cultural Trust is funded via a cultural license plate, some state assets, and individual and corporate donations that receive a 100 percent tax credit. The trust, which gathers arts, heritage, and humanities organizations together under its umbrella and incorporates a partnership with county and tribal cultural coalitions, has granted over $14 million to arts and heritage organizations and to each county and tribal association. It has a tax incentive structure that allows individuals and businesses to make donations to over thirteen hundred arts and heritage organizations. The donor then makes a matching grant to the Oregon Cultural Trust, which can be deducted back *in full* from state taxes. This means that individuals can double the impact of their giving, and in turn, that we can all do our part. It sets "a national model for government funding innovation," says Christine D'Arcy, former director of the Oregon Arts Commission. "It has created a powerful incentive for giving to culture—a tax credit that rewards increased philanthropy."

The Cultural Trust emerged out of a desire "to attract people who don't necessarily have the money to start a trust themselves. Arts and heritage support is always the first thing to be cut, and this trust means that anyone can be a Schnitzer or a Swindell because you're giving into this collective pot of funds," says former OCT manager Kimberly Howard. The OCT helps break down the urban-rural divide, too, because while the majority of

Public art in Joseph (famed for its bronze foundries). Photo by Kristin Anderson.

contributions come from Portland Metro area, the trust distributes funds to every county and tribal federation in the state. "We can't live in isolation," Kimberly explains, "and the Trust encompasses a much larger philosophical and geographical tapestry—it brings Oregon together, helps bridge some of those divides." One nonprofit director said that "one of the real patrons of the arts today is not one person, but hundreds and hundreds of people through the Cultural Trust."

But at OCT's current levels of funding, it can only distribute about a million dollars a year. The organization is working to build an endowment of $200 million, so that it could distribute a more significant $10–12 million per year in grants. Currently, their permanent fund stands at $20 million, which frustrates Kimberly. "If we could get at least half of Oregonians to buy in, they could buy in at $10 a year for ten years and at the end of that decade we'd have our $200 million . . . think of the impact that would come out of these small contributions!" Christine D'Arcy agrees. "Oregonians should support the organizations they care about. If we could create a culture of giving in our state, and help people understand that they can take personal action to make a difference, there could be real change," she says. "There is way more potential in the realm of individual giving."

A SHARED COMMITMENT

The struggles of the Oregon Cultural Trust—and its enormous potential— are mirrored in other government arts agencies and statewide arts organizations, including the Oregon Arts Commission, the Oregon State Historic Preservation Office, the Oregon Heritage Commission, and those cradles of education and discussion, Oregon Humanities and Oregon Public Broadcasting. Currently, low levels of arts funding for these and for arts nonprofits are accepted by the public as a matter of course, leaving most arts organizations in a position of channeling all of their resources and energy into raising the money they need to subsist. Established organizations are stretched so thin right now, and receive so few grant dollars, that fledgling organizations will struggle to get off the ground: a major new professional orchestra is unthinkable in the current arts climate, and few new theaters, community halls, or museums are being built or opened.

Raising levels of government funding—which will require citizen voices, letters, and votes—will help. But government funding is only half of the solution: private donors, volunteers, foundations, and corporations need to up their games. As Jerry Hulsman and others have noted, a healthy arts scene attracts employees and more business. "My vision for the future is no different from any arts organization right now," says Julie Vigeland of the Oregon Arts Commission and longtime advocate for Portland Center Stage.

"I hope that arts organizations who operate responsibly are able to carry on their craft and do so without fear of imminent demise, that they have stable funding, something that's adequate to get the job done. . . . It's not a grand vision, because we're not at the point where we can think of a grand vision yet." "What if we value arts, heritage, and culture as if it really mattered to our lives?" Kimberly Howard asks. "People see their value, and yet it's not yet translating into investment. Our society will be stronger for acknowledging that value with solid funding."

So what is that value? Why should we elevate cultural funding? The answer floods back in chorus. "The vast majority of what we know about past civilizations comes from their art and architecture. One of the things that Oregon's arts and heritage institutions are doing today is laying down a marker for what our civilization is about. Moreover, the arts work in the present, too: they can raise very important questions about our society that need answering, need addressing, and they can raise these questions in ways that create empathy, interest, and engagement rather than polarization or apathy," says Paul Nicholson. José González says, "Art is the big picture—it's our understanding of nature, of industry, of the environment, of society. Once you have an appreciation of art, you see things differently, more wisely. Because of this, it is a conduit for better understanding between and amongst people." Fishtrap's Ann Whitfield Powers agrees, and adds that we have an obligation to keep people's souls fed as well as their bodies. "Cultivating creativity is a conscious decision. Today, when there's so much pressure toward multitasking and technologies, in-depth thinking and true imaginative creation has to be a conscious commitment. I think cultivating the soul is as important as cultivating the body: we have to feed the mind and the imagination, and help people to realize that their creative selves are powerful. We all have an obligation to keep that creativity and that passion *alive*."

Ultimately, attitudes toward arts and heritage support may be changing, but they are changing far too slowly. Funding these sectors is a matter of urgency and survival. As Kevin Irving, artistic director of Oregon Ballet Theatre, puts it, "the arts can't fund themselves. We'll never earn enough money to make ourselves sustainable. We rely on stakeholders and donors to make up the gap: because of the nature of art, that's part of the business model." Put simply, arts and heritage need public and private subsidies just like teacher training needs subsidy: Oregonians need to support what society values and needs, not just what makes money.

The Oregon Public House's motto. Photo by Kristin Anderson.

7
Building the Future: Community Philanthropy, the Next Generation of Givers, and New Models of Giving

"Each of you might suggest different words, but our goal certainly is the same: a better Oregon."
—Tom McCall, inaugural message to the 1971 Oregon Legislature

"Our goal as concerned Oregonians is to increase the number of donors and the amount that people give."
—Sally McCracken

At the heart of this book are two pointed and related messages. The first is that nonprofits provide absolutely vital services to our state and are an essential pillar of our civic structure: we cannot take them for granted. Second is that their success relies on the generosity of donors and volunteers. Whether you help out as a soup kitchen cook or writing tutor or board member, whether you donate money to a scholarship fund or $5 a month to Friends of Trees, your contributions are essential to the function and progress of Oregon's society.

But there is a third key message: there is room for improvement in our levels of giving. According to Volunteering In America's 2012 survey,[1] only

34.1 percent of Oregonians volunteered in their community, which means that 65.9 percent didn't. The Oregon Community Foundation's *Giving in Oregon* 2013 report finds Oregonians donate an average of 2.25 percent of our income to charity.[2] While these volunteering and giving rates place Oregon above the national average in both categories, we still fall well below the top states in both volunteerism rates and the percentage of income donated.

We think Oregon can do better. With that in mind, this chapter looks toward the future, celebrating leaders in three areas essential to improving Oregon's philanthropic participation levels: community-wide grassroots fundraising; younger generations of givers; and ingenious new models of giving, including one that taps into another of Oregon's most lauded and vital cultural assets, beer.

INCREASING COMMUNITY PHILANTHROPY: GRASSROOTS PROJECTS, LOCAL LEADERSHIP

In the spring of 1994, a small group of civic leaders launched a thoughtful effort to increase charitable giving in Oregon. Leading this group was Sally McCracken, a founder of Central City Concern's alcohol treatment program, the chair of the Oregon Community Foundation's board, and, following in the footsteps of her mother, who had encouraged and nurtured her civic engagement, a volunteer and donor to nonprofits since she was very young.

Sally sensed that Oregon's levels of giving were not as impressive as they could be, but there were no objective indicators with which to test her assumption. Was Oregon above or below the national average? Did we give to education more than to arts or vice versa? Where were the gaps and the possibilities? In order to increase charitable giving, Sally thought, we first must understand what it is. To do this, she convened a group of civic leaders who together commissioned the statewide research that led to the first *Giving in Oregon* report, published in 1994 by OCF.

The press gave the report's findings front-page coverage, and philanthropist John Hampton said that it was like a light bulb being switched on. "We understood giving for the first time and the vital role it plays in Oregon," he declared.

Sally McCracken. Courtesy the Oregon Community Foundation.

In highlighting rates of giving to certain population demographics and nonprofit sectors, *Giving in Oregon* underscored the key role nonprofits play in shoring up our civic structure—and thus the vital importance of philanthropy to our quality of life. One of its findings was that while established donors should be giving at higher rates (as compared to national averages of giving), Oregon nonprofits also needed to develop a wider base of donors. As Sally put it, philanthropy needed to move beyond main street and reach new pockets of donors and volunteers who were not yet participating fully in building their communities. To expedite this process, Sally called for two key reforms: the founding of the Giving in Oregon Council to monitor and promote charitable giving, and increased access to training and support for nonprofit leaders seeking to attract a broader range of donors.

Raising levels of giving never just *happens*: it takes someone to push, to move a need into the spotlight. In the years since the first report, Oregon has managed to increase its levels of community philanthropy and broaden its donor base. Sally helped with this by campaigning for greater assessment and advocacy; others have helped by increasing levels of support for nonprofit and grantmaking professional organizations such as the Willamette Valley Development Officers, Philanthropy Northwest, Grantmakers of Oregon and Southwest Washington, the Nonprofit Association of Oregon, Emerald Valley Development Professionals, and the state chapter of the Association of Fundraising Professionals.

Across the last few decades, there have been many outstanding efforts to stoke community engagement and widen communities' sense of what is possible. Some community campaigns have raised eye-watering sums through broad support: in the mid-1990s, for instance, former executive director of the Portland Art Museum John Buchanan and his wife, Lucy, who was the museum's development director, raised over $125 million dollars in under ten years to fund the museum's renovation and expansion—by doing so, they opened the city's eyes to the levels of local giving that were possible with a little creativity, charm, and persistence. Elsewhere, the University of Oregon's Campaign for Oregon brought in record gifts for the school; Portland Center Stage's Gerding Theater campaign established a new arts center in the Pearl District; and the United Way has built a reputation on its ability to draw upon broad community support and to transform communities' contributions into significant new initiatives around education, income, and health.

But the amount raised is in some ways less important than the act of elevating community participation. The remainder of this section will look at efforts to broaden community engagement, both by celebrating grassroots community campaigns and by highlighting efforts to strengthen the local leadership that drives such campaigns forward.

PORT ORFORD PUBLIC LIBRARY:
100 PERCENT COMMUNITY-BUILT

Many fundraising campaigns are smaller than the Portland Art Museum's but are no less impressive in their ability to mobilize donors and volunteers. Port Orford's library is a fitting example. Although Port Orford has had a library

Tobe Porter (left) and two patrons of the library. Photo by Kristin Anderson.

since 1921, its collection had long outgrown the meager room allocated to it near City Hall. In 1995, locals formed the Library Foundation, a nonprofit established to find the collection a permanent home. Port Orford is not rich—54 percent of its inhabitants are low to middle income—but for them, having a good library was nonnegotiable.

Tobe Porter, who had directed the building of the Langlois library up the road, was recruited to take charge of the project. "I love to raise money, and I wanted to build this. I'm happy to be the person at the front—someone's got to be," Tobe says with a laugh. "For a project like this, you have to start small and start locally. The land that the building sits on was donated by Eldon Deen's daughter. Many of our books come from the community. The Girl Scouts troop gave $73. It wasn't about how much we raised, it was about how much we involved the community and made it their project." That level of community support made it easier for the Rose E. Tucker Trust to commit $15,000 in seed money to the project, which in turn validated the library foundation's application for a federal grant of $500,000. All told, the foundation raised $1.8 million, a third of which came from the people of Port Orford.

The construction bids came in higher than expected. Tobe and her crew "were dashed to the ground, we were done in. And we told that to the community, and they got behind us, even the ones who initially were opposed to the project." The foundation put a bond on the ballot for $450,000 that would only be issued if it were needed. About 70 percent of the community voted in favor of the bond, although in the end they did not need to use it: under Tobe's leadership, they raised the additional funds. Thirteen years after the process began, the library was completed, and on the day it opened in 2008, Tobe recalls, "four hundred or so people lined up outside, and they would just stop and look at it and cry with pride. It's a library that the community built 100 percent."

What's more, its day-to-day operations, furnishings, and functions reflect its grassroots origins. Sixteen volunteers run the front desk, and the library has only four paid staff, none of them full time, including Tobe, who says "I am humbled by the dedication of the volunteers to this, I really am." The library's shelves are lined with books, many donated by members of the community, and its walls are covered with art either donated or lent by the community. In its main corridor, a beautiful bronze girl stands raising a placard reading "Imagine," an appropriate sculptural donation from a local supporter, and a warm evocation of the building's purpose and origins. On the wall opposite hangs a quilted tapestry of brightly colored books. An eye-catching display, this is Port Orford Library's donor wall: each book's spine is inscribed with a key contributor.

One of these is Peggy Alessio, whose family has been in the area since 1901. "This library is the soul of the community," she declares, "and it's been

Peggy Alessio next to the Library's beautiful donor quilt. Photo by Kristin Anderson.

exciting to watch its progression. It's such a great story, and I'm proud of my little role in it." It is also, she observes, an indispensible gathering place for the community. It has resources for job seekers, Internet access, and meeting rooms that host everything from Italian and GED classes to yoga, bridge, and regional governance meetings. "Everyone's very proud of it," Tobe says. "We're open seven days a week, and I think people feel that it means we don't have to be called 'Port Awful' anymore. When visitors come to town, they're brought here as well as to the beaches."

The Port Orford Library is such a source of communal pride and value that the town is embarking on a new library fundraising campaign. Their goal is straightforward: they hope to build an endowment fund of about $500,000 so they can operate the library from the accrued interest. The endowment, housed at OCF, thus far holds about $60,000 raised through resourceful campaigning. "We're doing small creative fundraisers to get the idea of an endowment fund out into the community," says Tobe. "Our story now is that we have this treasure and we want to remain debt-free forever. As frugal as we are, we still need about $10,000 to $15,000 a year in operating funds." They have all sorts of strategies for raising money and awareness, she adds: an Un-Birthday Party, a Christmas Bazaar, a soiree drolly called "The Non-Event," a reader board that runs along the building's roofline and is available to rent for about $25, and a dry-erase board near the check-out counter celebrating the donor of the day. They also are one of Amazon.com's "Smile" partner charities: if you select the library as a recipient, the company will donate a small portion of the proceeds from your purchase to Port Orford Library. As Tobe points out, "the amazing thing about the library is that its story comes from all angles: volunteers, book donors, small donors, art donors, grassroots funders, foundations. . . . It's a great model; a successful, ongoing model. And it is something the community is really proud of."

SEED-FUNDING AND SUPPORTING LOCAL LEADERS: THE MEYER MEMORIAL TRUST AND THE FORD INSTITUTE FOR COMMUNITY BUILDING

Communities like Port Orford across Oregon have proven themselves capable of leveraging local resources for local and statewide good. While most leadership comes from within the affected communities, philanthropic foundations have often helped support these leaders and their budding initiatives. Especially noteworthy are the diverse efforts of two foundations: the Meyer Memorial Trust and the Ford Family Foundation.

The Meyer Memorial Trust is beyond doubt Oregon's largest source of philanthropic support for innovation and change through what is referred to as "venture funding." Much like a venture capitalist, Meyer is willing to support efforts with a higher level of risk but that also promise a higher level of reward. Much of their funding is directed to brave grassroots projects. Doug Stamm, Meyer's chief executive officer, attributes this entrepreneurial thinking to Fred Meyer himself, the retail giant who died in 1983.

Many local nonprofit leaders and organizations got started with a grant from Meyer. The foundation provided lead gifts to Malheur Field Station, BRING Recycling, Self Enhancement, Inc., and Baker City's Oregon Trail Interpretative Center. It has granted to NAYA, IRCO, CIO, the "I Have a Dream" Foundation, and the Salem-Keizer Coalition for Equality; to Medford's Jazz Festival; to the Elgin Health District to establish the area's only dental clinic, and to many other small but essential grassroots efforts. The diversity and success rate of Meyer's grants are impressive.

Doug Stamm attributes Meyer's success rate to several factors: extensive due diligence before a grant is awarded; working in close partnership with nonprofits and other stakeholders in the field ("they are the experts," says Doug); and allowing enough time for a grantee to achieve success. On this latter point, Doug feels that funders ask the wrong question when they ask "How long is too long to fund a project?" Instead, he says, the question should be "How long is enough?" The willingness to stick with an organization can be incredibly validating for a small or start-up project, and it can also liberate the organization to focus more of its resources on programming and problem-solving and less on fundraising, which surely is the whole point.

Doug Stamm feels that Meyer's willingness to take risks has helped establish some of their most important projects: a leadership development program that was a partnership with the Coalition of Communities of Color and six minority-led nonprofits; seed funding for an affordable housing preservation fund that attracted other funders and has grown to over $30 million; operating support for Stand for Children so they could work on policy rather than fundraising; and the Willamette River Initiative, where Meyer support was the catalyst for a new coalition of public and private entities to improve water quality, habitat, and wildlife along the Willamette River.

The Ford Family Foundation's Ford Institute for Community Building (FICB) complements Meyer's efforts. Where Meyer supports community initiatives with seed grants, the Ford Institute for Community Building helps those initiatives come about and succeed by investing in promising local leaders. It specifically targets leaders of rural and small towns of less than thirty thousand people. These individuals participate in a five-year mentoring program that increases their personal, organizational, and community development skills, with the goal of building the capacity of a community to define and achieve its own vision of vitality.

In the past sixteen years, FICB has graduated over five thousand Oregon leaders from small communities across the state and is now serving between four and five hundred leaders per year, according to its director, Joyce Aske. The Ford Institute for Community Building's mission is simple, she says: empower communities so they have the capacity to define their own futures, and promote collaboration within and between communities. The leaders chosen for their program represent a diverse spectrum of the community, with young and minority leaders highly represented. By directing resources at smaller communities and by encouraging grassroots leadership, the institute has not only helped erode the urban-rural divide but also has built up equity and inclusivity within communities.

Amy Callahan of Cottage Grove is a graduate of the program and describes it as transformative to her and to her town. "The program invests in our community at a time when it feels like all resources go to urban settings. This is an opportunity for us, in rural settings, to take the ball and run with it. . . . It provides us all with a sense of connection and hope. It will help us learn how to talk to each other so that we can combine resources, build efficiencies, and help shape the direction of our future instead of letting things happen to us."

LOCAL LEADERSHIP: TENACITY AND CREATIVITY

As both Meyer Memorial Trust and the Ford Family Foundation recognize, it's ultimately all about having people on the ground working from within their communities to lead community improvements. Without Tobe Porter, for instance, the Port Orford Library would not be the glowing success it is today. It is her type of creativity and passion that helps elevate levels of community philanthropy and change lives for the better.

(Left) Dale Thomas introducing himself to one of the Hanoverian foals he and his wife raise. (Right) Elgin Opera House, restored in the 1980s and 1990s after a huge grassroots community campaign. Photos by Kristin Anderson.

Across the state, local citizens are working to elevate levels of giving in their communities. For instance, John Sweet, cranberry farmer, Coos County commissioner, and general pillar of the Coos Bay community, is an outspoken advocate for his hometown's philanthropic vitality. "Even in tough times, philanthropy's been remarkable here. We have a fantastic Boys and Girls Club, a great art museum, the Coos Bay Municipal Swimming Pool, a community scholarship program that started off with $10,000 fifteen years ago and is now $2.8 million," John says. "Times are tough and yet people in the community continue to support these really worthwhile efforts—it never ceases to amaze me how generous the population is and how much good gets done."

It's not hard to raise philanthropic participation levels when giving is made fun and easy, says Dale Thomas of Gold Beach. Dale, who is a Rotarian and also a board member of the Curry County Health Foundation, says that 73 percent of the money they have raised for the Foundation comes from donors who are not Rotarians or previous Foundation donors. "We bring a lot of new people in, and we do it because we're making it fun," he explains. "We went to Costco, bought a load of wine for the silent and live auctions, and made it into a party. We roped in new community members to donate things—there's got to be a piece of art in your house you can live without, or an experience you can offer, or a skill you can teach," he says. "You can turn philanthropy into something entertaining, into a project. We have another fellow in town who owns the bookstore, and together we contributed an auction item that was fifteen manly movies and six bottles of single-malt: we called it the man-cave!"

Most people are ready to give and ready to be asked, says Penny Allen, who lives up the highway in Bandon. "There's a lot of neighbor-to-neighbor,

South Coast dunes framed by goldenrod. Photo by Kristin Anderson.

friend-to-friend help here. If there's a sick kid, or hospital bills, there's always a huge outpouring of support, and people always step up to the plate." All it takes is someone organized enough to make the ask, she says. "It's very gratifying to be involved in a community that is caring. There was a bank teller who fell ill, and the community raised over $30,000 for her medical bills and her family." Everyone gets involved in the community, she says. Like Dale Thomas. Or John Sweet, who donates to Coos Bay's Boys and Girls Club, has held multiple civic offices, volunteers with the Coos Art Museum, has been on the Ford Family Foundation's board, and helped drive the founding of OCF's Ready to Smile Program. Penny also contributes at multiple levels: she has been a PTA and school board member, a den mother for the Boy Scouts, and is a Rotarian, among other roles. "I work very, very, very hard," she says, "because I feel like I can make a difference and bring things to the table that help organizations to grow."

Across the state, local leaders like Penny, Dale, John, Peggy, and Tobe are mobilizing citizens ready and willing to create and sustain projects that not only better local communities, but make Oregon's broader social structure more resilient. Each region of Oregon has its own wellsprings of community philanthropy waiting to be tapped. Local needs are often best served by local responses, and there is no better way to unite a community, and to introduce a permanent culture of giving back to it, than to rally people around local causes.

THE NEXT GENERATION OF GIVERS

Some nonprofit professionals worry whether younger generations will be as generous as their predecessors. Today's youth face challenges that previous generations were often spared—crippling student debt, high costs of living, inaccessible house prices, decreasing job security and social mobility—yet they are nevertheless engaged and generous with their time and resources.

TRADITION BETWEEN GENERATIONS:
FAMILY PHILANTHROPY

The next generations of givers are already firmly established in Oregon's philanthropic landscape, partly because they have had such excellent role models in their parents and grandparents. Many of the volunteers and donors interviewed for this book have spoken about the powerful effect their own parents' volunteering and engagement have had on them. As the latest *Giving in Oregon* report notes, 52 percent of adults whose parents gave money to nonprofits do so themselves, compared with 24 percent of adults whose parents did not regularly give; rates of volunteering align similarly.[4]

One formalized way of establishing a philanthropic habit is the family foundation. According to a survey by the Center on Wealth and Philanthropy, $41 trillion will change hands from one generation to another by 2052, and $1 to $2.5 trillion of that will be intergenerational wealth transfer within the next three years.[3] Family foundations can be independently run or established as an advised fund at a community foundation. Great wealth isn't necessary for this: at OCF, for instance, the minimum amount for starting an advised fund is $25,000. Even though the parents often create the advised fund, foundation staff can work with the entire family to clarify shared family values and goals and to implement a program to achieve them. The agreements establishing a family foundation may require that all family members attend site visits and engage in other activities that bring kids into direct contact with those to whom they are giving.

In the preceding chapters, we've seen a number of great examples of intergenerational family philanthropy: the Gray family, the Hayes family, Gert Boyle and Kathy Deggendorfer, and several others. The Austins are another superb example. Led by Ken and Joan Austin (Joan passed away in June of 2013 at the age of eighty-one), they are the founders of Newberg-based company A-dec, the largest privately held dental equipment manufacturer in the world with over a thousand employees. The Austins have deep roots in Oregon: Ken's great-grandfather is buried in Champoeg Cemetery, and their love of the local landscape inspired Joan to start up the Allison Inn so that others could visit the region they love. They contributed $10 million to OSU, they gave land for the Newberg Library, they host annual summer concerts in Newberg by the Oregon Symphony, and they have given lead gifts to countless other projects. Perhaps most impressively, Ken and Joan banded together with their son, Ken III, and his wife Cecilia and their daughter, Loni Parrish, and her husband Scott, to create a family fund that now includes three generations of family members as advisors.

Of course, many families don't have the resources to establish a family trust or foundation. But there are steps we can all take to pass on a philanthropic tradition. Bringing your kids along when you volunteer can be an effective way to cement in them the habit. And encouraging them to follow their passions by volunteering with or donating resources to organizations that work in their interest areas is also helpful—giving your child $5 a month to distribute can be as instructional as a formal family foundation. Similarly, instead of an advised fund, a family can open a checking account and dedicate it to charitable giving: many parents give their children equal voting rights at the table when deciding upon recipients of charitable gifts. Family volunteering, independent family foundations, advised funds, checking accounts, or a giving allowance for children all create invaluable pathways to involve the next generations.

COMMUNITY 101

Outside of the family, a handful of formal programs exist to introduce young people to giving back. Some schools have a community service mandate as part of their curriculum. Others, like Community 101, incorporate grant-making as well. Started by the PGE Foundation and now run by the Oregon Community Foundation, Community 101 is a project based in high school classrooms throughout Oregon that gives students the tools to effect positive change in their communities. Its structure is simple: a class receives $5,000 from a donor or business for grantmaking in the areas of arts and culture, education, the environment, and healthy families. The students are asked to

A Community 101 class at Roosevelt High School in Portland distributing their grants to nonprofits Raphael House and Impact NW. Courtesy the Oregon Community Foundation.

Community 101 students volunteering in Cottage Grove. Courtesy Oregon Community Foundation.

identify community needs and to decide how to focus and implement the grant. Then, at the end of the term, they present their grant awards.

What is impressive about the program is that it requires students to actually get out into the community, assess needs on the ground, and acquire a wider perspective on local needs by volunteering with a local nonprofit for two to five hours per month. Even though the program is of limited scope and duration, that kind of eye-opening experience can inspire a lifetime of giving back, and the classroom programming provides in-depth opportunities to discuss civic engagement, critical thinking, and global literacy, which are put into practice when students do their research and grantmaking. In 2013, approximately thirteen hundred students from sixty-two Oregon schools awarded over $310,000 to nonprofits, provided ninety-eight hundred hours of community service, and raised an extra $8,450 to boot.[5]

The program has successfully created pathways into community engagement for a large number of Oregon students. The statewide program director, Jennesa Datema, says that it works because "youth are involved in real life experiences that engage their hearts and minds. It helps them to become advocates in their communities for themselves, their families, or for people who are underserved or underrepresented. Handing over the philanthropic reins to young people, so they are donating money to services they think are important (and possibly to services they received), gives them pride and a sense of responsibility to pay it forward."

Community 101 is not really about the money—although students agree that it's awesome to give it away. The beautiful thing about Community 101 philanthropy is that young people give freely—without technical vetting or the matrices that accompany professional grantmaking—to causes that are urgent, heartfelt, and increasingly dear to them personally. That warmth and enthusiasm sets them up well to be engaged citizens and future philanthropists.

NEW PHILANTHROPIES, NEW FACES

Plenty of Oregon's young people are finding their own paths into giving, some pioneering groundbreaking philanthropic strategies along the way. In 2007, for instance, thirteen-year-old Katelyn Tomac Sullivan received the Oregon Association of Fundraising Professionals Youth Philanthropy award for her fundraising for cancer research. When her mom was diagnosed with breast cancer several years earlier, then third-grade Katelyn created a flier that read "Me and my friends are razing money for breast cancer research" and began fundraising. She started a nonprofit, Kate's Kids for the Cure, which has twelve members ranging in age from eleven to thirteen. Through car washes, golf tournaments, concerts, and bake sales, they raised over $35,000.[6]

Five-year-old Madison Alexander won the American Red Cross Oregon Trail Chapter's Junior Philanthropist of the Year award in 2013 for similarly herculean efforts. Madison, who lives in Northeast Portland, asked that for her birthday, family and friends donate to the Red Cross instead of giving her gifts. With encouragement from her family, Madison raised $50 in quarters and one $20 bill for the Red Cross—a pretty amazing contribution from someone who won't even be able to give blood for another twelve years.[7]

Zoe Brown, a high school junior, gives back to the community through activism and advocacy. When a delegation from the nonprofit One Million Bones visited her school to teach about genocide, she knew she had found her own opportunity to make a difference. In order to raise awareness of conflicts in Somalia, South Sudan, Burma, and the Democratic Republic of Congo, Zoe organized her neighbors, family, and fellow students to create more than 1,450 papier-mâché and clay "bones" to show solidarity with the victims.

Young people are also organizing more formally and more collectively for charitable purposes. Kids Helping Kids is organized under the auspices of a national organization, but its origins are with one local student at South Eugene High School, whose punishment for misbehaving was to take a leadership course. The lesson stuck, and through the class he came up with the idea for a fundraising beauty pageant with a twist—*guys* would compete and girls would act as their managers. The first round was wildly popular, raised a lot of money, and spurred new competitions. Now, the program has operated for over twenty years and is still going strong, covering a large geographic area, from Coos Bay to Corvallis. A total of eighteen high schools are involved, and together they have raised well over $350,000 to help with the medical care and morale of sick children in hospitals.

The lessons of leadership, compassion, organizing, and community-building that these students have taught each other were proven in heart-breaking circumstances a few years ago. In February 2011, Conner Ausland and Jack Harnsongkram, two students in the program, were swept out to sea by a sneaker wave while celebrating a Kids Helping Kids pageant on a field trip to Yachats. Devastated, their fellow students rallied to celebrate their friends' lives by raising funds for a memorial courtyard at their school, for coastal warning signs about sneaker waves, and even for scholarships to a school one of the boys had volunteered with in Central America. Despite the tragic circumstances, these students' dedication to giving back is as laudable as their methods are creative.

LEVÉ: YOUNG PROFESSIONAL WOMEN UNITING TO LIFT UP PORTLAND NONPROFITS

Created and run by a group of early-career professional women, many of whom work for nonprofits, Portland-based Levé is another innovative example of an emerging group of philanthropists. Created in 2004, Levé was born out of a holiday party thrown by a group of college friends to raise money for a local charity. All of Levé's members have deep roots in Portland and feel obligated to give back to the community that they love. Levé leverages its social and professional connections each year to draw in young people with little experience of traditional philanthropic structures in the hopes of creating a new generation of givers.

Building on that initial holiday party, Levé has thrown a signature Charity Ball every year since 2004, and in the first ten years, raised over $410,600 for its nonprofit partners. Each year, Levé rigorously vets and then partners

Levé's 10th Annual Charity Ball. Courtesy Ben Pigao Photography.

Levé board and committee members. Photo by Ben Pigao Photography.

with an established local nonprofit, providing financial and volunteer support that culminates in the ball (motto: "Party with a Purpose"). And each year, Levé has watched its fundraising ability grow, its applications from potential nonprofit partners multiply, and its participant numbers swell from a handful in its first year to over eight hundred attendees at Charity Ball 2013.

For its tenth anniversary in December 2013, Levé invited back all nine previous nonprofit partners—P:ear, the "I Have a Dream" Foundation of Oregon, the Children's Cancer Association, Growing Gardens, Schoolhouse Supplies, Friends of the Children Portland, YWCA of Greater Portland, Mercy Corps, and the Meals on Wheels People—and raised a record-breaking $130,000 to be divided equally among them. The money they raised mostly came from small individual donations contributed by under-forties, a notoriously difficult age group to access. And they raised almost $14,000 internally from their board and committee members.

Because of Levé, each of these nonprofits received not only around $15,000 of unrestricted funds in 2013, but also many hours of volunteer labor. "We wanted to provide capacity building for our partner organizations," explains founding member Kendall Murphy, "so we started asking our members to volunteer a certain number of hours with our nonprofit partner, and then we extended that call for volunteers to our social media and professional networks. We hold volunteer happy hours every year and we help direct capable volunteers to organizations that can utilize their skill sets—we try to match volunteers to nonprofits with precise attention to the needs and capacities of both. . . . We've not only raised funds but also a lot of volunteers," she adds.

Levé's model has attracted widespread support and praise, and not just from the twenty- to forty-year-olds who are their core demographic. At eighty, Polly Grose is one of Levé's older donors: she contributed $10,000 to

2013's fundraising efforts and offers up a passionate reason for her support. "What I admire about Levé, why it fulfills such a need in this country," she asserts, "is that it empowers the younger generation to pay attention to community needs. Your generation is so professional and important, and there isn't a lot of time to spend on developing contacts within the community or to work for the community good," she continues. "Levé is such a strong organization with a strong mission. I believe it can spawn similar organizations throughout the country. That's why I donate to Levé."

Unlike Polly's contribution, the vast majority of Levé's funds are raised from within the twenty- to forty-something crowd. The donations are not large—the largest individual check Levé had ever received before Polly's was for $5,000, and most gifts hover between $20 to $100—but Levé's base of support is huge. Through its supporters, and through the dedicated volunteerism of Levé's driven and creative members, Levé has lifted itself into a unique position of leadership. Groups from Seattle, Canada, and elsewhere have contacted Levé for advice on replicating its model, and an all-male fundraising group, Portland's Wingmen (surely a *Top Gun* reference), have also sought Levé's support and guidance.

Kendall says that watching Levé flourish has been a wonderful experience. "We've really been able to grow together professionally and take this to a serious level. We get to support the community in which we were all born and raised, and we also are able to encourage our networks to get involved philanthropically," she says. "Programs like this reengage our generation, and let our peers know that philanthropy doesn't have to mean a huge dollar amount—smaller contributions, and volunteer hours, are highly valuable." Financially, she explains, "it is hard for twenty- and thirty-somethings, and those coming up below us, to support organizations: we just don't have a lot of money. But when you incentivize engagement with a good party, and when you show people an easy and gradual pathway to giving that includes volunteering, it's a good way of getting us to give back in the long-term." Kendall explains. "I think a lot of people in our generation have a passion for seeing the Portland community thrive, and they understand that it's important to give back. Levé helps them see that no matter the amount, their contribution *matters*, and that, far from being staid and old-school, philanthropy can be entertaining, progressive, and fulfilling."

A BRIGHT FUTURE FOR YOUNGER DONORS AND VOLUNTEERS

Regardless of their pathway into giving, young people's desire to give back is clearly evident. According to the Case Foundation's "Millennial Impact Survey," 72 percent of millennials (born between the early 1980s and the early 2000s) want to participate in a nonprofit young professionals group; 52 percent are interested in monthly giving; and a whopping 83 percent of millennial respondents made a gift to a nonprofit in 2012.[8] Almost 40 percent of Oregon's sixteen- to nineteen-year-olds volunteer, as do 20 percent of its twenty- to twenty-four-year-olds, 30 percent of its twenty-five- to thirty-four-year-olds, and 43 percent of its thirty-five- to forty-four-year-olds. All of these demographic groups set aside time in their lives and burgeoning careers to volunteer.[9] As a result, many in the nonprofit world are heralding this generation as one of the most engaged and attentive in their giving, even more so than previous generations. According to research, their philosophies of giving differ slightly from preceding generations. Young people are more committed to specific ideologies and ideals, contributing time or money not only because they believe in giving back but because they believe in the *cause*.[10] They also are likely to follow up on their donations and remain attentive to progress on an issue in ways that solidify their commitment to civic improvement and make them informed donors. Jim White, director of the Nonprofit Association of Oregon (NAO), explains that they are also flexible as to how they accomplish their altruistic goals. NAO held a focus group of millennial and generation Y nonprofit leaders, and learned, Jim says, that "young people are seeing the opportunity to do good through different avenues, whether they're working in private, public, or nonprofits. We are anticipating a lot more movement between and within sectors."

Through the combination of young individuals' passions for a cause, their own trailblazing routes into philanthropy, and established programs and family giving strategies, the next generation of Oregon philanthropists are off to a strong start. Still, there are large sections of Oregon's youth that have neither familial role models nor clear institutional routes into civic engagement and volunteering. These young people represent a huge untapped resource for Oregon's communal future, and more efforts like Community 101 and Levé need to be directed toward them. Parents also need to take the lead. Joyce White, director of Grantmakers of Oregon and Southwest Washington, reiterates the urgency of this work: "I think that some people have lost sight of the social contract, have lost touch with what their individual responsibility is to the community. I think that if we can engage even more young people in philanthropic activity, we can rebuild that social commitment to community."

FUTURE PHILANTHROPIES: NEW MODELS OF GIVING

As Oregon's relatively high levels of youth engagement indicate, giving back to one's community has never been more feasible or popular. High profile international philanthropists—the Bill Gates and Warren Buffetts—are turning their giving into public events and are working to make philanthropy something talked about, drawing everyday citizens into dialogue and action.

Increasingly, the public is becoming aware that not only can everyone give back, but there are multiple pathways for doing so. Requests for volunteers are everywhere, and volunteers are increasingly visible, from greeters at airports to petitioners on the streets. People of all ages are following little Madison Alexander's lead in requesting charitable donations in lieu of birthday, wedding, and holiday gifts, and it's remarkably easy nowadays to buy a loved one a museum membership or to donate in someone's honor a goat or a llama or a well for clean drinking water from Heifer International or Mercy Corps. Run/race/walk fundraisers have also been very effective at raising awareness, attracting new donors to a cause, and engaging with the public in a very entertaining way while also becoming fundraising cornerstones for the organizations they champion (often medical advocacy, research, and care nonprofits).

Modern technologies make it possible to give with the click of a button, and fundraising and social engagement websites like Kickstarter, IndieGoGo, StartSomeGood, and social media apps make raising awareness, attracting small donors, and getting fledgling nonprofits off the ground an easier business—although as a result there is also more competition for donors' attention. Of course, the perennial challenge for nonprofits is to translate these new ways of giving into a stable and committed donor volunteer corps: it's easy to click a button once, but the trick is getting folks to check back and subscribe. Nevertheless, Oregon nonprofits have been creative in their use of these new technologies: for example, the Urban League has launched a Kickstarter campaign to fundraise for the publication of a new *State of Black Oregon* report in 2014.

For the most part, these new avenues into giving have done much good: they have made giving something that is talked about, publicized, and commonplace. They have also helped to revitalize the notion that, at whatever level, donating and volunteering is part of a wider social contract and essential to a healthy, happy sense of self. However, creative ways of fundraising are as numerous as Oregon's communities, and a number of stellar homegrown innovations occupy pride of place.

SOCIAL VENTURE PARTNERS:
POOLING RESOURCES FOR GREATER IMPACT

In 1997, Seattle-based computer engineer Paul Brainerd had a simple yet brilliant idea. He reasoned that it would be more effective for a group of well-educated professionals to pool their intellectual and financial resources to make grants rather than doing so independently, and out of that concept,

Social Venture Partners (SVP) was founded. Now, to start this section with a Seattle-based organization might seem like cheating, but there is an Oregon connection: when co-author Greg Chaillé learned about what Brainerd was doing in Seattle, he invited him to Portland to present to a few civic leaders who were keen to replicate SVP's model in Portland. He came, and shortly thereafter the Portland branch of SVP, which now boasts over 140 members, was founded.

These Oregon leaders were interested because SVP's model is unique and highly interactive. SVP members (or partners) must contribute at least $5,000 a year to the organization, which is added to a pool and distributed as grants. Partners play a strong role in the process of selecting grant recipients, and once a grant has been issued, they volunteer their expertise in order to help nonprofits streamline and maximize their internal capacity and organizational strength. In this model, the relationship between donor community and nonprofit is hands-on, with the donor engaging at the beginning and volunteering with the organization for the duration of the grant and beyond. This benefits the partners as much as the grantees: the partners study community issues together, learn about nonprofit strategy and context, and are offered training opportunities and workshops to educate them about philanthropy and civic engagement. Meanwhile, the grantee nonprofits benefit not only from these partners' pooled financial resources but also from their business, science, education, technology, and other relevant professional expertise. This makes not only for a stronger bond between nonprofits and their funders, but also for a more enthusiastic and empathetic attitude toward giving and volunteering.

In Portland, SVP has recently targeted early childhood education as a priority and is working with nonprofits including NAYA, the Latino Network, and Adelante Mujeres to ensure that northwest Oregon's most disadvantaged children don't start their educations off on the wrong foot. Internationally, SVP has more than twenty-seven hundred global members based in thirty-four offices ranging (as they say) from Boston to Bangalore. That Portland's SVP can have a huge impact locally while being part of a significant global network means that they can appeal to a wider philanthropic base and draw on the expertise of a global community of donors, advocates, and authorities—an innovative model, and a great opportunity for Oregon.

THE *WILLAMETTE WEEK* GIVE!GUIDE

Whereas SVP was a model successfully imported to Oregon, *Willamette Week*'s Give!Guide is a philanthropic innovation as Oregonian as myrtlewood and McMenamins. The Give!Guide was the brainchild of Richard Meeker and Mark Zusman, the publisher and editor, respectively, of the weekly Portland newspaper *Willamette Week*. The newspaper occupies a fond space in many Portlanders' hearts, not least because it has a reputation as a watchdog against corruption and injustice. It was their concern for the community that caused Meeker and Zusman to create one of Oregon's most innovative pathways to philanthropy.

In 2002, they started thinking about the demographic cohort *Willamette Week* "owns," a fair number of whom are between the ages of eighteen and thirty-five. Not only is this group the future of Portland's civic life, Meeker and Zusman realized, but it is also the demographic with the least established giving and voting habits. At the time, there was little being done to get younger people to vote, outside from the brand-new Bus Project, which organized young people to discuss and advocate around issues of democracy and sovereignty. And there was also little being done to promote philanthropy widely among young people in Portland. So the two owners divvied up the assignments: Zusman took voting and Meeker giving. Zusman created Candidates Gone Wild, a beer-infused extravaganza that lured young Portlanders into attending political debates. On the giving front, Meeker decided to publish a giving guide by recruiting grassroots nonprofits to be profiled in a special holiday seasonal insert that included giving incentives to help attract young donors unaccustomed to giving.

After setting up a basic web page to facilitate giving, they established a number of prizes, including the Skidmore Prize, named after the fountain in Old Town that is emblazoned with C. E. S. Woods' encomium "Good Citizens Are The Riches of A City," which would be given to leading nonprofit workers under the age of thirty-five. The first Give!Guide went out in 2004, and when the dust settled, *Willamette Week* had raised a little over $20,000 for twenty-four local nonprofits and had distributed four $3,000 Skidmore Prizes. In the intervening years, the Give!Guide has expanded exponentially, now profiling 129 handpicked nonprofits, boasting a shiny new website, and offering fun incentives for different levels of giving provided by a long list of corporate in-kind donors (ranging from a taco or coffee to a bottle of A to Z Pinot Noir). In its first nine years, the Give!Guide raised $7.3 million dollars; in 2013, its tenth anniversary, it raised $2,453,083 dollars through about seventy-five hundred separate donations. This, Meeker and Zusman declared proudly, was over ten times as much per capita as a similar campaign run by the *New York Times* had raised. Now, the Give!Guide has become a year-round enterprise for the paper, with a full-time executive director to oversee it. It is gratifying that the Give!Guide has become a permanent fixture: with its proven track record of attracting young donors into philanthropy, the Give!Guide is a huge success for *Willamette Week* and a huge benefit to the community at large. Richard Meeker considers it the paper's "single greatest

The Oregon Public House. Photo by Kristin Anderson.

innovation" and said he "sometimes feel[s] like a proud papa."[11] His pride is justifiable: there are few more effective means of attracting young donors en masse to public giving.

THE OREGON PUBLIC HOUSE:
HAVE A PINT, CHANGE THE WORLD

Tucked away in an unassuming part of Northeast Portland is certainly one of the most diverting, as well as the most innovative, new nonprofit models. Like the Give!Guide, it is designed to encourage those who do not give regularly to do so; also like the Give!Guide, its demographic is relatively young.

This is the Oregon Public House, which claims to be the world's first nonprofit pub. Founder and Board Chair Ryan Saari met us at its bar—a gorgeous hand-hewn slab of hardwood that he sanded and installed himself—to tell us about the project. "My background is ministry," he begins, "I'm a pastor by day, and I've always framed my work in terms of giving back. But religion in Portland especially can be a polarizing topic, creating a lot of riffs and schisms, and I wanted to start a way of giving back to the community that was outside the walls of religion because I think a lot of people without a faith share the same values and priorities as I do."

He began brainstorming with some friends about the means to bring his vision to life. "We realized that Portland had enough nonprofits," Ryan explained, "so then we thought about how we could support them financially. This was in 2009, when the economy was tanking and nonprofits were really struggling. I wanted an accessible entry point for philanthropy, a way for people to give back even if they don't have a huge amount of disposable income." He bounced around a few ideas but kept coming back to the idea of a social means of giving back, a community center of sorts, and at one point they were having beers and he said, "How about a pub?" Ryan's friends didn't laugh him out of the room, nor did a few other respected advisors, so he and his friends got to work.

Ryan, who sports a dark beard and a low-key, flannel-and-jeans style, is a charismatic storyteller, and his passion for the pub comes through keenly. "We had no money, no business experience, and no resources to buy and convert an existing restaurant. Plus, we didn't want to take any loans out: you don't want your charity to be in debt before it's even started." Eventually, Ryan found the perfect venue: the Oregon Public House is housed in a beautiful early twentieth-century fraternal lodge and ballroom that had fallen on hard times. "It had been taken over by a medical marijuana dispensary and smoking club, and it was really nasty inside," Ryan says. "Before we could revamp the kitchen, we were literally mopping black, congealed weed smoke off the ceiling."

With the help of about two hundred volunteers, and after three years of construction and fundraising in which they raised over $200,000, the Oregon Public House opened its doors in May 2013. Ryan and his volunteer team ended up stripping the building down almost entirely. Its tables and booths were built by volunteers with donated materials; the bench padding was sewn by a former elementary school principal; barstools were donated by a local wood- and metalworker; and a brick accent wall was laid by volunteers. The space is inviting—the tall windows at the front let daylight filter deep into the pub's recesses.

Its approach to giving is straightforward: when ordering food and drink, each diner and drinker is given a choice of several rotating nonprofits to receive all of the profits from their order. The choice of nonprofits is pointedly diverse: the pub wants drinkers to think about their philanthropic priorities and to engage, however briefly, with an issue or need. In its short

(Left) Oregon Public House's Give-O-Meter. (Right) Ryan Saari, founder of Oregon Public House. Photos by Kristin Anderson.

Some of Oregon's finest beer, in this case from Astoria's Fort George Brewery. Photo by Kristin Anderson.

life, OPH has raised money for many nonprofits, including the Black United Fund, My Voice Music, the Columbia Land Trust, Habitat for Humanity, and the Leukemia and Lymphoma Society. "Our motivation started not with running a great restaurant or a high-end drinking establishment: it started with how do we give back to our city in a fun, social, and profitable way, so that while we have great products and great service, nonprofits receive as much from us as possible," Ryan explains. But the beer is *good*, and the food is tasty, and the atmosphere in the pub is uniquely warm and appealing, only partly because they advertise "aletruism" on tap.

Above the bar, there is a shelf lined with pint glasses and steins labeled "The Wall of Founders." These glasses belong to donors who committed certain amounts to the pub's founding; in exchange, they receive a free drink a day, week, month, or year depending on how much they contributed. Near the bar, a chalkboard lists the charities to which patrons can donate their proceeds, and next to the bar near the entry is the Give-o-Meter, charting each nonprofit's levels of contributions and reminding every drinker that this is not business as usual.

In its first year, the Oregon Public House gave over $36,000 to local nonprofits. Ryan hopes to eventually hit $10,000 a month in donations, a remarkable rate considering how much new ground the pub is breaking. "There was no model for this," Ryan explains. "As the nation's first nonprofit pub, we had to do it ourselves, but our structure is sound and incorruptible—like any nonprofit, our board of directors is all-volunteer, including myself. We have a few paid staff now—the cook, a restaurant manager, etc.—but we are still strongly volunteer-run: volunteers bus tables, help us clean up, help us with marketing and accounting, spread the word, and serve on our board." He dreams of taking the pub to scale, he says, and making it part of Portland's cultural landscape. "Eventually, I would love to see this in three or four big Portland neighborhoods. Basically everything we make goes back to the city, so I'd love to see the city take ownership of the idea. The idea was definitely born out of Portland being number one in both nonprofits and in breweries, and we're already getting national attention for this model. We would hope that, you know, visitors would come to town and go to Voodoo Donuts and then go for a drink at our pub."

Regardless of future ambitions, however, the Oregon Public House is an exceptional example of philanthropic creativity, and its robust and resilient mode of income generation taps into a wider trend within progressive nonprofits. The best thing about the model, Ryan explains, is not only that new donors are drawn into philanthropy and volunteerism, but also that the pub is self-reliant: Portland is never short of beer drinkers. "I don't know much about the traditional forms of philanthropy," he says, "but one of the things we're trying to create in terms of a different model is one that's sustainable and replicable. The funds that we're generating are ones that are continuing to reproduce. In the traditional philanthropic model nonprofits have to continually ask for money, and then ask again, and again. What we want to do is create the machine that's giving out money, create a perpetuating source of charitable contributions." As simple as the idea sounds, finding a model that can do this is challenging; Ryan, with a fresh perspective on nonprofit structuring and appreciation for the best facets of Portland culture, has managed to achieve it. "We started out thinking about how we could give back to the city," he says simply, "and we think we've found a way to do it."

OREGON PHILANTHROPY:
GROWING, ADAPTING, MENDING

As a state, we have never before had such potential to take on the significant challenges we face: we have new technologies, new models of giving, and new philanthropic ideas and voices arising daily. An abiding love for community unites all of these donors and volunteers, whether they give $500 million, $5, or five hours; donate time to a beach clean-up, go door-to-door for an advocacy organization, or grant conservation easements on their land to Ecotrust. Some register their weddings with charities instead of department stores or contribute to politicians who are advancing something they believe in. Some take smaller paychecks in order to continue working for the nonprofit whose work they love. Others volunteer their time with individuals, or at schools, governments, nonprofits, and other organizations across the state. In many cases, people donate to their communities through estate gifts and will never see the beneficiaries of their wealth.

Oregon philanthropy is a diverse affair, with stories of leadership and creativity originating from unlikely and far-flung sources. *State of Giving* demonstrates how essential Oregon's nonprofits are: they shore up our civic structure, our wellness and empowerment, our self-definition, and our land and culture. Filling gaps across sectors and demographics left underserved by government, by prejudices, or by sheer lack of awareness, nonprofits are indispensably part of what makes Oregon *Oregon*. Our nonprofits need philanthropists—those donors of time, talent, and treasure—in order to facilitate their good work. John Sweet of Coos Bay says, "this state just does a lot of good things. We tend to dwell on our problems, but philanthropy is part of what makes our state great."

John is absolutely right, but with government cuts, growing social and racial inequities, increasing environmental conservation needs, and a burgeoning population, it will take a lot more philanthropy, from a much broader cross section of our society, just to keep us at our status quo. And volunteers can only do so much: demand is outpacing nonprofit growth and outstripping philanthropic contributions, and we are actively losing ground in funding our essential nonprofits. In 2012, the Nonprofit Association of Oregon and Portland State University's Institute for Nonprofit Management released the first *Oregon Nonprofit Sector Report*, which surveyed 10,429 non-profits across diverse sectors, all constrained by recessionary austerity. The report showed that while 60 percent of nonprofits had recorded increased fundraising in 2011, the demand for their services had increased by 65 percent.[12] Moreover, while there are over 22,000 nonprofits in Oregon, only 8,519 had paid staff as of 2010.

The organizations and individuals profiled in this chapter have given us a glimpse of what is possible: they have used passion, creativity, and a belief in community to elevate levels of grassroots giving, to train up the next generation, to lead by example, and to change our civic structure for the better. For lasting improvements to education, poverty, social inequity, urban/rural unity, environmental conservation, the arts, and other essential concerns to take hold, Oregon needs the rest of us to take note of these actions and innovations, and to follow suit with similar urgency, ardor, and ingenuity.

Conclusion
Oregon's Present, and Its Potential

*"Never doubt that a small group of thoughtful, committed citizens
can change the world. Indeed, it is the only thing that ever has."*
—Margaret Mead

"I have found that among its other benefits, giving liberates the soul of the giver."
—Maya Angelou

Oregon nonprofits, volunteers, and philanthropists have much of which to
be proud. Homegrown organizations like the Vibrant Village Foundation,
Ecotrust, and MercyCorps are making a difference nationally and internationally. Oregon-focused nonprofits like the Chalkboard Project, Port
Orford Ocean Resource Team, IRCO, Levé, the Maslow Project, the Oregon
Public House, and countless others are being consulted and feted nationally
because of their innovative and successful models. And Oregon's nonprofits
have immeasurably improved our own lives: reforming the education system,
conserving quintessentially Oregonian landscapes, advocating for social
equity, feeding and sheltering our most impoverished neighbors, bringing
communities together across the state, enriching our cultural heritage, and
increasing our state's capacity for innovation and social cohesion.

Oregon philanthropists are also making waves. For instance, Peter Stott, longtime donor to Portland State University and to the Portland Art Museum, was honored in 2013 with investiture into the Horatio Alger Association, a national society that honors outstanding philanthropists of higher education. Fred Fields' landmark bequest propelled him into the top tier of American philanthropists. And Phil and Penny Knight's monumental $500 million dollar challenge grant for cancer research at OHSU has gained widespread national attention, both for the size of the challenge and the short two years OHSU has to raise the matching $500 million. If that amount can be raised, it will make Oregon an international center of cancer research, and it should also serve as a catalyst for more giving across the board.

Oregon's volunteers, although often under the radar, also deserve great acclaim. In 2012, the most recent year such data has been calculated, Oregon volunteers contributed the equivalent of an astonishing $3.6 billion of service.[1] Longtime Oregon Symphony supporter Jerry Hulsman won the Volunteer of the Year award in 2013 for his indefatigable, year-round fundraising efforts. In the past ten years, the all-volunteer ARCS Foundation Portland Chapter has raised over $2 million for scholarships to support 129 doctoral scholars in STEM fields at OHSU and OSU: the hundred women who make up its membership are making a difference in these students' lives and helping to build up Oregon's economic and educational future. Some, like retired Portlanders John Nagelman and Dick Hazel, tutor in low-income school districts; others stay at home tending to loved ones, or plant trees, or, like Jennifer Little of the Washed Ashore Project, help construct giant penguins and seals out of marine debris. These individual efforts, whether given in a few hours or across a lifetime of dedicated service, make a huge difference in Oregon's communities. As Harriet Denison reminds us, "guys who coach Little League—that's philanthropy. It binds communities together more than money can, and we need to celebrate their role as philanthropists as well."

Because of the successes of our nonprofit, donor, and volunteer leaders, we know what is possible with a strong culture of giving. But the successes of others do not excuse us from doing our part. Throughout this book, we have approached Oregon philanthropy with a critical eye, acknowledging our underwhelming rates of giving and calling for a broader and deeper social commitment. According to a 2012 Volunteering In America study, Oregon ranks eleventh in the nation for volunteering, with 1.1 million of us—just over a third of the state's population—donating hours of service.[2] Eleventh in the nation may seem laudable, but if only a third of us are volunteering, that leaves a whopping two-thirds who aren't. Oregonians pride themselves on localism, self-reliance, and a pioneering attitude, but for that to be an authentic characterization, we could demonstrate a bit more of the get-up-and-get-it-done spirit.

Similarly, our monetary giving is solid but uninspiring. We rank seventeenth in the nation in percentage of income donated.[3] Number one and two are strongly religious states (Utah and Georgia), but just because we are more secular as a state does not excuse our lower rates of giving. Admittedly, our 2.25 percent is better than California and significantly better than Washington, our West Coast neighbors, but there is still vast room for improvement.[4] If Oregon were ranked in the top five nationally for charitable giving, our state would be a very different place—stronger, more resilient, more united, more engaged civically. We aspire to have the best basketball and soccer teams, but where is our competitive spirit when it comes to the amount of money and hours we give within our own lives?

A large percentage of donations in Oregon are made to religious institutions and universities. How much more robust our communities would be if we could *add* to the amount that we give to and volunteer with our largest and most personally familiar institutions, by increasing our giving to include those smaller, often less marketed organizations that enrich the fabric of our communities in diverse and less familiar ways? Imagine, too, how vital a society we would have if we were funding nonprofits at levels that went beyond mere subsistence. If each of us could find organizations that represent our values and interests and really get behind them—not just for the big, splashy capital campaigns, but for the day-to-day operating support and consistent volunteer hours that keep them going—then the nonprofits that shore up our social foundations would themselves be anchored on bedrock.

State of Giving profiles many outstanding nonprofits undertaking transformational work on some of Oregon's most urgent issues—the urban-rural divide, education inequity, hunger and homelessness, environmental conservation, minority inclusion and equity, and cultural programming. We do not want these nonprofits to merely survive—we want them to grow and flourish and provide their services in more effective and comprehensive ways; we also want them to work progressively toward permanent solutions. As David Rockefeller once said, "Philanthropy is involved with basic innovations that transform society, not [with] simply maintaining the status quo or filling basic social needs that were formerly the province of the public sector."

Far from being the province of the rich and privileged, giving back to our communities is a social obligation we all share and can all, in our own ways, *do*. Adrienne Livingston, former director of the Black United Fund, notes that "when people hear philanthropy, they think they need to be a millionaire. But philanthropy can be food, or a free music gig, or some accounting work." Giving is a kind of gateway drug, luring us into longer and

Mount Hood. Photo by Kristin Anderson.

more fulfilling commitments to causes and organizations. Your entry point is irrelevant—philanthropy's varied arms are entwined.[5]

We hope that *State of Giving*, in highlighting some of the organizations worthy of your support and engagement, has solidified your sense that there is something qualitatively wonderful and unique about the crazy patchwork of our state. Most of all, we hope it moves you to action. The Appendixes that follow provide some tips and resources to help you find meaningful volunteer and donor work at all commitment and ability levels. And finally, please spread the word. Whatever your mode of giving, publicly recognizing and discussing the importance of giving back encourages every citizen to make philanthropy and volunteerism a part of their daily ritual and raises awareness of the seminal role nonprofits play in our lives and communities. While there is much excellent philanthropic work going on right now in Oregon, for new sources of philanthropy to emerge, we need to keep talking about the diverse challenges we face as a state, and to keep celebrating those contributions of time, treasure, and talent that support the nonprofits working toward their amelioration.

If we can move beyond philanthropic minimalism, if we can take more risks with the organizations we support, if we can see past our neighborhood priorities to contribute to wider and more diverse needs, and if we can increase the number of Oregonians giving in whatever way is right for them, then Oregon will progress and thrive. We already have a strong sense of being Oregonians, whether we came here yesterday or 150 years ago. We are creative, innovative, passionate people. Now, we need to come together under a statewide vision and a lasting commitment to each other.

Acknowledgments

Our thanks to the many great folks—interviewees, advisors, and cheerleaders—who helped us with this book, including:

INTRODUCTION: Arlene Schnitzer and Barb Hall of the Harold and Arlene Schnitzer CARE Foundation, Kerry Tymchuk and Geoff Wexler of the Oregon Historical Society, Jamey Hampton, Vicki Shaylor of Hampton Affiliates, Mike and Sue Hollern, Loren Irving, Steve Stewart, the Oregon Department of Parks and Recreation, Duncan Campbell of Friends of the Children, Don Vollum, Joe Weston, Mike Keiser of the Bandon Dunes Golf Resort, Charlie Swindells, Sherrill Kirchoff.

CHAPTER 1: Don Frisbee, Bill Thorndike, former Secretary of State Norma Paulus, Charles Rouse, Gretchen Pierce, Kathy Deggendorfer and Brad Tisdel of the Sisters Folk Festival and the Americana Project, Jonathan Nicholas, Bob Moody, Sally McCracken, Melissa Hochschild and John Furgurson of the High Desert Museum and the rest of the Museum's staff, Charles Sanderson and Jodelle Marx and Donovan Jacob of Slamboo.

CHAPTER 2: John Tapogna of ECONorthwest, Ken Lewis and Sophie Phillips of the Oregon "I Have a Dream" Foundation, Ron Herndon and Elaine Harrison and Julie Antinonou and Leslie Mathies of Albina Head Start, Tony Hobson and Jeanette Lewis of Self Enhancement, Inc., Eli Morgan, Dave Hatch of Salmon Camp, Sue Hildick and the staff of the Chalkboard Project, Chris Otis of SMART, Eduardo Angelo and Annaliva Palazzo-Angulo of the Salem-Keizer Coalition for Equality, Dick Withnell, Chief Justice Edwin Peterson, Chief Justice Paul De Muniz.

CHAPTER 3: Beverlee Hughes and Denise Wendt of Food for Lane County, Mary Farrell and Roger Stokes of the Maslow Project, Monica Beemer and Genny Nelson and Brenda Morgan of Sisters Of The Road Café, Aleita Hass-Holcombe of the Corvallis Homeless Shelter Coalition, Teresa and Jay

Bowerman, Anna Jones and Andy Catts of the Clackamas Service Center, Pam Slater of ACCESS, Sherm and Wanda Olsrud, and Steve and Shelly Olsrud.

CHAPTER 4: Russ Hoeflich and Mark Strand of the Nature Conservancy, Nick Walrod and Joan Gray of the Gray Family Foundation, Susan Allen of Our Oceans, Julie Daniel and Sonja Snyder of BRING Recycling, Julie Rogers, Bob Jones, Ardyth McGrath, Peter Hayes of Hyla Woods, Leesa Cobb and Aaron Longton of Port Orford Ocean Resource Team, Larry Nixon, Jim Martin of Berkley Conservation Institute, Rachel Shimshak of Renewable Northwest, John Shelk of Ochoco Lumber, Truman Collins of the Collins Foundation and Wade Mosby of Collins Companies, Jim Walls of Lake County Resources Initiative, Duncan Evered and Lyla Messick of Malheur Field Station, Robin Engle of Oregon League of Conservation Voters, Doug McDaniel, Nils Christoffersen of Wallowa Resources, director emeritus of Sustainable Northwest Martin Goebel, Angela Haseltine Pozzi and Frank Rocco and Mary Johnson of the Washed Ashore Project, Jennifer Little, Tom and Kris Bowerman of the McKenzie River Trust.

CHAPTER 5: Harriet Denison, Jaime Arredondo and Laura Isiordia and Larry Kleinman of CAPACES Leadership Institute and PCUN, Matt Morton and Darla Hilmoe of NAYA, Joe Finkbonner of the Northwest Portland-Area Indian Health Board, former director of the Black United Fund Adrienne Livingstone, Midge Purcell and Julia Delgado of the Urban League of Portland, Sokhom Tauch and Djimet Dogo and Lee Po Cha and Margaret Mularkey of IRCO, Baher Butti and Kayse Jama and Stephanie Stephens of the Center for Intercultural Organizing, Nicola and Meg Cowie, Jeana Frazzini of Basic Rights Oregon, Robin Castro and John Halseth, Scott Hatley and Dan Friess of Incight, Jerry Carleton, Mair Blatt, Susan Johnson of Project Dove in Ontario.

CHAPTER 6: Paul Nicholson of the Oregon Shakespeare Festival, Julie Vigelund of the Oregon Arts Commission, Kerry Tymchuk of the Oregon Historical Society, Jarold Ramsey of Jefferson County Historical Society, Lynn Longfellow of the Oregon Nikkei Legacy Center, Willie Richardson and Gwen Carr of Oregon Black Pioneers, Christine D'Arcy, Kimberly Howard, John Olbrantz of the Hallie Ford Museum in Salem, Maribeth Collins and Truman Collins of the Collins Foundation, Theo Downes-LeGuin and Bryan Suareth of Disjecta, José Gonzales and Dañel Malan and Julieth Maya Buri of Miracle Theatre Group, Andrew Proctor of Literary Arts, Gwyneth Gamble Booth, Tom Booth, Diane Ponti, Gary White, Ann Whitfield Powers and Rich Wandschneider and Janis Carter of Fishtrap, Sara

Miller, Kevin Irving of Oregon Ballet Theatre, Jamey Hampton and Una Loughran and Jonathan Krebs of Bodyvox, Charlie Walker and Jane Boyden of Neskowin Chamber Music, Lindsay Berryman, Lorna Spain of the La Grande Symphony Orchestra, Allandra Emerson of the Port Orford Arts Council, Reena Evers, Dan and Priscilla Bernard Wieden and Addy and Big Bird and Tricia Snell and Michelle Meyer of Caldera.

CHAPTER 7: Sally McCracken, Joyce Akse of the Ford Institute for Community Building, Doug Stamm of the Meyer Memorial Trust, Tobe Porter of the Port Orford Library, Peggy Alessio, John Sweet, Dale and Jo-Ann Thomas, Penny Allen, Amy Callahan, Alexa Sharps of the Children's Miracle Network, Kendall Murphy and Megan Dobson of Levé, Paul Brainerd, Richard Meeker, Ryan Saari of Oregon Public House, Martha Richards of the James F. and Marion L. Miller Foundation.

AT THE OREGON COMMUNITY FOUNDATION: Max Williams, Kathleen Cornett, Wendy Usher, Joan Vallejo, Laura Winter, Arlene Cogan, Lara Christensen, Michele Boss Barba, Hirut Yehoalashet, Amy Cuddy, Carly Brown, Cristina Sanz, Jennesa Datema, Dianne Causey, Dorothy Jamison, Cynthia Hayes, Roberto Franco, Eric Parsons, Eric Vines, Amy Rainey, Sara Brandt, Joan Kerns, Mike Wallace, Sue Miller.

SPECIAL THANKS TO: Joyce White of Grantmakers of Oregon and Southwest Washington, Jim White of the Nonprofit Association of Oregon, Kathleen Joy of Oregon Volunteers, Jim Pasero, Eric and Holly Lindauer, Ashley Campion, Susan Lindauer, Amy Brown, Jerry and Beth Hulsman, Tony Leineweber, Sarah Nevue, Lori Sweeney, Lyn Hennion, Mary Wilcox, Hal Snow, Dr. Fritz Fraunfelder, and Janet Fratella. Huge thanks to Eleanor Sacks, who read the entire book in draft and improved it greatly. And the heartiest of thanks to everyone at OSU Press: Tom Booth, Marty Brown, and especially to Micki Reaman, for her editorial rigor, patience, and intelligence.

THANKS FROM KRISTIN ANDERSON: Unending thanks to Greg Chaillé, who introduced me to some of the most admirable and interesting people in Oregon; who allowed me to glean from his expertise; and who honored me with his trust and confidence. Greg, it has been a pleasure to work with you and a joy to call you my friend. You deserve every millimeter of that beautiful Joe Weston rose. Thanks also to Wendy Usher, who kindly introduced us.

Thanks to Dick and Cheryl Hazel for the crackling fires, pubs, and friendship. Thanks to my brother, Taylor; to my grandfather, Jerry Nudelman, for his love and support; and to my grandmother, Joan Anderson, for being an intrepid and loving research companion. Thanks also to my parents, Michael and Jamie Anderson, whose perpetual encouragement, curiosity, humor, intellectual and editorial rigor, and friendship have together been a cornerstone to me—and whose philanthropy deserves its own recognition. And finally, thank you to my husband, Michael O'Brien, for his wit, strong cups of Assam, cheese-filled oatcakes, muddy hikes, bone-dry martinis, and love.

THANKS FROM GREGORY CHAILLÉ: I want to thank Oregonians throughout the state who showed me time and again the tremendous commitment they have to their communities and to making Oregon a better places to live. You are an inspiration! Life in Oregon would be dreary indeed without you. We truly live in a "state of giving."

Thank you also to the board members of the Oregon Community Foundation who had the confidence to hire me in 1980 as the Foundation's first program officer and as the Foundation's president in 1987. We accomplished much together. Through the years, this board's enthusiasm for philanthropy propelled countless projects on to success. They have been the real champions for giving and are the unsung heroes of philanthropy in Oregon. Combined with OCF's great and hardworking staff and volunteer corps, the OCF board has been a catalyst for philanthropy. Special thanks go to Bob Chandler, whose love for Oregon and concern for its future made him a wonderful mentor, and to Ned Look who was the executive director when I first arrived at OCF. With few resources and lots of vision, Ned took me under his wing and taught me about philanthropy in Oregon. And he was an expert.

And to Kris Anderson, my co-author—you made this book go from idea to reality. Thank you for being a hardworking and enthusiastic partner. Your insights, intellect, and creative ability made this book come to life. You took abstract ideas and turned them into clear prose. And a thank you to my colleague Wendy Usher, who introduced me to Kris and helped with "the book project" in many other ways.

Finally, special recognition to my son, Peter, and daughter, Adrienne, who have been my closest advisors over the years. From attending dozens of events to critiquing speeches and annual reports to listening to initiative ideas, they have been an invaluable sounding board and source of wisdom for me. Thank you, Peter and Adrienne.

Appendixes

In his introduction to SOLV's *Oregon Owner's Manual* (2002), Governor John Kitzhaber wrote:

> Now more than ever we must renew our commitment to preserving these treasures that make Oregon special. . . . Oregonians take seriously their responsibility to manage their environment and their society. They give of their time and their personal resources to ensure that this place lives up to the promise that drove the pioneers to endure the hardship of the Oregon Trail. . . . As William James said, "act as if what you do makes a difference. It does."

If the stories in this book have motivated you to take up Kitzhaber's challenge, the Appendixes—which include resources for potential donors and volunteers, as well as a guide to evaluating nonprofits and an additional reading list—have been compiled to help you to act.

Portland, with Mount St. Helens in the distance. Photo by Kristin Anderson.

Appendix I
Types of Donations

Any support that you can give to an organization will be gratefully received. If in doubt, ask the organization what it needs or offer what you have to give. But if you'd like to learn more about different types of donations and different options for establishing a charitable routine, read on. Not all organizations will be able to accept all types of donations (for example, not all organizations have a members corps), but the examples that follow are widely known and widely used. If you're unsure what your giving priorities are, or if you want to indicate your unqualified support of an organization, consider making an unrestricted (unspecified) gift to an organization: it will allow your gift to be used where it will be most useful. Or consider volunteering your time with the organization to learn more about its operations and needs.

NON-MONETARY DONATIONS

VOLUNTEER SUPPORT

Any contribution of time and talent to an organization or cause is considered volunteer support. Most nonprofits rely on a backbone of committed volunteers to serve as advocates, labor, and consultants. Volunteer contributions of time can amount to thousands, hundreds of thousands, or millions of dollars given to an organization; Project Dove in Ontario and Food for Lane County in Eugene, for example, have both acquired the equivalent of multiple staff people (and hundreds of thousands of dollars in saved salary payments) through the dedication of their volunteer corps.

IN-KIND DONATIONS

Related to volunteer time, in-kind donations can be services that you provide from within your professional field—for example, pro bono legal work or bookkeeping—or goods you donate—for example, food and wine for fundraisers, auction items, facilities, advertisements, and promotional assistance.

MONETARY DONATIONS

There are a number of categories of monetary gifts, including cash gifts (currency, money orders, checks, etc.), appreciated property (appreciated securities or real estate, etc.), or other assets, including stock and personal property (art, cars, etc). These can be collected in a number of ways, and they can also be designated for a number of different purposes.

MEMBERSHIP DUES OR MONTHLY CONTRIBUTIONS

Many nonprofits have membership or subscription bases that guarantee them a steady, base level of income. Memberships often come with benefits for the member, such as free or discounted admission or access to insider information. Other nonprofits request that you sign up for a regular contribution timetable (monthly, quarterly, or yearly) which also provides nonprofits with the security of knowing what's coming in when. These regular contributions are usually set up as automatic payments from your credit card or your checking account.

GENERAL PURPOSE OR OPERATING SUPPORT

Most dues or regular contributions go into an organization's general operating support fund, which is a nonprofit's bread and butter. A donation or grant for operating support can be used by a nonprofit at its discretion: uses may include rent, salaries, endowment, or program expenses as well as other operating needs. Nonprofits work very hard to maintain their operating support donors and to grow this base of support, and most organizations could not survive without a strong corps of general operating donors.

While individual donors most often contribute to general operating funds, many foundations have specific policies against granting for general operating purposes, believing this is the responsibility of the community where the nonprofit is located. This frequently is a point of tension between the nonprofit community and foundations. Nonprofits often feel they are doing all they can to raise money from individuals, and that the added support of foundations for general operations could mean the difference between a good and an outstanding organization, or between survival and thriving. Foundations, on the other hand, often feel that they do not want to get locked into funding just a few nonprofits that might become dependent on their grants. Some foundations are now realizing that a blanket ban on general operating grants may not be beneficial, but nonprofits still rely upon individual donors for the bulk of their general operating support, so if you can give unrestricted funds, we encourage you to do so.

RESTRICTED SUPPORT

When an individual, business, or foundation specifies the purpose of a donation, the donation becomes restricted and funds cannot be used for any other purpose without first obtaining the donor's permission. There are a number of different kinds of restricted program donations. The most common are:

PROGRAM/PROJECT SUPPORT

Some people and institutions donate to specific programs or projects within an organization: for example, you could contribute to Write Around Portland's prison workshops or to Parkinson's Resources of Oregon for their caregivers' support program or to Saturday Academy's robotics classes. Program/project grants are the most common type of foundation grants.

SEED FUNDING

Whether it is for a new organization or a new program, seed funding is like the venture capital of the nonprofit world. Seed funding supports innovation and change. Involving more risk than the average donation, seed funding is an important part of the nonprofit funding world. We can be thankful there are donors and grantmakers willing to take risks with seed funding, although due diligence is recommended.

CAPACITY-BUILDING DONATIONS

Capacity-building donations are made to help strengthen a nonprofit organization's capacity or ability to achieve its mission. This support might be targeted to strengthen management, technology, staff training, volunteer training, or the fundraising capabilities of an organization. Donations to improve capacity can have long-term benefit.

CAPITAL SUPPORT

Many donors like to support what is often referred to as "bricks and mortar" campaigns—support that goes to build or purchase tangible assets for an organization. Capital support often goes to new building projects, expansions, renovations, or other facility or equipment upgrades. These campaigns tend to be short-term and high-profile. Many donors find satisfaction in knowing that they gave something visible, physical, and lasting. Naming rights to new buildings and renovations can be attractive incentives for some larger donors and corporations.

ENDOWMENT DONATIONS

Many nonprofit organizations create endowment funds to provide a permanent source of revenue by investing a sum of money and using the investment earnings as income. Endowment funds can support an organization's general operating budget or can target specific programs or positions in the organization: for example, Albertina Kerr Center for Children, Port Orford Library, and Planned Parenthood of Southwest Oregon have endowments to support their day-to-day expenses; whereas the Jordan Schnitzer Museum of Art in Eugene has an endowment for education and outreach and Literary Arts has an endowment to support the creation of new literary work in Oregon.

If you're uncertain of the kind of giving you'd like to undertake or the nonprofits to which you'd like to donate, you can also consider contributing money to a respected foundation or other grantmaker who can do the research for you and either contribute your money where it is most needed or provide you with a curated list of recommendations. Many community foundations and other grantmakers—for example, United Way, the Oregon Community Foundation, the McKenzie River Gathering Foundation, and the Oregon Cultural Trust—have made it possible for you to donate to their general funds so that they can use their expertise in distributing your contribution. We advise you to consult licensed tax and/or investment professionals.

Friends greet one another at Sisters Of The Road. Courtesy Sisters Of The Road.

Appendix II
Charitable Giving Options

For most people, charitable giving means writing a check or sending a credit card donation to a few charities on an annual basis. Membership or subscription dues are other common means of contributing. And fundraising sites like Kickstarter provide an easy, spontaneous way to donate to causes.
But there are many alternative forms of giving that can benefit both the donor and the nonprofit. If you're considering giving over a longer time period or donating larger amounts, we recommend you discuss these options with your tax advisor, as many types of gifts will provide tax benefits to the donor and/or to the recipient organization.

In general, there are two main categories of gifts: current and deferred. A current gift comes from your current income or other assets on hand. A deferred gift is to be made in the future, most commonly through a bequest from one's will.

CURRENT GIFTS
- Provide immediate support for the nonprofit.
- Come in the form of cash or other assets (retirement assets, royalties, debt financing, art or other property, stocks, a car, subsidized or waived rent, donated land/property, in-kind donations such as legal/tax work).
- Provide the donor with an income-tax deduction.

DEFERRED GIFTS

- Bequests from a will can be significantly larger than current gifts, as the donor is deceased and no longer needs the funds.
- Charitable Remainder Trusts, another common type of deferred gift, are created by the irrevocable transfer of property to fund a trust that distributes at least annually to beneficiaries (the donor, spouses, or others). Upon the beneficiaries' deaths or a fixed number of years, the trust assets go to the nonprofit.
- Charitable Lead Trusts pay either a fixed dollar amount or percentage to one or more nonprofits during a fixed term, after which the remaining assets are transferred to the donor or family.
- In Gift Annuities, a donor irrevocably transfers a gift to a nonprofit or foundation, in exchange for which the nonprofit or foundation pays the donor or beneficiary a fixed sum for life. Like a trust, a gift annuity provides a life income to the donor or designee, with the remainder going to the nonprofit.
- Life insurance or retirement account beneficiary: a nonprofit can be named as the irrevocable beneficiary of a life insurance policy or an individual retirement account.

An effective giving strategy involves a thoughtful combination of current and deferred giving. From a nonprofit's perspective, current giving provides the much needed revenue for today's expenses, while deferred gifts can build the additional asset base for things like cash reserves, endowments, and building maintenance. After consulting your tax advisor, you can either contribute to these directly or talk to philanthropic managers, such as community foundations or the United Way.

Duncan Evered of the Malheur Field Station talking with students about bird biology, migration, and conservation issues. Photo by Lyla R. Messick. Courtesy Malheur Field Station.

Appendix III
How to Evaluate a Nonprofit

Most of us give to the causes that we care about. This is a good thing: donating by the heart is always a great way to ensure that you'll keep on giving. Few of us need or want to conduct in-depth research on an organization before we contribute; however, taking steps to learn about its programming, structure, and how your contribution will be put to use can be both reassuring and engaging—a way to reinforce your passion for an organization's good work. Most research around an organization will focus on two key questions: Is an organization responsible with its finances? and, Is it effective in enacting its mission and goals? The following criteria and considerations may help you answer these questions.

A CLEAR MISSION

Critical to any organization's success is a clear mission. Too often, nonprofit organizations gradually expand their missions because of their dedication to serving the community, a problem known as "mission drift." This mission drift, occasionally catalyzed by grantmakers' overemphasis on program funding, can decrease organizational effectiveness.

ACTIVE AND DIVERSE BOARD OF DIRECTORS

Donors should expect to see an active board that meets at least quarterly and has a diverse set of skills and experience. Areas of special expertise include finance, fundraising, and leadership. When possible, a board should include representatives from the community being served. Other things to look for are effective board leadership, a leadership succession plan, and clear bylaws.

A DEDICATED AND TRAINED STAFF

While a board of governors monitors an organization's progress toward its goals, it is the staff who usually get things done. The staff should be dedicated to the mission and be trained in the areas of expertise needed for success. Ongoing training for the staff is critical and the organization should be continually investing to increase staff capabilities. For smaller and newer organizations there may be limits—financial or otherwise—as to how much staff training can occur. Nevertheless, there are some training opportunities that do not cost very much. Taking advantage of these opportunities indicates a serious commitment toward mission fulfillment and organizational development.

A STRATEGIC PLAN

Where is the organization going over the next few years and why? What are its priorities, and how will they be funded? These and other critical questions about the future are best answered through careful planning and documentation of why and how the organization will operate in the future. Many organizations have a written strategic plan; others may have a clear sense of where they are going without an actual written document. A strategic plan is one assurance of clear direction.

DUPLICATION OF SERVICE

This is a key question in the nonprofit community because there is nothing to prevent one organization from duplicating the services of another. Keep your eyes open for duplication, but also recognize that two different organizations providing the same service may not be duplicating each other: they may be teaming up to address a significant problem, or serving different communities, or simply working separately to fulfill needs that could never be met by just one organization.

FINANCES

Does the organization have clear financial statements that are regularly reviewed by the board? Do these financial statements show you, the donor, that the organization understands its financial position? Are the financial statements reviewed by an outside independent agent or auditor? Smaller organizations with fewer resources may resort to a statement of financial position presented by an accountant or auditing firm. It is important for donors to ask for financial statements and to expect those statements to be accurate and complete. By doing this, we not only understand an organization's financial position before we invest, but we are also demanding high standards of the nonprofit community. Outside sources, such as the IRS, and websites such as Charity Navigator and Guidestar, may also provide more objective, if superficial, insights.

If you're donating online through crowdsourcing, bear in mind that, as Jim White, director of the Nonprofit Association of Oregon, explains: "the crowdsourcing model relies on an organization or cause to hold itself accountable, [whereas] when you're giving through [established] institutions, there are regulatory and ethical standards." If you're giving to an organization located abroad, finding transparent information about an organization's structure, finances, and efficacy, or the laws and regulations governing such things, might be more difficult. This doesn't mean you shouldn't give via crowdsourcing or to nonprofits abroad: it's just more complicated to assess them.

Finally, it is worth remembering that an American nonprofit's existence—provided that its existence has been verified, of course—means that it has been subject to regulations and laws, that it endures checks and balances. Moreover, for better or worse, Oregon nonprofits are subject to the nation's toughest law (HB 2060) on nonprofit spending: a nonprofit will no longer be eligible for the state charitable tax deduction if it cannot prove that at least 30 percent of donations to it "support their mission." The nonprofit community also holds itself accountable, guided by professional organizations such as the Association for Fundraising Professionals, the Willamette Valley Development Officers, Grantmakers of Oregon and Southwest Washington, and the Nonprofit Association of Oregon.

TAKING RISKS

Charitable giving always involves some risk, and very few organizations are perfect. The size and developmental stage of an organization may determine to what degree the above criteria are met. And the amount spent on programing might not reflect a nonprofit's effectiveness: organizations with higher overheads might be investing in staff development/retention and other capacity building initiatives that increase overall effectiveness. When investing in people, you have to trust your intuitive sense of their character and ability to get things done. Risk-taking is part of a complete philanthropic strategy—too much of an emphasis on proven success, effectiveness, and stability can mean that start-up projects and new nonprofits would never have an opportunity to grow and make a difference.

USEFUL WEBSITES

There are many online resources a potential donor can employ: most will help you to assess an organization's financial responsibility, but it is more difficult to find sites that will help you to assess its efficacy and impact. Guidestar (www.guidestar.org) and Charity Navigator (www.charitynavigator.org) are two fairly encyclopedic sites for financial assessment; both are working to find ways to better assess nonprofit efficacy and impact. The IRS also maintains a list of registered charities (for tax-deductible contributions): apps.irs.gov/app/eos/. GreatNonprofits (greatnonprofits.org/) lets users review nonprofits, a subjective measure of efficacy. And the *Oregon Business Journal* also publishes a yearly list of Oregon's 100 Best Nonprofits to Work For, a good marker of employee happiness and perhaps organizational health.

Other digital philanthropic resources include:

The Chronicle of Philanthropy, www.philanthropy.com
Philanthropy Roundtable, philanthropyroundtable.org
Nonprofit Times, thenonprofittimes.com
Philanthropedia, myphilanthropedia.org/
The Better Business Bureau's Wise Giving Alliance, www.bbb.org/charity
Oregon State University Center for Civic Engagement, oregonstate.edu/cce/
Oregon Involved, www.oregoninvolved.org
Grantmakers of Oregon and Southwest Washington, www.gosw.org
Nonprofit Association of Oregon, www.nonprofitoregon.org
GiveWell, www.givewell.org
Gifthub, www.gifthub.org
Oregon Foundation Databook, www.foundationdatabook.com
Bolder Giving, boldergiving.org
The Foundation Directory Online, fdo.foundationcenter.org
The Council on Foundations, www.cof.org
Forum of Regional Associations of Grantmakers, www.givingforum.org
The National Center for Family Philanthropy, www.ncfp.org
Worldwide Initiatives for Grantmaker Support (WINGS) Philanthropy Data Network, www.wingsweb.org

ALS Association of Oregon and SW Washington's 2013 Walk to Defeat ALS. Photo by Kristin Anderson.

Appendix IV
Volunteer Resources

Kathleen Joy, director of Oregon Volunteers!, says that Oregon communities "have always had an interdependence—in a rugged environment, humans need to help each other out. That will to help out, that connectedness, that independent, problem-solving, I-can-help-make-it-better attitude, makes Oregon volunteers a centerpiece to our nonprofit culture. . . . They help us to build better communities."

As the profiles throughout *State of Giving* demonstrate, the nonprofit sector depends on volunteers for everything ranging from highly specialized professional support to basic services and frontline assistance. Through volunteering, you can further an organization's mission, improve and connect to your community, meet new people, and demonstrate your values. Here are a few matters to consider as you think about becoming a volunteer:

- What kind of volunteer work would you like to do? What can you bring to an organization? Do you have specific skills—medical, legal, financial, educational, etc.—that you could share with a community or organization? Or do you want to do something completely new and different?
- What organizations match your interests? Is the mission one you feel truly passionate about?
- What is the time commitment you are willing to make? Don't get overwhelmed. Select two or three organizations that interest you the most and set up a visit with each.

• Does the organization have a volunteer coordinator or at least utilize its volunteers well? Do the organization's literature and website acknowledge volunteers? Do volunteers have opportunities to take on increased responsibility? Are there volunteer training programs and opportunities to grow into different positions? Not all organizations are able to meet all these standards: some organizations are more grassroots and simply need all hands on deck. Still, you are giving the organization one of your most valuable possessions: your time. In return, the organization should give you a positive experience.

In your research, you may find that volunteers seem to be celebrated and supported less consistently than donors or nonprofit workers. Little grant money is available to help nonprofits better train, use, and support their volunteers, which means that some organizations struggle to deploy volunteers effectively. Advocacy is needed to help correct this imbalance and to raise awareness of the crucial role volunteers play in American society. Please regard this imbalance as a call to arms rather than a disincentive—volunteer, and spread the news about yours and others' good work!

USEFUL WEBSITES

Oregon Volunteers, www.oregonvolunteers.org

Volunteers of America, www.voa.org

Volunteer Match, http://www.volunteermatch.org/

Oregon State University Center for Civic Engagement,
    http://oregonstate.edu/cce/

Oregon State University Nonprofit Jobs & Volunteer Opportunities listing
    http://oregonstate.edu/career/nonprofit-jobs-volunteer-opportunities

Sparked, www.sparked.com

HandsOn Network, a national organization with chapters across Oregon,
    www.handsonnetwork.org/actioncenters/map

United Way, www.unitedway.org

Central Oregon: Volunteer Connect, www.volunteerconnectnow.org

Clackamas: Clackamas Volunteer Connection,
    www.clackamas.us/socialservices/volunteer.html

Mac's List, a job and volunteer listing site mainly for Portland and statewide
    positions, www.macslist.org

United We Serve, www.serve.gov

Idealist, www.idealist.org

International Volunteer Programs Association, www.volunteerinternational.
    org

United Nations Volunteers, www.unv.org

Rotary Clubs, www.rotary.org

Lions Clubs International, www.lionsclubs.org

Kiwanis International, www.kiwanis.org

Wallowa County farm. Photo by Kristin Anderson.

Appendix V
Additional Reading

What follows is a selected list of texts, with either national or local perspectives, that might help you navigate and explore the waters of volunteerism, philanthropy, and nonprofits. For more in-depth or issue-specific sources, please consult the book's endnotes.

Arrilaga-Andreessen, Laura. *Giving 2.0: Transform Your Giving and Our World.* Hoboken, NJ: Jossey-Bass, 2011.

Provides an extensive review of the multiple ways to give, with clear examples and stories about volunteering and giving money.

Bouchard Boles, Nicole. *How to Be an Everyday Philanthropist: 330 Ways to Make a Difference in Your Home, Community, and World—at No Cost!* New York: Workman, 2009.

A great guide, and call to action, for those interested in civic service, with a strong emphasis on types of volunteerism.

Brest, Paul, and Hal Harvey. *Money Well Spent: a Strategic Plan for Smart Philanthropy.* New York: Bloomberg, 2008.

Focuses on the importance of having a clear strategy for your philanthropy and how to develop one. Provides case studies and real world examples.

Connors, Tracy D. *The Volunteer Management Handbook: Leadership Strategies for Success.* Hoboken, NJ: Wiley, 2011.
> A guide mostly for nonprofits, but also useful for volunteers looking to assess or improve volunteer programs' capacity.

Crutchfield, Leslie, et al. *Do More Than Give: The Six Practices of Donors Who Change the World.* Hoboken, NJ: Jossey-Bass, 2011.
> This book is change oriented and shows the reader how to move from just giving money to nonprofits to becoming an active participant in setting policy, advocating, and creating more support for the causes you care about.

Crutchfield, Leslie, and Heather McLeod Grant. *Forces for Good: Six Practices of High Impact Nonprofits.*
> The authors identify six key practices employed by twelve nonprofits that have achieved an extraordinary level of success in creating positive change.

Fader, Sunny. *365 Ideas for Recruiting, Retaining, Motivating, and Rewarding Your Volunteers: A Complete Guide for Nonprofit Organizations.* Starke, Fl: Atlantic Publishing, 2010.
> A resource mainly for nonprofits, but also useful for volunteers looking to learn more about nonprofit volunteer strategies.

Friedman, Eric. *Reinventing Philanthropy: A Framework for More Effective Giving.* Dulles: Potomac Books, 2013.
> A businessman's approach on how to identify and select nonprofits that are achieving results consistent with your goals.

Friedman, Lawrence, and Mark McGarvie, eds. *Charity, Philanthropy, and Civility in American History.* Cambridge: Cambridge University Press, 2004.
> A fascinating compendium from professional historians on the history of American philanthropy and its role in American society.

Gary, Tracy, et al. *Inspired Philanthropy: Your Step-by-Step Guide to Creating a Giving Plan and Leaving a Legacy.* Hoboken, NJ: Jossey-Bass, 2007.
> Explains how to make a difference by creating giving and legacy plans, suggests questions to ask nonprofits, and spells out how to partner with advisors and nonprofit leaders for successful outcomes.

Hibbard, Michael, et al. *Toward One Oregon: Rural-Urban Interdependence and the Evolution of a State.* Corvallis: Oregon State University, 2011.

Focuses on the urban-rural divide and strategies for overcoming this problem through political, economic, and social actions.

McGill, Lawrence T., and Seema Shah. *Grantmaking to Communities of Color in Oregon.* Portland: Grantmakers of Oregon and Southwest Washington, 2010.

A thorough analysis of foundation grantmaking to communities of color and its trends, omissions, successes, and failures.

Meier, Julia, et al. *Philanthropy and Communities of Color in Oregon: from strategic investments to assessable impacts amidst growing racial and ethnic diversity.* Portland: Coalition of Communities of Color, 2011.

Available to download for free, this is an in-depth examination of how philanthropy is targeting—or failing to target—the specific needs of Oregon's marginalized communities of color.

Purcell, Midge, et al. *The State of Black Oregon, 2009.* Portland: The Urban League of Portland, 2009.

Seminal report on inequities in the black community throughout the state: an educational, sobering, thorough call-to-arms. Available for free download. A new report is scheduled for release in late 2014/early 2015.

Schröer, Andreas, et al. *Oregon Nonprofit Sector Report: State of the Nonprofit Sector in Oregon.* Portland: Portland State University/The Nonprofit Association of Oregon, 2011.

A useful and sobering assessment of need and provision in Oregon's nonprofits. Available for free download.

Tierney, Thomas J., and Joel Fleishman. *Give Smart: Philanthropy that Gets Results.* New York: PublicAffairs, 2012.

A highly regarded guide for philanthropists and nonprofits on how to be more effective in understanding each other and achieving mutual goals.

True North: The 2013 Oregon Values and Beliefs Survey. Portland: Oregon Values and Beliefs Project, 2013.

A fascinating overview of the diversity of beliefs and values held by Oregonians. Available for free download at www.truenorthoregon.org

Weeden, Curt. *Smart Giving Is Good Business: How Corporate Philanthropy Can Benefit Your Company and Society.* Hoboken, NJ: Jossey-Bass, 2011.

This book demonstrates how to strategically plan, manage, and evaluate corporate contributions so that giving benefits society and delivers a return to the companies making the contributions.

Zeiler, Freddi, and Ward Schumaker. *A Kids' Guide to Giving*. Norwalk, CT: Innovative Kids, 2006.

A clearly written and engaging guidebook on how to give money and time and how to research and select charities to support. Written by a kid for kids.

Zunz, Oliver. *Philanthropy in America: A History*. Princeton: Princeton University Press, 2011.

A scholarly account of philanthropy's development within and impact upon American life from the nineteenth century to the present.

Photo by Kristin Anderson.

Notes

INTRODUCTION

1 The Portland Foundation, started in 1920, was Oregon's first community foundation, but it did not survive the Depression.

2 Anonymous, "Donna Woolley Obituary," *Oregonian* (6 March 2011), http://obits.oregonlive.com/obituaries/oregon/obituary.aspx?page=lifestory&p id=149110713.

3 Anonymous, "Timber and Generosity: Donna Woolley made use of her gifts," *Eugene Register-Guard* (2 March 2011), http://projects.registerguard.com/web/opinion/25950816-47/woolley-oregon-eugene-board-foundation.html.csp.

4 Jean Nave, "Michael P. Hollern," *Sisters County Historical Society* (2006), http://www.sisterscountryhistoricalsociety.org/People/MikeHollern.htm.

5 Elizabeth Ueland, "Mike Hollern: Real Estate Developer with Vision," *Cascade Business News* (17 April 2012), http://www.cascadebusnews.com/news-pages/business-spotlight/2181-mike-hollern-real-estate-developer-with-vision.

6 Anonymous, "Duncan Campbell," *Encore.org,* http://www.encore.org/duncan-campbell-purpose. See also: David Boarstein, "For Children at Risk, Mentors Who Stay," *New York Times* (6 October 2011), http://opinionator.blogs.nytimes.com/2011/10/06/for-children-at-risk-mentors-who-stay/?_r=0.

7 Ibid.

8 Ilene Aleshire, Sherri Buri McDonald, "Business trailblazer Chambers dies at 79," *Eugene Register-Guard* (9 August 2011), http://projects.registerguard.com/web/newslocalnews/26679580-41/chambers-business-carolyn-communications-community.html.csp.

9 Paul Haist, "Harold Schnitzer Passes from Scene," *Jewish Review,* vol. 53, no. 20 (1 May 2011), 1, 30.

10 Leonard Laster, M.D., *Life After Medical School* (New York: W.W. Norton, 1996), 318, 307.

11 Sara Planecki, "Historical Notes from Walt Reynolds: Reminiscences of an African-American Physician," *OHSU Archival Blog* (23 May 2007), http://ohsu-hca.blogspot.com/2007/05/walt-reynolds-reminiscences-of-african.html.

12 Anonymous, "*Giving in Oregon Report,*" Oregon Community Foundation (2013).

13 Anonymous, "Volunteering in America: Volunteering and Civic Engagement in Oregon, Trends and Highlights Overview," Volunteering in America, http://www.volunteeringinamerica.gov/OR.

14 See Chapter Five and the Appendixes for more discussion of the 501(c)3 and 501(c)4 categories.

15 "Giving in Oregon Report," Oregon Community Foundation.

16 "Volunteering and Civic Engagement in Oregon," Volunteering in America.

CHAPTER 1

1 Michael Hibbard, Ethan Seltzer, et al.,*Toward One Oregon: Rural-Urban Interdependence and the Evolution of a State* (Corvallis: Oregon State University Press, 2011), 19.

2 Ibid., 121.

3 "American Fact Finder: Oregon," United States Census Bureau (2010), http://factfinder2.census.gov.

4 Anonymous, "Obituary: Robert Chandler, Prominent Editor of Small Ore., Calif., Newspapers," *Seattle Times* (13 July 1996), http://community.seattletimes.nwsource.com/archive/?date=19960713&slug=2338995.

5 Jackman Wilson, "Bob Chandler taught lessons his students won't forget," *Eugene Register-Guard* (31 July 1996),12A. http://news.google.com/newspapers?nid=1310&dat=19960731&id=u0lWAAAAIBAJ&sjid=IusDAAAAIBAJ&pg=3281,7842026.

6 Bob Chandler, "The bad guys aren't bad at all," *Bend Bulletin* (4 November 1978), 6, http://news.google.com/newspapers?nid=1243&dat=19781104&id=kj9YAAAAIBAJ&sjid=1_YDAAAAIBAJ&pg=6831,6598257.

7 Bob Chandler, "Reorganizing Oregon," *Bend Bulletin*, 29 December 1991. http://news.google.com/newspapers?id=XZxTAAAAIBAJ&sjid=HocDAAAAIBAJ&pg=5449,1933839&dq=bob+chandler+bulletin&hl=en. Accessed 8 July 2013.

8 Marie Deatherage, "Baker County Comes Back: How the Meyer Trust is Working to Help Rural Oregon Survive" (Portland: Meyer Memorial Trust, 1998–1999), 31. http://www.mmt.org/sites/default/files/BakerCountystudy.pdf

9 Terri Harber, "New life for Richland's school," *Baker City Herald* (31 August 2011), http://www.bakercityherald.com/Local-News/New-life-for-Richland-s-school.

10 Bob Boyd, "High Desert Museum," *Oregon Encyclopedia*, http://www.oregonencyclopedia.org/entry/view/high_desert_museum/ Accessed 5 July 2013.

11 Statistics taken from "Cycle Oregon History." Accessed 12 July 2014. http://www.cycleoregon.com/about/history/.

CHAPTER 2

1 These are five-year "cohort" graduation rates: if four-year cohort rates are used, the numbers drop even further in all categories. Oregon Department of Education, "Summary of 2011–12 Five-year Cohort Graduation Rates," http://www.ode.state.or.us/wma/data/schoolanddistrict/students/docs/summarycohortgrad1112.pdf.

2 "Oregon State Annual Report Card," Oregon Department of Education (2012), http://www.ode.state.or.us/data/annreportcard/rptcard2012.pdf.

3 Editorial Projects in Education, "Oregon State Highlights: Code of Conduct—Safety, Discipline, and School Climate," *Education Week's Quality Counts* (January 2013), 2, 8. http://www.edweek.org/ew/qc/index.html.

4 EcoNorthwest staff, "The Economic Impacts of Oregon's Achievement Gap," EcoNorthwest & Chalkboard Project (25 October 2010), http://chalkboardproject.org/wp-content/uploads/2010/10/Economic-Impact-of-the-Achievement-Gap1.pdf.

5   Nigel Jaquiss, "The Firebrand: Ron Herndon," *Willamette Week* (10 November 2004), http://www.wweek.com/portland/article-3823-the_firebrand.html.

6   Nancy Cook, Ron Herndon, and Glenn Bailey in interview with Craig Melvin, "Head Start, social welfare programs suffering from sequester cuts," *Hardball with Chris Matthews* (12 May 2013), http://www.msnbc.com/msnbc/watch/head-start-social-welfare-programs-suffering-from-sequester-cuts-29955651732.

7   "Testimony of Ron Herndon, Chair of the Board, National Head Start Association Before the Committee on Education and the Workforce Subcommittee on Education Reform, U.S. House of Representatives, July 31, 2001," http://archives.republicans.edlabor.house.gov/archive/hearings/107th/edr/earlychild73101/herndon.htm.

8   "About the ASPIRE Program," Office of Student Access and Completion, State of Oregon, http://oregonstudentaid.gov/aspire-about.aspx.

9   Merlin Vanderay, "Tony Hopson, Founder of Self-Enhancement inc." *About Face Magazine.* 22 March 2013. http://www.aboutfacemag.com/interviews/community/tony-hopson-sr/. Accessed 4 April 2013.

10 It is also a member of the Oregon Alliance for Education Equity discussed above in conjunction with SKCE.

11 Its main funders are the Collins Foundation, the Ford Family Foundation, JELD-WEN Foundation, the Meyer Memorial Trust, the Oregon Community Foundation, and the James F. and Marion L. Miller Foundation.

12 Daniel Fallon, "Case Study of a Paradigm Shift: The Value of Focusing on Instruction," Education Research Summit, Education Commission of the States, 2003.

13 The CLASS Dashboard, April 2014.

CHAPTER 3

1   "HUD reports slight decline in nation's homelessness in 2012," US Department of Housing and Urban Development (10 December 2012), http://portal.hud.gov/hudportal/HUD?src=/states/oregon/news/HUDNo.2012-12-10.

2   "Far Too Many Oregon Students Still Facing Homelessness," Oregon Department of Education (15 November 2012), http://www.ode.state.or.us/news/announcements/announcement.aspx?ID=8701&TypeID=5.

3   Oregon Food Bank Network Stats, "Record Numbers Seek Emergency Food," Oregon Food Bank, http://www.oregonfoodbank.org/Understanding-Hunger/OFB-Network-Stats?c=130183968782465900.

4   "Oregon hunger rate remains high, but begins to budge," Partners for a Hunger-Free Oregon, http://www.oregonhunger.org/files/News_2012_USDA_Food_Security_report.pdf.

5   The bill did add $200 million of funding for food banks, but this will scarcely compensate for the $8 billion cut. Nevertheless, it is important to note that nutrition programs remain by far the largest funding allocation on the bill. (Rob Nixon, "House Approves Farm Bill, Ending a Two-Year Impasse," *New York Times* [29 January 2014].)

6   David Sarasohn, "An Oregon magazine cover we'd rather cover up," *Oregonian* (17 December 2011), http://www.oregonlive.com/news/oregonian/david_sarasohn/index.ssf/2011/12/an_oregon_magazine_cover_wed_r.html.

7   A challenge grant helps an organization to raise additional money by pledging to give a certain amount to an organization only if it raises a certain amount by a certain date. Matching grants work much the same way, with matching funds donated by a certain ratio (usually 1:1). Both are thoughtful and effective philanthropic strategies to help engage and motivate other donors.

8   Suzanne Stevens, "No. of homeless Portland families up 29%," *Portland Business Journal* (15 December 2011), http://www.bizjournals.com/portland/news/2011/12/15/number-of-homeless-portland-families.html.

9   Genny Nelson, University of Portland Honorary Degrees Commencement address, May 2010, http://www.up.edu/commencement/default. aspx?cid=8305&pid=3144.

10 Rebecca Koffman, "Sisters Of The Road Café in Old Town serves up nourish-ment, dignity," *Oregonian* (28 December 2012), http://www.oregonlive.com/ portland/index.ssf/2012/12/sisters_of_the_road_caf_in_old.html.

11 Ibid.

12 Joanne Zuhl, "Genny Nelson, Sisters' co-founder, retires," *Street Roots* (10 December 2009), http://news.streetroots.org/2009/12/10/ genny-nelson-sisters-co-founder-retires.

13 John Foyston, "Genny Nelson served up dignity at the Sisters Of The Road Café for 30 years," *Oregonian* 10 December 2009. http://www.oregonlive.com/ portland/index.ssf/2009/12/genny_nelson_served_up_dignity.html. Accessed 24 February 2013.

14 Paris Achen, "Medford's second in state's homeless student count," *Medford Mail Tribune* (23 September 2010), http://www.mailtribune.com/article/20100923/ News/9230323.

15 Not designated for a particular program or purpose. Undesignated funds are very useful to nonprofits: they can direct these funds where they're needed most. They indicate support of an organization's overall mandate and trust in an organization to spend wisely.

CHAPTER 4

1   Writers' Program of the Work Progress Administration, *Oregon: End of the Trail* (Portland: Binfords & Mort, 1940), vii-viii.

2   Wallace Stegner, "Coda: Wilderness Letter," *The Sound of Mountain Water* (New York: Penguin, 1980 [1969]), 145.

3   Aldo Leopold, *A Sand County Almanac* (New York: Oxford University Press, 1989 [1947]), viii.

4   The Pacific lamprey is a migratory fish and an important ceremonial food for the Columbia Basin tribes. As with salmon, the numbers of lampreys have declined, in part due to hydropower dams on the Columbia.

5   Mark Zusman, "John Gray, the Quiet Lion, Dies at 93," *Willamette Week* (23 October 2012), http://www.wweek.com/portland/blog-29348-john_gray_the_ quiet_lion_dies_at_93.html.

6   Sunriver was much smaller under Gray's development; it has since expanded under subsequent owners.

7   Editorial, "John Gray and Oregon, 1919-2012", *The Oregonian* (22 October 2012), http://www.friends.org/latest/remembering-john-gray.

8   Passed in 1973, Senate Bill 100 established zoning laws and a statewide planning infrastructure in order to ensure that Oregon's land was being developed in accordance with public interest. Measure 6 would have ended the state's land use planning laws, returning them to local authority; Measure 37 provided compensation strategies for those whose private properties were subject to environmental restrictions; and Measure 49 lessened aspects of Measure 37's impact and jurisdiction.

9   "John Gray," *Oregonian* (22 October 2012).

10 This quadrant of Oregon has seen hot debates between two usually aligned par-ties: species conservationists—who are worried about the growth of wind farms in the area as threatening to the sage grouse—and renewable energy advocates, who assert that not only is this area perfect for wind power generation, a very clean energy source, but that it also could bring much needed rental income to agrarians and ranchers on whose land the turbines and transmission lines could be sited.

11 Reynolds School District services areas of Portland, Gresham, Troudale and a few other communites: it is predominantly urban.

12 Our Ocean is a Pew-funded coalition of conservationists, scientists, businesspeople and other stakeholders who advocate for more marine reserves in Oregon's coastal waters and whose good works have led to the creation of three other reserves in addition to Redfish Rocks. They deserve to be mentioned herein far more than they have been.

13 *"Oregon Economic Summary, August 27th 2014,"* Oregon Office of Economic Analysis, http://www.oregon.gov/DAS/OEA/docs/economic/oregon.pdf.

14 See: Associated Press, "Oregon Forestry Board may tighten logging rules," *Oregonian* (9 January 2012); Lisa Arkin, "Oregon Forest Practices Act needs to be updated," *Oregonian* (14 October 2013). http://www.oregonlive.com/opinion/index.ssf/2013/10/oregon_forest_practices_act_ne.html.

15 "Oregon's Forests: Some Facts and Figures," Oregon Department of Forestry (2009).

16 The Collins Foundation, the company's charitable arm, is discussed in Chapters Six and Seven.

17 For an overview of Oregon's forested lands and their ownership, see Oregon Department of Forestry's "Oregon Forestland Ownership" map: http://www.oregon.gov/odf/resource_planning/forestatlas/forestland_ownership.jpg.

18 See: Peter Hayes, "Understanding Hyla Woods" (12 October 2013), http://hylawoods.com/?p=266.

19 Over the decades, the Forest Service has attracted controversy with prolific road-building through its forests as well as through some of its stewardship policies and budgetary decisions.

20 Doug McDaniel, "Letters to the Editor: Kudos to Wallowa Resources," *Wallowa County Chieftain* (20 January 2011), http://wallowa.com/opinion/letters_to_editor/letter-kudos-to-wallowa-resources/article_61be55dc-24c5-11e0-b98e-001cc4c002e0.html

21 *"Giving in Oregon Report 2013,"* Oregon Community Foundation (Portland: OCF, 2013).

CHAPTER 5

1 American Community Survey, US Census Bureau, 2012. This takes into account equal education and experience.

2 According to Incight, a disability empowerment and advocacy organization.

3 APANO, Basic Rights Education Fund, CAUSA, et al. "Facing Race: 2011 Legislative Report Card on Racial Equity—Oregon," 16, 7, http://www.westernstatescenter.org/tools-and-resources/Tools/facing-race-2011-legislative-report-card-on-racial-equity.

4 "Philanthropy and Communities of Color in Oregon: from strategic investments to assessable impacts amidst growing racial and ethnic diversity," Coalition of Communities of Color (Portland, 2011), http://www.coalitioncommunities-color.org/docs/Philanthropy_Communities_of_Color_in_OR.pdf.

5 "Grantmaking to Communities of Color in Oregon," The Foundation Center (2010). (Data from 2008.) This report notes that this number is complicated: grants given to the broadly targeted programs also reach minority communities, and at the same time, minority communities are consistently undercounted, underreported, and mis- or cross-listed by ethnicity. They use as their determinant organizations/programs in which people of color are at least 51 percent of their clients. Tribal foundations have a slightly higher rate of giving to communities of color.

6 Ibid., 20.

7 Unpublished anonymous survey response, Grantmakers of Oregon and Southwest Washington, 2010.

8   "Better Schools, Better Oregon: Conditions Report," Chalkboard Project (Portland, 2013), http://www.chalkboardproject.org/images/PDF/Chalkboard_cond_final.pdf.

9   501(c)3s are nonprofits that are not explicitly political or lobbying, instead typically providing education, outreach, or services: contributions to these are in most cases tax deductible. 501(c)4s are political advocacy nonprofits: contributions to these are typically not tax deductible. Many social justice organizations have both a 501(c)3 and a 501(c)4 arm. Philanthropy is important to both categories of organization.

10 Affiliated Tribes of the Northwest Indians et al (27 other native and native-serving organizations). "Making the Invisible Visible: Portland's Native American Community" (2009). A highly recommended, well-referenced two-page overview.

11 Oregon Department of Education.

12 A practice common amongst tribes from Matt's home region farther north.

13 "*The State of Black Oregon,*" The Urban League (Portland, 2009); Kristian Foden-Vencil, "Racial Disparity Emerges in Oregon Unemployment Data," Oregon Public Broadcasting (16 January 2013), http://www.opb.org/news/article/racial-disparity-emerges-in-oregon-unemployment-data/.

14 Anna Griffin, "Braiding African American hair at center of overregulation battle in Oregon," *Oregonian* (11 August 2012); Urban League, "Amber Starks: Empowerment Advocate," http://ulpdx.org/news-archive/amber-starks/.

15 For more on Jerry Carleton's volunteer work with Incight, see here: http://leve-nw.org/blog/incight-profile-jerry-carleton .

16 Bitten the Kitten. "Don't blame us: she came with that name," says Nicola.

17 Reid Wilson,"Gay marriage initiative leads by wide margin in Oregon," *Washington Post* (8 May 2014).

18 *Grantmaking to Communities of Color in Oregon* (2010), 14.

19 By some definitions, because of the diversity of its varied tribal members, NAYA would not count as culturally specific. IRCO and CIO certainly are not, and yet these organizations all offer targeted knowledge, access, and culturally sensitive services.

20 Basic Rights Oregon operates both as a political lobbying group (a 501(c)4) and as an education organization (a 501(c)3), and thus contributions given to its lobbying side are not tax deductible . . . but are essential.

21 Nicole Hannah-Jones, "Oregon's 2010 Census shows striking Latino and Asian growth," *Oregonian* (23 February 2011), http://www.oregonlive.com/pacific-northwest-news/index.ssf/2011/02/2010_census.html.

22 Nicola Cowie, "Uniting to win for us all," *Proud Queer Monthly* (13 June 2013), http://www.pqmonthly.com/opinion-uniting-to-win-for-us-all/15130.

23 Ibid.

CHAPTER 6

1   Washington and California fare even worse, at 45th and 46th respectively, but that hardly constitutes a victory for Oregon. See: "State Arts Agency Legislative Appropriations Preview, Fiscal Year 2014," National Assembly of State Arts Agencies (15 August 2013), http://www.nasaa-arts.org/Research/Funding/State-Budget-Center/FY2014-Leg-Approp-Preview.pdf.

2   "Grants Almanac," National Assembly of State Arts Agencies (2012), http://www.nasaa-arts.org/Research/Grant-Making/index.php. Rachel Goslins, executive director of the President's Committee on the Arts and Humanities, reports in a *Washington Post* article that "sixty percent of schools say they've cut arts education in the last 10 years." Anne Midgette, "After years of crouching, arts ed is raising its hands again," *Washington Post* (21 February 2013).

3   "Profile of Oregon Nonprofits," Nonprofit Association of Oregon; National Assembly of State Arts Agencies.

4   "Profile of Oregon Nonprofits," Nonprofit Association of Oregon.

5   *Giving in Oregon Report, 2013.* Oregon Community Foundation.

6   "Arts & Economic Prosperity IV," Americans for the Arts. Eugene's results available here: http://aftadc.brinkster.net/AEPIV/OR_CityOfEugene_AEP4_SummaryOfFindings.pdf and Portland's are available here: http://aftadc.brinkster.net/AEPIV/OR_GreaterPortlandArea_AEP4_SummaryOfFindings.pdf.

7   Mark Golden, "Note to Business Leaders: The Arts Deserve More Than a Nod From Your Philanthropic Budget," Americans for the Arts, http://www.americansforthearts.org/blog-feed/note-to-business-leaders-the-arts-deserve-more-than-a-nod-from-your-philanthropic-budget.

8   Terry Richard, "Oregon Travel Experience installs Robert Gray historical marker, notes first African visitor." *Oregonian* (11 September 2013), http://www.oregonlive.com/travel/index.ssf/2013/09/oregon_travel_experience_insta.html.

9   "STEM" is an acronym for Science, Technology, Engineering, and Mathematics. "STEAM" adds arts into the mix.

10 They were not moved elsewhere, unlike many tribes.

11 Richard Speer, "Portland2014: Oregon only, please," *Willamette Week* (5 March 2014), http://www.wweek.com/portland/article-22085-portland2014.html.

12 See the Introduction for a profile of John and Carol Hampton.

13 Coyne, John, "Talking with Rich Wandschneider," Peace Corps Writers (July 2002), http://www.peacecorpswriters.org/pages/2002/0207/207talkwandsc2.html.

14 Ed Battistella, "An Interview with Rich Wandschneider," *Literary Ashland* (1 October 2013), http://literaryashland.org/?p=3655.

15 Excerpt from April 14, 1986, letter from Brian Booth to Ursula Le Guin.

16 Steve Duin. "Oregonians mourn Brian Booth, founding partner of Portland's Tonkin Torp law firm and community leader," *Oregonian* (7 March 2012), http://www.oregonlive.com/news/oregonian/steve_duin/index.ssf/2012/03/steve_duin_oregonians_mourn_br.html.

17 National Assembly of State Arts Agencies, http://www.nasaa-arts.org.

18 Richard Deasy, ed., *Critical Links: Learning in the arts and student academic and social development* (Washington, DC: Arts Education Partnership, 2002), http://www.gpo.gov/fdsys/pkg/ERIC-ED466413/pdf/ERIC-ED466413.pdf.

19 James. S. Catterall, et al., "The arts and achievement in at-risk youth: findings from four longitudinal studies," National Endowment for the Arts (Washington DC, March 2012), http://arts.gov/sites/default/files/Arts-At-Risk-Youth.pdf. As cited in www.theartscan.org "Why Arts Education Matters."

20 Edward Fisk, ed., *Champions of Change: The Impact of the Arts on Learning,* Arts Education Partnership and the President's Committee on the Arts and Humanities, http://artsedge.kennedy-center.org/champions/pdfs/ChampsReport.pdf.

21 "The 50 Most Generous Donors of 2012," *Chronicle of Philanthropy* (2 October 2013), http://philanthropy.com/article/The-2013-Philanthropy-50/137153/.

22 The Fields gift is not the first fund at OCF to prioritize arts. The Bonnie Bronson Fellowship for female artists was created out of small donations from Oregon artists in memory of painter and sculptor Bonnie Bronson, who died in a climbing accident on Mt. Adams in 1990. The creation of the Bonnie Bronson Fellowship reminds us that you don't have to be contributing at a Fred Fields level to make a difference to Oregon's artists.

CHAPTER 7

1   "Volunteering and Civic Engagement in Oregon," www.volunteeringinamerica.gov.
2   Highly religious states like Utah and Georgia top the list: contributions to churches count toward this rating.
3   As quoted in the Forum for Sustainable and Responsible Investment, 2012.
4   *Giving in Oregon 2013*, Oregon Community Foundation.
5   "Community 101," Oregon Community Foundation, http://www.oregoncf.org/ocf-initiatives/civic-engagement/community-101.
6   Lucy Burningham, "Katelyn Tomac Sullivan, Youth in Philanthropy," *Oregon Business* (December 2007), http://www.oregonbusiness.com/articles/31-december-2007/626-the-oregon-philanthropy-awards.
7   "Northeast Portland young people recognized for philanthropy, activism," Larry Bingham, *Oregonian*, 19 June 2013. Accessed 26 December 2013. http://www.oregonlive.com/portland/index.ssf/2013/06/northeast_portland_young_peopl.html.
8   Derrick Feldmann et al., "The 2013 Millennial Impact Report," Achieve/The Case Foundation (2013), http://www.themillennialimpact.com/2013RESEARCH.
9   *Giving in Oregon 2013*.
10 This can mean that nonprofits struggle to retain donors, losing them to others doing similar work; therefore, nonprofits are having to work on clearly associating their own work as definitive to these causes about which young people are passionate.
11 Richard Meeker, "A Note from Willamette Week Publisher Richard Meeker," *Willamette Week* (6 November 2013). http://www.wweek.com/portland/article-21485-a_note_from_the_publisher.html.
12 *Oregon Nonprofit Sector Report: State of the Nonprofit Sector in Oregon* (Portland State University; The Nonprofit Association of Oregon, 2011), http://www.nonprofitoregon.org/sites/default/files/uploads/file/ONSR.pdf.

CONCLUSION

1   "Volunteering and Civic Engagement in Oregon," http://www.volunteeringinamerica.gov/OR.
2   "Volunteering and Civic Engagement in Oregon, 2012," http://www.volunteeringinamerica.gov/OR.
3   *Giving in Oregon 2013*; "Sharing the Wealth: How the States Stack Up In Giving," *Chronicle of Philanthropy* (19 August 2012), http://philanthropy.com/article/Sharing-the-Wealth-How-the/133605/.
4   *Giving in Oregon 2012*, Oregon Community Foundation.
5   Donors are more likely than non-donors to volunteer and give in-kind gifts to nonprofits; of donors, 42 percent also volunteered with a nonprofit, compared to 20 percent of non-donors; and 82 percent of donors also gave goods. Sources: *Giving in Oregon 2013*; Volunteering and Civic Life in America, Corporation for National Community Service.

Index